Child Psychology :
Anti - Social Behaviour

Child Psychology : Anti - Social Behaviour

K.S. Moorthi

2008

CYBER TECH PUBLICATIONS
4264/3, Ansari Road, Daryaganj, New Delhi-110002 (India)
Ph.: 011-23244078. Fax: 011-23280028
E-Mail: cyberpublicationsdelhi@yahoo.com

Child Psychology : Anti - Social Behaviour

First Edition 2008

Published by G.S. Rawat

For Cyber Tech Publications

4264/3, Ansari Road, Daryaganj, New Delhi - 110 002

E-mail : cyberpublicationsdelhi@yahoo.com

Phone : 011-23244078,

Fax : 011-23280028

Printed at

Amit Enterprises, Moujpur, Delhi. Ph. - 9810878184

Preface

The present study bad social surroundings and bad company have been found as major factors responsible for producing and perpetuating anti-social behaivour amongst the children. Here the police may prove of much help in preventing and controlling the problem directly as well as indirectly. This is very easily possible for then as they have vast resources, sufficient knowledge on the subject of crime and delinquency, reliable information about delinquents as individual, greater exposure and association with the public etc. to accomplish the task.

The anti-social child does not constitute a unique type of human being. They have the same human desires and natural yearnings as anyone else. They are also human beings though the victims of faulty upbringing and poor school and social environment. Therefore, to prevent the children from failing into as such habits and to control and cure those who have already caught into this phenomena, some remedies have been suggested/recommended under this study. In the first place parents should try to provide a congenial atmosphere at home for the child's study and relaxation/recreation, give him his rightful place in the family, show sympathy, love and favourable attitude, provide sense of security, fulfill his basis requirements, make proper supervision along with necessary freedom to the child and keep constantly in touch with the school. The role of school and teachers is equally important in tackling the problem. The school should try to create an environment in which the child can be kept usefully busy and provide all the necessary facilities to him, according to his interest and aptitude, which are helpful in the all round development of his personality. It should seek help and co-operation from the parents and the community.

We recc·d our grateful acknowledgements to national and inernational scholars and institutions for excellent contributions on the subject.

The publisher and their staffmembers have assisted in every possible way and have worked hard for its timely completion of the book.

—Editor

Contents

1

Introduction

The child guidance movement started formally n this country about fifty years ago. During this half century there have been many changes not only in the child guidance clinics but also the professions working in these clinics. Child psychiatry, which did not exist at that time, has gradually accumulated a body of knowledge and skills of its own so that it is now recognized as separate special field within psychiatry.

The children with marked anti-social behaviour are categorized as juvenile delinquents. Broadly a juvenile delinquent is a child generally between the ages of seven to eighteen years and whose anti-social tendencies are so grave that they become or ought to become the subject of official action. Delinquent behaviour is a rebellion and an expression of aggression which is aimed at destroying, breaking down or changing the environment. The definition of a delinquent various according to community attitudes, the state of law and the policies of law enforcement agencies and the kind of behaviour which led to a delinquency level depends upon the kind of society in which one lives. "Juvenile deviance has been an important issue in every society in time and space. Therefore this phenomenon has been giving rise to extremes of emotions in affected people and non-conforming act of a juvenile has been evoking mixed reactions against concerned depending upon the area, cultural norms, social attitudes, position, placement, relationship with the perpetrator or victim, responsibility, interest, knowledge, discipline, orientation and outlook of the people defining and applying social standards on the activities of the juvenile."

Indian society has achieved considerable progress and development in different spheres of social activity. But this rapid advancement has also brought many socialevils in its stride. Indulgence in anti social activities by the students at a very delicate (adolescent) age is one of the major evils. The principles of secondary schools have confronted with problems pertaining to anti-social activities like, gambling, stealing and drug abuse among the students of their schools. The speed with which such behaviour is spreading among the student community is the most dangerous aspect of it. Future planners and administrators of schools are in general worried about the intensity/magnitude of the problem. The resettlement colony in question, is generally inhabited b the people of the lowest strata of society.

It is also feared that in such colonies anti-social elements like gamblers, pick-pockets, drug addicts etc. lie in good numbers. The students coming from such homes and surroundings are likely to be more prone to these anti-social activities as compared to the students residing in other colonies. The problem does not concern schools only. Seen from a wider angle, it is a social problem which concerns everyone in the society. But school is supposed to be an institution where there children are taught about the good and had behaviours. More so to the children coming from parents who have not been able to set a model to their children. These children are a part of the society and the country is equally dependent upon this section of the population. Such problematic children may prove to be cancerous to the growth of the society and weaken the foundations of the countries future. It is a sheer waste of humanresources and miscues of manpower. In school, it leads to other serious problems like breaking school rules, damaging school property, redeness and misbehaviour with teachers etc. The net result is the entire atmosphere of the school is spoiled and other innocent students may suffer the consequences. The problem in its serious form does not spare the home as well. The parents are worried over the behaviour of their sons when they (sons) return late at night, use abusive and filthy language, are caught eve-teaching stealing, gambling, pick pocketing and indulging in other violent activities. It is a disgrace to the society and demoralizing for the nation when children start indulging in anti-social activities and criminally waste their talents and energies by putting it in undesirable directions. The school as a temple of learning and the teacher as a nation builder, is duty bound to use his influence and act in a manner which not only prevents the problem from originating but also checks and cures it and enables the spoiled children to adjust in the new circumstances. This is as matter of fact, progressive function of education which ultimately results in national strength and social uplift. It is therefore, imperative to examine the factors responsible for such anti-social behaviour and to find out possible and suitable remedies for quick solution of the problem.

The major objectives of the study are: (a) To identify the nature and magnitude of the problem, (b) to analyse the major causes of the problem, and (c) to suggest suitable remedies for overcoming the problem in schools.

The study covers only few anti-social activities such as stealing, gambling drug abuse and smoking reflecting anti-social behaviour. Except smoking the other three activities are considered as of anti-social nature form legal point of view also. But the investigator includes smoking also as an anti-social activity on the following grounds.

smoking works as a seed for growing plants of various anti-social behaivour viz. drug addiction stealing gambling etc. Smoking is injurious to health, is an statutory warning and this slogan is invariably printed on all the cases of cigarettes. The World Health Organisation in Geneva has banned smoking in particular areas on an experimental basis.

2

Child Nature Place and Origin of the Problems

During this time much has happened in analytic work to throw added light on the problems concerned and to influence the conditions of life for young people, whether normal or abnormal, Nevertheless, in spite of partial advances, the position with regard to the analytic study of adolescence is not a happy one, and especially unsatisfactory when compared with that of early childhood. With the latter period, we feel sure of our ground, and in possession of a wealth of materials and information which enables us to assume authority and apply analytic findings to the practical problems of upbringing. When it comes to adolescence, we feel hesitant and, accordingly, cannot satisfy the parents or educational workers who apply for help to us and to our knowledge. One can hear it said frequently that adolescent is a neglected period, a stepchild where analytic thinking is concerned.

Place of Origin of the Problem

The parents have stated that their children had acquired the bad habits at the school in the company of their friends. The place of originating these habits is not the school but the home and social surrounding in which the child lives and moves and spends about 80 per cent of his total time. It can be noted form that 100 per cent cases of stealing. 80 per cent of gambling, 75 per cent of smoking and 20 per cent of drug addiction originated from society and percentages in case of home for the above cases are zero, 20, 25 and 80 respectively, whereas none from the school campus.

Table 2.1: Place of Origin of the Problem

Nature of Problem	*No. of Cases*	*Home (percentage)*	*Society (percentage)*
Smoking	20	25	75
Drug Addiction	5	80	20
Gambling	5	20	80
Stealing	3	0	100

It is, therefore, established that home and society are equally responsible in generating these bad habits and are the breeding grounds of anti-social behaviour.

The cases investigated under the present study ranged in the age group of 15 to 19 years and the age of origin of the problem ranged between 11 to 17 years.

Nature of the Problem

The problem identified under anti-social behaviour were mainly four in nature. They are smoking, drug addition, gambling and stealing. Smoking leads to drug addiction followed by other antisocial activities like gambling and stealing.

When the smokers fall into the trap of drug addicts, they first start with a very small quantity of the substance placed inside the cigarettes etc. After sometime they start enjoying the 'kick' and need more. Since the drugs are very costly and beyond their reach, they start stealing money and materials from home to satisfy appetite for drugs. Very soon they learn the art of stealing and start laying their hands over other people's property and pockets. Money earned through this way is misused for gambling in the greed of earning more money and the circle is complete. Once they become addicts or slaves of the drugs, they cannot live without it. Then in the absence of drugs they feel severe pan in the stomach and the whole body, and the eyes stat lacrimating and nose starts flowing. The adverse effect of the drugs surfaces very soon. The fingers get burnt, black spots appear around the eye lids, the body becomes while and the child looses all interest in studies, games or any other work. It is estimated that there are eleven lack drug addicts in Delhi alone. This has created greater risk for our children who may fall victim to this evil habit in the company of such people.

Causes of the Problem

According to their higher percentages some of the factors can be put in the category of major cause. They are bad social surroundings, lack of EVGC facilities, bad habits of family members, bad company, illiterate parents, poor living conditions at home, lack of child's interesting studies, and lack of activities in the school The knowledge of these causes can prove of immences help in finding out suitable remedies.

Causes of Anti-Social Behaviour

Causes	*Percentage*
Bad Social surroundings	95
Bad company	85
Lack of Proper guidance and counselling facilities in the schools	95
Lack of activities in the school	40
Rudeness and Indifference of teachers	5
Lack of Interest in studies	65
Indiscipline	25
Poor Health	15
Poor Living conditions at Home	65
Bad Habits of Family Members	85
Illiterate Parents (both or either of the two)	85

The various cases of the problem have been analysed under the following broad categories:

(a) Individual and Behavioural, (b) Home, (c) Social (d), School.

The child himself with his attitudes and behaviour is responsible for learning bad habits to certain extent. The that child's lack of interest in studies contributes to the problem to the extent of 65 per cent, his disobedience, unruly behaviour and in disciplined attitude to 25 per cent and poor health to 15 per cent. The percentages mentioned above do not suggest any great intensity in this particular cause. This means this cause can be effectively routed out by taking suitable remedial steps.

This dimension examines the living conditions at home in terms of housing accommodation, size of the family, education of the family, income of the family, habits of the family members and other facilities at home. Looking at the large size of family members ranging from 5 to 9 with an average of 7 the accommodations in respect of 90 per cent families are badly overcrowded and insufficient.

In addition to all this, the behaivour and habits of the family members do not seem to be condusive to the proper formation of habits of the child. It can be clearly seen from that 85 per cent fathers and 20 per cent clearly seen from that 85 per cent fathers and 20 per cent mothers are smokers, 45 per cent fathers and 5 percent mothers are drug addicts, 5 per cent fathers, and 5 per cent mothers are gamblers while 5 per cent fathers and 5 per cent fathers and 5 percent mothers are gamblers while 5 per cent fathers and 10 per cent mothers indulge in stealing. In short a large number of houses lack minimum facilities, are over crowded and their earnings are meager that means poor living conditions are found at home.

The behaviour of the child already infected with such habits produces tremendous influence over the behaviour of other innocent children around them. The study shows that some of the cases acquired these habits at the school possibly because of lack of spare time and also non-availability of safe and lonely place – which are essential requirements at the initiation stage.

However, when the same children move in their social surroundings they come into contact with other children while playing or simply loitering around. During the course of investigation undesirable social surroundings and bad company have been found to be the major causative factors responsible to the extent of 95 and 85 percent, to the problems respectively. The two are also interdependent and supplementary teach other. For example, bad company produces bad environment (or bad social surroundings) and in the same way bad social surroundings lead to bad company. The children there, naturally, move around for playing and other purposes.

Some of them due to individual, home or school problems are easily attracted towards other children or even grownups, who have already acquired bad habits, and are thus initiated into such habits and anti-social behaviours. Such habits have invariably started with smoking in the first place. It can, therefore, be concluded that the influence of societal factors, such as bad social surroundings and bad company, are more pronounced over the behaviour of the children than any other factor.

The school has not been found directly responsible in originating the problem. However, it has been causing and contributing to the problem to some extent by failing to take preventive measures and also by creating situations under which the child becomes vulnerable to fall prey to these problems very easily. That means had there been these facilities a good number of students could have been prevented from falling in to the trap of bad habits right at the beginning. In the same way lack of activities created scope to the extend of 40 per cent while rudeness and indifference of teachers produced negligible effect i.e. only 5 per cent. Lack of interest in studies has been responsible in causing the problem to the extent of 65 per cent. Lack of interest in studies has been responsible in causing the problem to the extent of 65 per cent. Though it is an individual factor but the schools are also responsible for this individual indifference to the extent it was caused due to bad teaching and lack of other facilities in the school. This view has also been and lack of other facilities in the school. This view has also been confirmed by a recent study on anti-social behaviour which concludes thus, "the teachers and people in management themselves might be poor in prosocial value and behavioural orientations. They might be loving to terrorise the students by enjoying dominant position entrusted to them by the society and by getting its support."

Recommendations

The problem of anti-social behaviour of the children has been the cause of concern of not only the parents but also many other professional groups. The educators, administrators, clinical Psychologists, guidance counselors, social workers, sociologists, psychiatrists, the criminologists, the police and judges and at one time or other it has "captured the attention of many different types of citizens from the man on he street to the president.."

There are a number of child welfare institutions functioning in Delhi correcting/curing and reforming the problem of children and putting them on the right path. They swing into action only when the child commit some criminal offence i.e. when he is declared a proved juvenile delinquent. Barring a few, no organized and systematic effort has been made by any agency or institution to go deep into the causes of the problem and take steps to prevent the problem of occurrence and to check and control it, if it is already in the process of growth in certain children. Only the preventive measures supported b curative efforts may succeed in routing out the problem from our society. This preventive programme starts at home, goes to the neighbourhood, extends to the school and covers all other community institutional structures. Here the role of individuals and institutions/agencies has been examined with a view to prevent, control and eradicate the problem of anti-social behaviours of the secondary school children:

- Parental Role
- Role of the School
- Role of the Teachers
- The School Counsellors
- The Police

Parental Role

It is incumbent on the parents to set an example of good behaviour at all times to children since a child draws his main identification from the parents he loves and regards best. Responsibility for the children vests with both mother and father. It would therefore be appropriate to identify the major roles of the parents, who even by their mere presence at vicinity – or distance through their latent or indirect support to the child – provide a protective umbrella thereby still a sense of security and confidence in a child. This reality plays an over bearing role in shaping and providing direction to the personality of the child.

The parent should show discipline by their own conduct. Mother and father should always present a united picture. They are expected to act as models not only in regard to ideals but also in terms of responses and reaction patterns of varies life situations and for this first of all they should give up their own bad habits.

Appropriate status should be accorded to the child among the members of the family. This satisfies adolescent's instinct of recognition and develops qualities like obedience, feeling of responsibility etc. in him.

Any reward or punishment given to the child should be justified and the purpose properly understood by the child to avoid any kind of malice from the parent-child relationship.

According to his age, potentiality and reflexes, the need,

importance and efficiency of social values and norms along with roles and responsibilities should be explained.

Proper supervision and control should be exercised over the child – to have a close watch at his activities, interests, company of friends, his movements etc. and apply preventive measures wherever necessary without putting unnecessary check on his freedom.

The basic requirements of the children should be fulfilled as far a possible.

They should be treated with due sympathy, affection and consideration.

The parents should keep in constant touch with the school and the teachers in order to keep themselves abreast of the progress of the child and also to find out solution of various problems facing the child.

But the parents of the colony under consideration are mostly illiterate and belong to a very low income category, therefore, they may not be expected to follow all the suggestions given above. Under the circumstances the responsibility of other agencies (outside home) becomes greater in dealing with the problem and the school in particular is supposed to play greater role in this direction.

School

School has not been found directly contributing to the problem yet it can play a very constructive role in the prevention and control of anti-social behaviour of the children. The school may succeed in their efforts in this direction only when they become good schools and are able to coordinate their efforts within the framework of total community endeavour. The school should create favourable condition for attracting and creating interest amongst the children and for the balanced growth and development of their personality by observing the following suggestions:

Should provide all necessary facilities which help in the all round development of the child.

Should differentiate instructions to suit the interest and abilities of the problem of child in order to ensure some measure of success and notification for them.

Should provide special services such as remedial instructions, counseling, testing, medical examination, home visitation case work, special health services etc.

Should maintain reasonable class and school size say for example, aroudn30 students per class and 500 per school.

should provide opportunities for school – community interaction by organising P.T.A., open day for the parents and society, playing matches between school and community inviting community members to participate in various activities of the school and vice-versa. Closer cooperation between parents and teachers will certainly help in moulding the children on correct lines.

Should identify the problem children through cumulative school records, tests, medical examinations, mutual confidence, home visits etc. and should accept them as a person as they are normal human begins though victims of circumstances.

However, the problem can not be solved by the school alone or for that matter by any single agency – be it home, clinic, or any other institution. The problem is of complex nature and calls for coordinated efforts of all community forces of which the school represents an important segment.

Teachers Role

Adolescence is a period of extreme in behaviour. Emotions of adolescents are intense in nature. On the basis of emotions an individual develops sentiments, values of life, ideals and virtues, which are the basic ingredients of character. This is the period when child is very much vulnerable and receptive to any kind of good or unhealthy effect/behaviour. The teachers' proper guidance and control is very necessary during this period.

"The teacher should organise and control emotions of an adolescent from the very beginning instead of repressing them. He should take care to explain the real situation to an adolescent and create a better environment avoiding all sorts of strains and mental conflicts otherwise he will develop a particular temper, movement, posture or clumsiness. Teacher should be on guard in relation to this type of children and treat them sympathetically.

The teacher should:

— Aim to develop self imposed control within the child

— Counsel problem children regarding their educational, vocational and personal problems

— Identify problem - prove youngster and refer them to E.V.G.C. of the school.

— Develop and use cumulative education and other records.

— Help the problem children from time to time, to appraise his own growth and achievement, providing thereby a sense of security through success.

— Have working knowledge of child's physical, emotional and mental growth and development which will enable him to collaborate with remedial, psychological and social work professions

— Present an acceptable attitude towards the problem child and also show an effective example for imitation through is behaviour habits and emotional maturity.

— Make effective use of knowledge of the basic human, physical and psychological needs and to establish specific and meaningful goals within the range of child potential.

The role of school counsellors is being progressively recognized in the achievement of individual educational excellence. In America the "Policy makers and special interest groups recommended an expansion of such services, a sharpening of counselors roles and planned an interaction between school counselors and parents, teachers and others as well as setting priorities in how counsellor's tie and skill will be used in a particular school and with particular group of students.

The counselors may prove of immence help to the school in particular and society in general by providing necessary guidance and help to the needy children, who are facing the problem or are prone to the problem in the following manner:

* He should keep a close track on the activities of such children, on daily basis, in all classes when the child moves from one class to another through Daily progress report (DPR) and case study.
* Should identify and teat drug dependency, aggressive behaviour and other bad habits.
* Should enable the student to cope with a wide range of development and social dilemmas.
* Should help the students to plan, choose and succeed in vocational education and in higher education.
* The counsellor's functions in general should include cooperative activity with teachers, the use of group guidance techniques, computer assisted guidance, comprehensive career information system and related methods designed to provide career guidance to all students.

The National Commission on Secondary Education (1984) held the view that the school counselors were important to excellence in vocational education.

In India though he importance of the services of councellors in the field of education is well organized but the face of expansion of school guidance and counselling service far from satisfaction. For example, out of the five schools selected for the present study educational and vocational guidance counselor was found in one school only.

A survey conducted by Perin H. Memta reveals that

only 55.28 per cent (i.e. 504 schools were covered by some kind of guidance service in 1981 and that only 78 counsellors were diploma holders in guidance. Some urgent steps should therefore be taken to provide efficient guidance service in all the schools.

- The counselling function should be discharged by professionally trained counselors.
- The counsellor-student ratio should be about 250 students for counselor, so that they could discharge their duties effectively.
- A separate guidance and counselling room along with all the necessary facilities should be provided to the counselors in every school.
- Relevant literature should be made available to the counselor for his/her small library and proper display on the wall boards of the guidance room.
- Heads of the schools should also be properly oriented about the guidance services, so that they may properly supervise and guide the counselors and may not assign them any other work of the school apart from the work for which they are meant. In other words, they should not be expected to do everything.

Keeping in view the importance of counseling service with regard to the benefit of school children in general and problem children in particular, a clear-cut long term policy for providing guidance serving and provision of sufficient funds by the Govt. for implementing the policy are essential prerequisites. One healthy and happy child will make a healthy and happy nation and no other charge of a Government can be more important than to take care of its children.

The police plays an important role in all the stages of behaviour modification of a delinquent, i.e. during location apprehension, custody, prosecution, treatment and rehabilitation. But their role at the stage of prevention is crucial.

The present study bad social surroundings and bad company have been found as major factors responsible for producing and perpetuating anti-social behaivour amongst the children. Here the police may prove of much help in preventing and controlling the problem directly as well as indirectly – by cleaning all vice-dens. This is very easily possible for then as they have vast resources, sufficient knowledge on the subject of crime and delinquency, reliable information about delinquents as individual, greater exposure and association with the public etc. to accomplish the task.

The anti-social child does not constitute a unique type of human being. They have the same human desires and natural yearnings as anyone else. They are also human beings though the victims of faulty upbringing and poor school and social environment. Therefore, to prevent the children from failing into as such habits and to control and cure those who have already caught into this phenomena, some remedies have been suggested/recommended under this study. In the first place parents should try to provide a congenial atmosphere at home for the child's study and relaxation/recreation, give him his rightful place in the family, show sympathy, love and favourable attitude, provide sense of security, fulfill his basis requirements, make proper supervision along with necessary freedom to the child and keep constantly in touch with the school. The role of school and teachers is equally important in tackling the problem. The school should try to create an environment in which the child can be kept usefully busy and provide all the necessary facilities to him, according to his interest and aptitude, which are helpful in the all round development of his personality. It should seek help and co-operation from the parents and the community.

The teachers command tremendous regard in the heart of students. They should know every child in their classes and should teach and help them wit full sincerity, devotion and affection. Their own attitude, behaviour and personality, should present a model of virtues for the child to emulate. They are really capable of doing miracles if they are willing to do so. The school counellors are trained lots in tackling the problem-children. They should follow a treatment procedure which fits in individual offender and not merely the offence, for which knowledge of working of the mind of the individual offender is very essential. The school counselor can prove to be of immense help in shaping the behaviour of problem children; but still they are found in a very few schools and there too they lack basic facilities for performing their jobs efficiently and skillfully. The education department is, therefore, advised to give this job top priority and allocate necessary funds to post such counselors in all the schools.

The police can also play a very important role in prevention, identification, treatment and rehabilitation of problem children. It can help in improving he social-environment and removing/reforming bad characters-which are the major factors causing the problem of anti-social behaviour. The police should, therefore, be given suitable training in order to bring a change in their attitude and to enable them to do this social defence work with full cooperation from the society and others engaged in this work. Any programme which aims to identify the potential problem at an early age, which tries to study and diagnose needs of the child, before and after the problem and which aims to provide treatment suited to individual diagnosis, may be expected to succeed to a great extent. But this is only possible when all the agencies/institutions and individuals concerned with the welfare of the child make a well knitted and coordinated effort in this direction. The problem of anti-social behaviour amongst the students cannot be successfully tackled unless thorough investigation is made into the causes, leading to this evil not only in resettlement colonies but also in different settlements inhabited by the people of varied socio-economic status.

3

Causes and Conditions of Psychological Etiology

The Alexander and other similar psychiatric classifications limit the dynamics of law violation too narrowly in focusing attention solely upon the neurotic offender. Various other relationships of the individual's subjective states to his misconduct will be considered below. First, however, the neurotic delinquent should be examined more closely. The neurotic offender is usually the product of an atmosphere of over rigid parental restraint, of overprotection and over restriction, frequently of perfectionism and inconsistency; the child's ego lacks the strength to sublimate his impulses into socially acceptable channels. But instead of attempting complete repression, which often leads to ordinary neurotic symptoms of hysteria (such as functional blindness, deafness, lameness, etc). Anxiety, obsessions, or compulsions, the individual here commits offenses which offer release to his only partly inhibited drives. Neurotic delinquency may, as Freud suggested, develop out of a sense of guilt in reference to socially unsanctioned wishes (Oedipal, Homosexual, or heterosexual); the individual may be seeking punishment to dissolve his guilt feelings. Where the impulses are wholly unacceptable to the ego (rather frequently in the homosexual personality, for example), a substituted expression-often itself painfully, repugnant-may be permitted as an unconscious preference. Thus such compulsive offenses as exhibitionism (indecent exposure), voyeurism (peeping), kleptomania (compulsive theft), pyromania (compulsive arson), extreme sadism (erotic pleasure in inflicting pain upon any object), masochism (Pleasure in receiving pain), or other sexually expressive behaviour may reveal the individual's repressed and pervertedly redirected drives). The following cases are illustrative:

The case of Albert Thornley, studied intensively by Ben Karpman and presented in detail frcm the records of his psychoanalytic therapy, illustrates very well the behavior dynamics in a neutotic individual "entangled in a maze of complicated mental states from which criminally sometimes offers an immediate, albeit wholly unfit, means of escape."

Thornley had an extended criminal history, including theft, extortion, fraudulent enlistment in the army, repeated drunkenness, and many minor offenses, though these were only a continuation of the delinquencies which developed in his youth. His problems of adjustment were mainly a product of the distortions in his intrafamilial relationships, serious enough to a lead to series of commitments to psychopathic institutions. A combination of an excessively close attachment to the mother and hate of the father wee at the root of his psychoneurotic and psychopathic trends. Through pout the history one finds repeated evidence of the patient's remarkable emotional attachment to the other, an attachment which influenced much of his subsequent behaviour, as his penchant in later years to associate with women old enough to be his mother. He displayed some insight into this fixation: "A short time after I finished school, my mother died, and when she left us it seemed as though something had gone out o my life and nothing has ever come into if to fill the empty space. Like most boys, I had grown to depend on her for advice; but, unlike many bys, I was more than willing to do what she asked e to do, and perhaps, I Loved her too well." Of his relationship to his father, Thronley cites a traumatic instance:" My parents once had a family quarrel and I ran out of the house and told the neighbors all about it.. After father's return from work, we were sitting down to the evening meal when mother told him what I had done. He said nothing to me during rest of the meal: but immediately afterwards told me to remove my clothes and then tied me to an old bed and started to whip, I have been whipped many times since then, but never like this. Can one imagine how it seemed to a boy scarcely more than a baby to be whipped by one be should love instead of hate? Little did I know that of all the less I have been taught, this one would stay with me long after the other had been forgotten. After this whipping my back was sore for a week, but strange to relate I did not run to my mother when I came downstairs down stairs; I went to a corner, sulked for awhile, and then went to bed where I cried myself asleep."

When Thornley was arrested for a minor offense his father recommended his reform-school commitment; there he learned all he did not already know about crime and sex. In the ensuing years his emotional dependence on the mother he had lost and his psychologically incestuous sexual relationships with older women caused him much pain and anxiety.

"In later years I regretted this trait in my disposition, but I honestly can't help it. I have always felt that a woman with whom I have had intercourse was not worthy of any man's consideration. From this you can see how much I loved my mother, both while she was living and after her death. His own marriage was rather naturally an incompatible failure and contributed to his neurotic escapes. The main reason for his social conflicts appears to have been the degradation of his personality consequent upon the breaking up of the home, allowing him to sink lower and lower in his industrial adjustment, often reaching an impasse at which some sort of antisocial activity seemed to him the only avenue of escape." The compulsive character of the illegal acts committed by some neurotic offenders, particularly where there is a distorted psycho-sexual history, is illustrated by the following excerpt from the public press:"

A lovesick young man, who lit fires to ease the loneliness after bidding his girl good night, was arrested in Newark early yesterday while kindling a flame in the cellar of a Forest Hill home.

Jersey police charged the prisoner, identified as J-S-, with arson, According to police, S-told of having started "at least four fires in Newark since November I." Assistant Police Inspector John Dolan estimated the damage at $20,000. S-was caught starting a blaze in the basement of [a building] by a tenant who was returning to his home after watching another fir ea block away.

The amorous arsonist told the cops he always got lonely after saying good night to his girl friend. He would yearn for some excitement and he'd start the fires to ease the strain and warm himself up inside, the police said. The following case illustrates very well the consequences of an over-rigid training in a "good home" that resulted in a high degree of moral anxiety:

Years ago I was consulted about making plans for a six-year-old girl because she insisted upon being skipped to a higher grade in school although she had started school earlier than the average child. She seemed bored with the low educational standards of the class, and she showed signs of severe social maladjustment. She was born in luxury, the only child of a foreign diplomat. Although the parents had continual social engagements, the mother tried very hard to give the child all the care that she needed. She had a nurse who surrounded the child with loving care and attention. The mother, who was a very intelligent and beautiful woman, emphasized that the child never had given any trouble up to the time of consultation. In fact, Bardber had been "a lady" almost since birth. She never had to be reprimanded, was always compliant. Thee never was a commotion in the nursery. Barbara never indulged in any childish mischief; she was always serious. It was not necessary, the mother stated, to punish Barbara because she always did every thing perfectly. If her mother or her nurse, both of whom she seemed to adore, explained it to her, she would accept everything without opposition. I never could find out how this smooth development could have been brought about in the earliest ego development, when verbal understanding is not yet possible. Indication of deep-seated emotional antagonism between child and mother seemed to have started in the form of a incompatibility at breast feeding. This was both unsuccessful and tormenting to mother and child. Nevertheless the mother continued her deliberate effort to be a model mother. Although Barbara never liked to eat, she made a great effort to consume large amounts of delicious food. If the food were removed, she would be discouraged because she felt people would be dissatisfied if she did not eat it. She was never really forced to eat in an overtly aggressive way, but she was told that she would growing and strong, and wasn't tat what she wanted? In Barbabara's case the unnaturally overprotected, exacting, and polite atmosphere from which aggression in its overt manifestations was completely abolished, compelled the child at a very early age to take, without overt anger or protest, the attitudes and unspoken commands of her environment (in her superego). Thus she had no opportunity to express her aggression and to release her tension in motor manifestations.

Barbara was forced to repress her aggression early and completely, whereas children need a chance to obtain control over their aggression and to repress the motor manifestations gradually and piecemeal. Barbara could not let herself be aggressive, because everybody around her was soft-spoken and mild. The danger of being diametrically different from the environment made her feel to keenly that impulsive behaviour would case loss of love...the ego-ideal erected was beyond what her comparatively weak ego could ever truly hope to live up to. Her ego was further weakened because, in order to keep in check such strong and abruptly executed repressions, she had to put up strong secondary defenses, so-called "reaction formations." She had to be a model child, a little lady. All that was at the expense of her ego, because the psychic energy in such cases is used up n keeping up the defenses instead of being utilized for constructive active functions. Psychoanalysts call this process the impoverishment of the ego...Barbara's ambition was infinite, but ambition is not ego strength. Such ambition is the superego' expectation that the ego achieve miracles. Such an ego gets continually discouraged; the gap between the ideal and the capacity is very wide; the discrepancy is felt as an inner sense of discouragement, dissatisfaction with oneself. This is the anxiety, which Freud called moral anxiety, that is felt as conscious or unconscious guilt. Superego anxiety, in fact, is that type of inner far that characterizes most children with primary behaviour disorders of the neurotic type.

The Psychopathic Delinquent

The Alexander and Staub schema too narrowly limits the varieties of offenders with a psychological eatiology, for there is no doubt that other types of psychogenic influences deserve a more important position that those promoting neurotic delinquency. One additional variety that has been prominent in recent psychiatric and psychoanalytical investigations is the psychopathic personality. The psychopath has been interpreted is the psychopathic personality. The psychopath has been interpreted as definition inhibition through the absence of an effective, coherent superego. He is a most unsocialized aggressive child-cruel, defiant suspicious, egocentric, unfriendly, vindictive, primitive, and hypersexual (or sexually uncontrolled). In extreme manifestations, he shows an utter lack of capacity for sympathy; he is quite without compunction for his ruthless exploitations and injuries to others. Such a person usually comes from a home situation defective in affection and control. He is an unwanted child, unloved, consistently rejected; his response is uninhibited hostility and overt aggressions. Characteristically a deprived person, his most serious deprivations are emotional. Because of the seriousness of his misbehaviour and his lack of identification with others, the psychopath is a difficult problem in treatment; the therapist requires infinite patience to provide him the consistent. Close, and warm understanding a that he needs. His history of rebellious responses to chronic rejection makes it almost impossible to come into touch with him. Usually committed to a disciplinary institution, the psychopath merely becomes more embittered and callous. Even if he receives therapeutic attention, the structure of his personality has ordinarily been too rigidly fixed from his earliest days to achieve much success with him.

Among various writers it has been customary to apply the term "conduct disorders' to the sort of symptomatology found in the psychopathic personality, especially in relation to children. John Van Ophuijsenis quoted in Lewis and Paccella as follows:

It is customary to speak of a conduct disorder whenever there is a deviation from the accepted code of morals. This is why conduct disturbances are also referred to as character disorders; the term, however, includes the "bad" habits and should not be substituted. In accordance with the before-mentioned criterion we find listed as conduct disturbances; lying, truanting, stealing, disobedience, running away, destructiveness, fighting, sexual activities, etc. In typical cases one or more of these disturbances are mentioned as the reason why parents or their substitutes or school authorities seek the help of the psychiatrist or of a child-guidance clinic. The invariably add information to the effect that the child is disobedient, unmanageable, and disrespectful and that the does not respond to punishment or show any sing of guilt. In many cases they also add tat the difficulties started at an early age, at three years of even before. "The child was always bad." Even at that time there was marked disobedience and rebelliousness; even then they had noticed the child's tendency to run away from home, or to lie, or to steal (e.g., pennies from the mother). Sometimes they mention that the child was not punished at first or at least very little, but the story always ends similarly; even severe physical punishment produces no improvement at all...

In the mind of the expert the constant conflict with the environment and the absence of guilt, which characterize every single typical case, very soon begins to appear as two sides of one abnormality. This abnormality seems to lie in what has happened to the child's aggressiveness: he shows much more aggressiveness than the average child in his contact with the environment, i.e., much more external aggressiveness, and he shows much les aggressiveness than the average child in his attitude toward himself, i.e., much less self criticism and reproach, which are the expressions of internalized aggressiveness,. Correlated with this and related to it, the examiner finds a narcissistic self-evaluation. The child appears to think of himself as come thing exceptional, great, strong, a "Big sot," etc., always with the expectation of being able to accomplish his aims regardless of the impediments formed by laws, customs, and moral code.

Abnormal aggressiveness, absence for defective development of guilt feeling, and narcissistic self-evaluation form the triad that characterizes the child with conduct disturbances.

A further contribution to the theory of the psychopath has been made by David M. Levy n his study of types of maternal overprotection, wherein he divides psychopaths into two groups, he indulged and the deprived, each with its somewhat distinct characteristics. It is generally agreed that the parent's rejection of his child is the basis either of indulgence or deprivation, though in the former mechanism, the guilt feelings experienced by the parent produce exaggerated and sporadic reactive efforts to display love. Levy points out that indulged children, undisciplined b their mothers, display infantile demands and expectations, but they are not characterized by emotional shallowness. They are capable of forming warm human relationships, although exploitation is the usual consequence of these relationships with the over protected. The deprived psychopath, on the other hand, is unable to establish identifications with person in his environment because of the emotional coldness that marked his early life. In the absence of sympathetic relationships the psychopath fails to develop a conscience or a capacity for warmth.

The case of Isaac represents the pattern of the psychopath in his typical manifestations; he differs from others mainly in having responded to treatment:

Issac, a boy of fourteen and one-half, with high intelligence, was committed for stealing, truancy, vandalism, sexual perversions and general incorrigibility. He was a handsome boy who always made a good impression until people got to know him; and only child whose mother died and whose father abandoned him when he was two years old. Reluctantly cared for by relatives, he as passed from one branch of the family to another, and finally to an orphan's home. From his very infancy he presented serious behavioural disorders.

In the institution he had no regard for routine or discipline; he made the most unreasonable demands. He was bitter and antagonistic, even to two people whom he processed to like the farmer and his social worker. His pleasure in farm work was encouraged even at the expense of formal school work in which he had no interest. Both these people spent a great deal of time with him remained consistently patient and sympathetic, and made no comment on his general misbehaviour. His poor behavioural was discussed with him when it was directed against these two people. They would stress their desire to continue to be his friends, but would point out that behavioural such as this provoked others into disliking him. Continuous exposure to this kind of handling brought out a good deal of self-blame on his part, and some expression of doubts as to his worth-whileness. He hung to these two contacts and made conscious efforts to see their, advice and to follow their guidance. As he was able to achieve some success in adjusting, higher and higher standards wee presented, and he was stimulated to meet them. The farmer and the social worker frequently shared experiences and ideas about him. These people became no only his ideals, but his conscience.

By the end of the second year he was able to do well, but this past reputation appeared to be against him. He was tried in a new cottage and told exactly why the change was made. Progress was then more rapid, the new cottage parents supplementing his two meaningful friendships.

The social worker then helped the boy reorient himself to his own past. By eliciting memories and piecing them together, the worker was able to help the boy understand that his misconduct was a consequence of his deprivations. He was told that while these explained his bad behaviour, society did not excuse it on that account.

He then became concerned about planning for his future. Farming was his vocational choice. In order to earn admission to a farm school he turned to academic schoolwork with a new interest. He went to a farm school after three years in the institutional an prepared himself there for a job.

He experienced some difficulties on a role but continued to maintain his friendship with the same social worker who helped stabilize him. He succeeded in being reasonably happy and self-supporting. On Dec. 9, 1941 at the age of twenty-one, he felt impelled to enlist in the United States Air Corps, three and one-half years after leaving the institution.

The Functional Psychotic

The functional psychotic deviates more widely from psychological normality than either the neurotic or psychopathic types, but he is also a product of a psychogenic etiology. Schizophrenia (or dementia paradox), the manic-depressive psychosis and paranoia, the major forms of functional psychosis, are found rather frequently among adult offenders. For the most part, however, they are disorders of maturity, less often found in the child and adolescent. In the first-named class of psychosis, however, and more especially in the hebephrenic form of schizophrenia, onset frequently occurs during youth. Hebephrenia usually begins before the age of twenty. Whether in the milder and nonpsychotic manifestations of the schizoid personality or in the more extreme break from reality that constitutes schizophrenia, these individuals tend to be socially unadjusted, withdrawn, and disorganized in their intellectual, emotional, and volitional functioning. They do poorly in school, at work, and generally in their personal relationships. Particularly, however, because of the lack of emotional stability, or integration, and their diminished self-control, these individuals may commit a wide variety of delinquencies. Often detectable in childhood or youth as increasingly disoriented prepsychotics, the excessively introverted schizoid should received early psychiatric treatment; with the progress of the disorder, any form of psychological therapy becomes increasingly difficult until, when he is completely disorganized, only medical help can possibly be effective) (mainly metrazol and insulin shock). Whether or not schizophrenia should in fact be considered psychogenic rather than constitutional in origin is a subject of dispute between the functional and neurological psychiatrists; there are strong evidences, at any rate, that organic changes do accompany the development of the disorder and some experts have attributed the pathology to hereditary origins. Whatever its roots, it constitutes a most serious disorder, not only psychologically, but in the delinquent and criminal manifestians that not uncommonly flow it. This case is illustrative:

A while, native-born American man, twenty-two years of age, single, attended school irregularly, lived a nomadic life, and worked only for short periods in a number of places.

As early as ten years of age, he was the source of a great deal of trouble both in his home and in the school. He rejected parental authority, resented the regulations of the school and was frequently in conflict with the principal, school teacher, and his schoolmates, he quite school at the age of fifteen or sixteen, but doesn't know what grade he had attained.

He had an uncontrollable temper and would become agreed at very slight causes. When agreed, he would leave home, sleep in the park, on the side walk, indoor ways, or go out in to the country. He would return in a and debilitated condition, sometimes after a few days and at other times dirty remaining away for two or more weeks. He was suspicious of his employer and fellow employees and frequently became involved in fistic s well as verbal combat. He would become dissatisfied ad quit or be discharged because of his uncooperativeness.

He had been in conflict with the law on tow occasions previous to the one preceding the psychiatric examination. On one occasions in an altercation he struck a man under the chink knocking him to the side walk, The patient insists the man died of fractured skull sustained from striking the side walk. The other appearance in court was the result of his driving to the adjoining state of Illinois in company with two other men in stolen car.

The offense for which he appeared in court previous to the psychiatric examination was attempted robbery in association with another man. He and his associate attempted to rob a filling station. The police department, having been advised of the possible robbery, had stationed officers in the filling station. When the would-be robbers had stationed officers in the filling station. When the would-be robbers came in, the officers opened fire. The patient's associate was killed, but the patient escaped unhurt. He was tried and sentenced to fifty years in the penitentiary despite the medical testimony, which was to the effect that he had dementia paradox and was limited in mental capacity to a level of high-grade feeble-mindedness.

Because of the customarily later onset, the manic-depressive affective or circular) and paranoiac insanities are less a problem with the juvenile than with the adult offender. But here, too, it is some times possible to diagnose the incipient manic-depressive in the school, the court, or the mental-hygiene clinic, in the moody adolescent whose affective and behavioural states display excessively wide variability. It is the opinion of the experts that the psychosis does not occur in children, but mature adolescents have been found in manic disturbance who are recalcitrant disorderly, rebellious, and aggressive. Similarly with the suspicious and ego-centric paranoid personality, the hazard of a more complete psychotic syndrome may be predicted from the incipient development of delusion a beliefs or the grandiose and persecutory trends a youth may manifest (Apparently no cases have been found of paranoid delusions in children.) Paranoid individuals, through they retain their intellectual powers intact, may be led to aggressive offenses against their imagined pesecutors. Juvenile delinquency is very rarely the product of a fully developed functional psychosis. However onset of mental illness does occur in youth-fairly often in the case of schizophrenia-and may be followed by laws violations resulting from the disturbed function. The following case illustrates the effects of a manic condition in a young man the exaltation and diminished self-criticism of this state commonly lead to this pattern of irregularities, extravagances, practical joking, and sometimes abusive and aggressive behaviour. A young man was charged with a breach of the peace by recklessly discharging a pistol at a ticket collector in a railway station. He had been in the habit of travelling to business every morning by a sub urban train. As a rule, the ticket collector did not ask him to show his season ticket, but on eh morning on which the offence was committed, the ticket was demanded, the patient refused to comply with the ticket collector's request, and when the latter insisted, the patient flew into a range and in a loud imperious voice demanded how the ticket collector dared ask a gentleman of his standing for his ticket when he knew quite well that he had a season ticket. When the ticket collector persisted in his demand for the ticket, the patient produced what after wards was discovered to be a toy pistol which made a loud explosion when it was forced, and discharged it in the direction of the railway official, who, thinking that his life was in danger, fled down the platform.

When examined by a psychiatrist, the patient was over talkative and exalted. He related with great pride and satisfaction the trick he had played upon the ticket collector, and also told of other practical jokes of a similar nature which he had recently carried out. For instance, on one occasion he told how he had thrown a bag of flour at a friend 9whoc was dressed up to go to a wedding) while they were both traveling in the same railway compartment.

The patient was clear in his mind. He had no delusions, and his memory and his intellectual functions were not in any way impaired. It was quite clear, however, that his behaviour was greatly influenced by his exalted mood; that his offence was the direct outcome of mental illness

The offender in the following case displayed paranoid trends inschizophrenia, which were primarily responsible for the murder he committed:

A young man twenty-two years of age was charged with murdering his sweetheart by striking her on the head with an iron bar. His history showed that there was no history of mental illness in his family. He was dully at school, and his teachers noticed that he was very timid and easily frightened. He worked for a time as an office boy, and later he obtained a post as an assistant store man in an engineering shop, which he held until his arrest. His parents had noticed that his behaviour had been peculiar for years. He had always been extremely as social and reticent. He spoke very little at home and when visitors came to the house, he either stayed in a corner by himself or he left the room. Before he left the house, he was in the habit of looking to make sure there was no one in the street. If he saw anyone standing near his house, he would turn back and wait until he could go out unobserved.

He had also been observed by his parents to stand in front of a mirror, partly undressed, grimacing, talking to himself, and masturbating. He had a violent explosive temper. Some time before his arrest, in the course of an argument with his mother, he picked up the pocket and struck her on the leg. On another occasion his sister criticized the manner in which he was cutting bread, and the patient rushed at her with the break knife and attempted to stab her.

Another member of the family described the patient as "the kind of chap you never knew what he would do if her got into a temper." "His mind seemed to be miles away from the conversation."

A neighbour described how she had looked upon the patient as queer, and how she had seem him laughing to himself, and how at times when she met him in the street he would greet her cordially; at other times he would pass her without recognition. She had noticed that sometimes when he was walking along the street, he would take a curious little run. His employer thought that he was below the average intelligence. He had noticed that he was inclined to be dreamy, and that he seemed to have difficulty in grasping instructions. He was very moody, and given to violent outbursts of temper in which his language was obscene and threatening.

When examined, the patient was clear in his mind. His memory seemed unimpaired, and he was able to give an account of his history and of the events connected with his crime. He professed great affection for the girl he had killed, but he said that for some time he had been very disturbed in his mind because she would not agreed to marry him. She seemed fickle, and he felt that she had him "dangling on a string." It occurred to him that if he gave her "a fright" it would bring her to her senses, and so for some time before he killed her, he was in the habit of carrying an iron bar in his pocket with which he intended to threaten her when a suitable opportunity occurred.

On the night when the crime was committed he met the girl. He had the iron bar in his pocket. They ha a quarrel, and the girl said that she would not gout with him any more. She laughed at him in a scornful way. He struck her on the head with the iron bar which he had brought with him, and after that he said that he "lost his head completely." The patient's manner was very childish. He showed a complete lack of appreciation of the seriousness of his position. He said that when he saw any one bending down in the street, he had an impulse to strike him on the head. He also said that sometimes he go t out of bed in the middle of the night to look at himself in the mirror. He said that his own family regarded him as peculiar, and that his brother and sister sometimes called him "looney." While in prison awaiting trial, he developed further symptoms of mental disorder. He was observed to laugh and to talk to himself. He made peculiar gestures and grimances in a foolish way. He complained that the prisoners and the warders were talking about him and commenting about the shape of his nose, and he expressed the fear that he would be attacked. He said that he had written a song which he was going to submit to a composer for his opinion.

Emotional Disturbance and Intra-familiar Tensions

Finally and the most important of the among the classes of psychological etiology that motivate delinquency, there are the psychological etiology that motivate delinquency, there are the affective responses of the individual to the thwarthing of basic needs in his personality. Emotional insecurity, feelings of inadequacy and inferiority, affectional undernourishment, extreme submissive or aggressive responses to rigid domination, these are among the common denominators not only of personal unadjustment but behavioral disorder and delinquency as well. The child needs an adequate and wholesome outlet for the expression of is psychic drives and wishes; as W.I. Thomas as pointed out, he requires particularly some satisfying implementation of his social drives or "wishes." Frustration of these basic psychological demands or the impossibility of securing socialized satisfactions may channelize them into law violative activity. Lack of affection and security easily lead to sexual delinquency, to theft, and incorrigible behaviour in children. Too, delinquencies provide an easy and often very full and exciting outlet for the boys' demands for status and adventure. If he lacks normal gratification in he home, school, and church, a child may discover in delinquency a fulfillment of his wishes beyond anything his moral elders can provide; and once a course of illegal conduct has been established in discharge of his psychic wants, their redirection into social sanctioned patterns is often very difficult.) The first case below illustrates the possible results of deprivation of security and affection:

Joe, aged fourteen, was referred to the juvenile court for stealing. He and a friend a year older had stolen guns, camping equipment, and an assortment of other articles, including a typewriter and fill in cards. The material had been taken over a period of months and had been stolen from various houses and stores, Joe, when questioned, explained that they had planned a hideaway in the woods for storage of the goods until they could be sold, Joe was obviously not the leader but he had been greatly intrigued with the details for their business venture. The typewriter had been taken from the school library so that all materials might be properly catalogued.

A study of the home disclosed that Joe was the older of two brothers. The father, an office worker, had shown little interest in him but had centred his whole affection upon the brother who was a year and a half younger than Joe and a quiet, confident child who felt secure in his position in the family. Joe was talkative, moody, and resentful by turns at home. At school he was smiling and popular, receiving high grades in his work. The mother had been a music teacher before her marriage and music was still her only great interest. One showed considerable ability along that line an his mother continually nagged him to practice on the piano. Both parents believed in strict discipline but disagreement in regard to methods led to constant bickering and inconsistent treatment of both boys. The father enforced his demands through threats and whipping while the mother scolded and entreated.

Joe, feeling insecure in the home and rebelling at the whole situation, readily accepted the plan of escape into the woods. On first contact with the probation officer he assumed a hostile attitude, reaction as he had towards his parents. When the probation officer ignored the challenge and asked him how he thought he could make the best of the difficult he was in, he appeared surprised, but he discussed his problems in a mature manner and offered constructive suggestions. He would work in the school library to pay for the material taken. He would spend his time reading in the evening, since the court restrictions would not allow him to go out. He did not like to be treated like a kid and if his parents would trust him with a gun he could go hunting with his uncle. He like music and he had been thinking about joining the glee club at school, but the wouldn't tell his mother so.

This study, from the cases of the Chicago institute for Juvenile research, reveals a delinquency ensuring largely from the desire for adventure and recognition:

When I was eight years old, I did my first job in the racket. This job was the biggest thrill I ever got in my life. It happened in April. That day I Was hanging around with the oldest brother and his gang. They had been playing baseball all afternoon and I was watching them.

When it got too dark to play ball well went into the alley to have a smoke and tell stories. The big guys got to talking about stealing, and my brother said he had good place spotted where he could get some easy "dought." The place was a butcher shop in thirty-first Street. The big guys planned everything, and I only listened. These guys were seven or eight years older than me and had pulled off a lot of big jobs before. They would never let me go with them on big jobs; but this might I went along and they didn't say a word We all when to the butcher shop about 11.30 o'clock. It was very dark and everything was quiet, and I was nervous and stayed close to my brother and another big guy went up to the building to see if the doors were unlocked. My brother had been in the place a few days before to see how to get in and where the cash register was; and so he led the way. I and two other guys waited close to the alley between two buildings. We were going to give "jiggers."

In a little white my bother came back and said everything was locked tight. The owner live over the butcher shop so we couldn't make much noise by breaking the glass or jimmy the door. We all went up to the back door, and then my brother got a box and stood on it and tried the transom and it opened. It was too little for my brother or the other guys to get through. Then I was thrilled when they said I'd have to crwawl through the transom. That was the kick of my whole life.

I was only eight and always was very little, so I could get through the transom easy. I was scared but made up my mind to go through anyway. I was too thrilled to say no. My brother lifted me up on his shoulders and I crawled through the transom. I hung down on the inside and stood on an icebox and then crawled down on the floor. The door was looked with a padlock and chain, but I was able to unlock the window and let the bi guys in that way. The big guys looked for money first and found $22. Then we all got everything we wanted to eat and several cartons of cigarettes and ditched the place.

When we got out, my brother divide up everything and I got $4 and a lot of cigarettes. I felt like a "Big shot" after that night and the big guys said could go with them every time they went Robbin." Almost every night we went robin." And many times I had to craw through transoms and one time through an icebox hole. That's hole. That' why they big guys called me he "baby bandit." The significance of the role of emotional discomforts, of the frustration of basic psychological needs, which so commonly reflects affective inadequacies in the child's home, has been given all too little attention in etiological research because of the preoccupation with the objective factors in the environment and the more behaviours traits of personality. John Dollard, However, has attributed a primary importance to the mechanism of frustration and consequent aggressive reaction s against the environment." The pattering emphasized in his work is a crucial determinant of delinquency in many cases, but this explanation is too pat in its simplicity for universal applicability. Healy and Bronner's more analytical investigation of the diverse chancelling of emotional requirements that may be thwarted in the family and of the valid reactive mechanisms that reflect the psychic-constitutional differences among children responding to their equal various situational milieux provides a more adequate appraisal. This research is considered in some detail below, with its implications for the psychological and social influences upon misconduct.

Intrafamiliar Tensions

In their work New Light on Delinquency and Its Treatment, William Healy and Augusta Bronner have expounded a theory of delinquent behaviour based upon psychological, psychiatric, and casework investigation. Although the sample of offenders selected for study was small (153), it nevertheless constituted an excellent group for the purposes of their study, since it represented delinquents in three cities (Boston, New Haven, and Detroit), studied clinically by three teams of experts (psychiatrists, psychologists, and psychiatric case workers) who pursued their analyses far more intensively and extensively than is customary in etiological research. The cases selected all had non-alignments siblings to whom comparison could be made as a control group with social back grounds similar to those of the offender sample. So selected, these cases did not make up a representative sample of delinquents. This limitation was not of primary importance, however, since the main purpose of the study was not o describe a typical group of offenders, but to analyze in depth the conduct motives and resultant in delinquents and to discover the differences marking their nondelinquent brothers whose general situational patterns in the home were similar. Thus it was hoped that more light might be thrown on the significant, but in the main obscure, problem, why two or more children in the same family, exposed to roughly similar influences, should behave very differently. The study has the additional virtue of putting its analytical findings into numerical terms for comparison with the nondelinquent brothers and with other samples of offenders. Thus combining the virtues of careful ongitudinal and cross-sectional research and permitting subsequent check by ofter investigators on the accuracy of their finings and the validity of their conclusions.

To limited extent the observations made in this research overlap the analyses of other students who have found causation in both individual and social factors. This study, however, highlights, as does the procedure of the psychiatric clinic itself, the interrelationship between the two categories of influence, their inseparability in the process of causation. Thus the study finds, and attributes an important significance to the deleterious social factors that appeared in man of the cases: In only twenty-two instances of their 153 delinquents did they find the child living in a favourable situation as to the following:

1. Reasonably good home conditions from the standpoint of stability, living conditions, normal recreational opportunities.
2. Reasonably good family attitudes from the standpoint of avoidance of friction, rational treatment of children, and being law abiding
3. Neighborhood not distinctly bad from the standpoint of inimical influences.

In only nineteen additional cases were two of thee categories of influences favourably. They found evidence of the importance of these situational variables in the fact that there were significantly fewer cases (a proportion of one to nine) of multiple delinquency in the family, when the family and neighbourhood conditions were favourable.

The workers also investigated the a subjective personality factors in the sample an offered striking data on developmental history, psychological deviations, and physical habits in contrasts drawn between the delinquents and the controls. These gave rater clear evidence of the relevance of constitutional and psychological factors in the making of the delinquent, revealing the much higher frequency of defect and disorder among the delinquents.

These findings as to social and individual circumstances add confirmation to the discoveries by other scholars of frequently recurring elements in delinquent histories. However, this study proceeds further to focus attention upon the emotional adjustments of the offenders, the quality of their subjective responses to the external milieu. Considerably more striking than the data above was their observation that 91 per cent of the delinquents suffered from major emotional disfunbances, 75 per cent displayed a marked antipathy to parents fro to school, whereas only 13 per cent of the no delinquents experienced any form profound emotional distress. The main forms of maladapted affective responses among 143 delinquents accepted as cases for treatment were these.

— Deep feigns of being thwared in self-expression and other self-satisfactions—45 cases

— Feelings of being rejected, unloved, or insecure in affectional relationship –53 cases

— Marked feelings of inadequacy r inferiority in some situations or activities—62 cases

— Emotional disturbances abut family disharmonioes, discipline, etc.—43 cases

— Great persisting sibling jealousy or rivalry—43 cases

— Deep-set internal emotional conflicts-19 cases

An unconscious sense of guilt and feeling of need for punishment-discovered in 11 cases.

Healy and Bronner conclude, after detailed analysis and comparison of their cases and controls, that the delinquents, more often thwarted, rejected, and disturbed, find substitutive satisfaction for their psychological needs in channels that lead to delinquency. The nondelinquents, less often from vicious homes and rarely disturbed emotionally, express their less distorted needs in socially acceptable ways, without excessive or escape techniques. Their greater docility and lesser gregariusness, as revealed in the study, facilitated outlets and reactive manifestations of their needs that are socially defined as moral and legal. Evidence for the soundness of this theory that delinquency is a channel from is directed drives is presented in abbreviate case history comparisons. The following is enlightening particularly as to the combination of constitutional and emotional influences.

There were eight pairs of nonidentical twin in the Healy and Bronner sample. IT was hoped that through this group they might uncover factors that would permit better prognostication of delinquency. Conceivably, what with the similarities between the twins, the differences significant for delinquency might be segregated. Here again, however, they could find no clearer composite for prediction than the combination of abnormal personality with deeply felt thwartings and inimical family situations. These twin studies also pointed up the close relationship between emotional disturbance and the onset or continuation of delinquency. This case is illustrative:

We may begin with our six-year-old twins. Although so young the delinquent had already definitely run away twice and on numerous occasions had wandered from home, having been picked up by the police several times. On one occasion he made a serious attempt to set the house on fire. He was a truant from school and had repeatedly stolen, even considerable amounts, from teachers as wells from his parents. He had also stolen money from a neighbour's apartment, a hospital, and a gasoline station Moreover, his parents complained of his disobedience, impudence to his mother, and his temper tantrums. In general, he was regarded as being extremely trouble some at school and incorrigible home. The control was an eve-tempered, obedient, thoroughly well-behaved 'model child."

The twins in this family of three children were the result of a welcomed pregnancy; the control was born first and without instruments; the delinquent was delivered by instruments during a difficult labour. They weighed about six pounds each; they were both bottle-fed from the time o birth. The delinquent was a fussy crying baby; the control was not. They both had an uneventful health history and were of about equal size and in good physical condition at the time of our study; they both exhibited occasional enuresis, but neither had any nervous habits. Our psychologists gave the delinquent an intelligence rating of I.Q. 82, commenting that probably he would have done considerably better if his attention could have been fully held. The I.Q. of the control was 95. The summing up of the personality characteristics of the delinquent shows that was exceedingly restless, active, impulsive, uninhibited, continually running off to play with other boys, among whom he was regarded as a follower. He frequently acted as a "show off," being specially delighted with the attention he received because he was such a small boy when he was held in the detention home for a new days, and he was especially proud of his grinning picture in the newspapers, which had appeared once after he bad been found by the police. At home he was said to be extraordinarily inquisitive, "into every thing". In the physical examination he appeared to have some shame about his body.

The control was an amenable, pleasant youngster, much quieter, self-reliant, and easily amused at home, preferring to be with his mother rather than to play with other boys, although he did sometimes gout to play.

The family lived in crowded quarters, but there was no great financial stress. Earlier they had lived in better homes and in decent neighbourhoods, though they moved much because the father frequently sold the home. The parents were thoroughly in compatible, engaged in much open quarreling and often, been before the children, made counter accusations and threatened divorce. There was violent disagreement about discipline; the mother charged her high tempered husband with whipping too severely and he maintained that although she was rather well educated, she was really dull, incompetent, and too lenient.

An amazing difference of attitude on the part of the father towards the delinquent and the control was reported to us and acknowledged by him. He maintained that the cause of it was the stubborn lack of response to him shown by the delinquent when an infant, only two months old. He said he detested they boy then and had ever since—"I can't bear to have him touch me. I would rather have a snake around me than have him." Though the mother stated that the father always repulsed the boy when the latter attempted to climb on his knee, both parents insisted that the child had never given expression to any strong feelings about being is liked by his father.

The older boy of eight had been very jealous of the twins from the time of their birth and cruel to them. He suffered from epileptic attacks for two years and afterward simulated attacks in order to gain attention. Though particularly hating our delinquent, or perhaps because of this hatred, he entered into delinquencies with him and inducted him into sex practices. Asia result of frequent beatings and the family disturbances, this older boy had emotional tensions of his own and, besides, gave evidences of being an epileptic personality.

Both the delinquent and the control had plenty of toys and at times had a playroom to themselves. They both went to Sunday school fairly regularly and willingly. The delinquent freely unburdened himself to the psychiatrist, telling many of his delinquencies, some of which were not known. About stealing a considerable sum from his teacher, he said rather demurely that his dad had to pay it back. In childish fashion he told of "other kids" inciting him to set the house on fire. His story included "another boy" with a name Similar to his own- "a bad boy" "He was mad at my dad and set the house on fire. Then I was afraid, and we got the first mostly out b stepping on the curtains before the firemen came." He went on to give in the plainest language the vile epithets which his father called him and also the equally opprobrious terms that his parents applied to each other. He showed much feeling about all this, saying that he was going to hit his father "right on the chin" some day. He also evidenced great dislike of his older brother and shame about their sex play together. The control, he said never did such things. It came out very clearly that the boy felt extremely insecure in his family relationships and that he greatly created recognition and affection.

The control, on the contrary, was very sure of himself and quite well satisfied with things as they were. In speaking of his brother to the psychologist he priggishly boasted, "I am the good boy."

New Light on Delinquency and Its Treatment has been criticized on the ground that "emotional disturbances" are too vaguely defined and too easy to discover in or project upon a sample of individuals known to be offenders. Here one encounters the familiar and apparently inescapable problem discussed in Chap. III: in any investigation of cause, whether case history (or other longitudinal method) or statistical (cross-sectional), one must rely on the observations of imperfect investigators. It is true, more cover, that this study focuses attention on subtile variables of feeling and relationship that do not lend themselves to easy or exact measurement. While ship that do not lend themselves to easy or exact measurement. While it must be recognized that clinicians do operate with such intangibles an undoubtedly with certain biases implicit in their frames of reference, yet this study must be accredited with an unusual amount of case in the analysis and comparison of the delinquents an their controls. Here the expertly trained investigators were looking for no single factor or set of factors; they sought widely, intensively and empirically, it appears, for any deficiencies and advantages that might be discovered as significant in distinguishing the etiologies of delinquent and nondelinquent. Though the size and selection of their sample limitstatistical validity, the study was primarily concerned with the dynamics of the individual offender, not description of the mass. Further studies of this sort, costly as they are, and badly needed to extend knowledge of causal processes. But the conducting of this study in more than one community with a number of experts functioning independently in the investigation lends additional weight to the Healy and Bronner conclusion, it is improbably that their observations could be the product of similar consistently erroneous diagnoses by a series of trained psychiatrists, clinical psychologists, and psychiatric social workers. This provides a check of internal consistency, although the authors did not exploit it in proof of their findings. Their research has been an excellent corrective to the simplified and particularistic explanations that still permeate thinking on causation. The skepticism of situationalists about the accuracy of psychological observation, however, will not be dissolved either by this study or repeated studies of this sort, it would seem. You may count broken homes, unemployed fathers, slum dwellings, I.Q's, grade retardation, etc., fairly precisely in delinquency description, whereas the subjective reaction states associate with the environment are less tangible.

REFERENCES

Bhadury, J. et. al., "Some negative correlates of Anti-social Behaviour", *Indian Journal of Criminology*, Vol. 15. No. 1, January 1987.

Mosavi, S.M., "Emotions and their utility forTeacher" *Education*, 44 (5) May, 1965.

Herr, L. Edwin, "The Relevant Counsellor," *The School Counsellor*, Vol. 34. No. 1 September, 1986.

Shea, T.M. *Teaching Children and outh with Behavior Disorders*, Saint Louis: The C.V. Mosby Co, 1978.

Rogers, C.R. *Clinical Treatment of the Problem Child*, Boston: Hougton and Mifflin, Co. 1939.

Shanmugam, T.E. *Juvenile Delinquency*, Madras: University of Maras, 1979.

4

Evaluation of Pupil Qualities and Characteristics of Educational Psychology

Some other activities can be observed by an experimenter's instrument. A doctor can observe the activities of your heart by means of an electrocardiograph. You are angry at something or Somebody. You alone know what it feels like to be angry. Or, you praise your student for some good work. He alone knows what it feels like to be praised. An individual has his own *Conscious experiences.* He has his own joys and sorrows, private thoughts and dreams, of which he himself is aware. These are Conscious mental processes. The individual can make a verbal report of his conscious experiences. Thus, conscious mental processes are accessible to others through verbal report or by way of inference from other behaviour. Any form of reporting on subjective conscious events or experiences is *introspection.* Included within behaviour are verbal reports made about subjective conscious experiences. A process is a series of activities. Besides conscious mental processes, *unconscious mental processes* exist in us. Generally, we are not aware of them. They are not readily accessible to voluntary control. They may prove harmful if we become aware of these unconscious mental activities.

The contents of the unconscious come from two sources. A part of it are the individuals inheritance. They are primitive brutal ideas and strivings that have never been conscious. The second part consists of buried thoughts, emotions and impulses, memories and wishes that were once conscious but have been pushed back into the hinterland of the mind because they were too shocking, painful or shameful to tolerate. While the conscious mental activities are internally consistent, the unconscious mental activities are internally chaotic. From the discussion carried on so far, all the activities of an individual are classified as observable activities, conscious mental processes and unconscious mental processes.

Thus, psychology is the systematic study of the fundamental laws that govern the observable activities and the conscious and unconscious mental processes of an individual. To serve our purpose, we may take into account two definitions of Psychology. One: "Psychology can be defined as the science of the activities of the individual." To define education is not that easy. Complexity of human nature and environment, different schools of psychology and philosophy, different political ideologies and cultures lead to different definitions of education, ultimately turning it into a rainbow. The existing definitions we come across are too broad or too narrow; each definition is tinged by a particular 'ism' or it emphasizes a particular aspect. While some believe education to be a life-long process, others limit it to instruction and training in the academic institutions. When Gandhiji speaks of education as, "By education, is mean an all-round drawing out of the best in the child and man—body, mind and spirits," he emphasizes upon the inner potentialities of the individual. On the other hand, when Dewey say, "Education I the development of all those capacities in the individual which will enable him to control his environment and fulfil his responsibilities," he emphasizes upon the social and environmental aspects of education.

What we need is a sharp and precise definition of education, useful and it possible, functional in nature that should fit in the theoretical framework of the present text. Of course, Peters (1967, p.1) impresses upon us the difficulties involved in aiming at such a definition of education when he says: "in exploring the concept of education a territory is being entered where there are few signposts. To use Ryle's phrase, the 'logical geography' of concepts in the area of education has not yet been mapped...'education' is a concept which is not very close to the ground. Yet, we have to choose a definition to suit our purpose.

So, *'education' is a "Concept"*. "Equality," "justice," "democracy" "education"—all these are concepts. When a symbol stands for a class of objects, events or ideas with common properties or relationships, we say that it refers to a *Concept.* "Vegetable" is a concept based on common elements. "Equality" is a concept based on common relations. Concepts may be of concrete things, for example, the concept "stallion" refers to a given variety of horse. They may be of abstract ideas, for example, "equality, "justice," "mass", implying relationships common to many different kinds of objects or ideas. (Hilgard et al., 1976, p. 273 & p. 602). To express the same things in a different way, A Concept expresses an abstraction formed by generalisation from particulars. "Weight" is a concept; it expresses numerous observations of things that are more or less "heavy" or "light'. A Concept that interests us much is "achievement," it is an abstraction formed from the observation of certain behaviours of children. These behaviours are associated with the mastery or "learning' of different school tasks—reading words, doing arithmetic problems and drawing pictures. The various observed behaviours are put together and expressed in a word – "achievement."

A definition consists of a statement of equivalence between the concept to be defined and a set of other concepts whose meanings is presumed to be known on other grounds. This means, we can define one concept with other concepts. For instance, we can define "weight" by saying that it is the "heaviness" of objects. Or we can define "anxiety" as "subjectified fear." In both cases we have substituted one concept for another. First, education is a "*human enterprise*." It is confined to human beings only and has nothing to do with inanimate objects, plants or animals. Man is distinguishable from all other things, both living and non-living on account of his special nature. We can train a dog but we cannot educate it. We can surely educate a human being.

Second, education is a "*process.*" It is not a thing which persons possess or which is a part of them. You can possess a pen or have black hair, but not education. Even knowledge, skill or character are not in themselves education. They stand as evidence that one has been educated. Education is not a thing but a process. It is a kind of activity or a series of activities in relation to human beings. To educate a boy or girl is to engage him or her in a process. If you say, you 'have an education', it means that you have undergone a process. Thus, education is a "*person-related process.*"

What kind of person-related process education is? Third, education is concerned with the "*development*" of human beings as persons—physical, mental, emotional and social development. It is a process involving personal becoming, and growth resulting from personal experience. It is concerned with the real an in- most nature of the person. The process of acquiring property or becoming famous is not education. Education is a process of personal growth or learning and also a process of bringing about changes in people for good.

Not all processes involving human development are education. Genetically determined growth, that is, maturation is not education. A need is a state of tension forcing a person to activity; but it is not education. Education is only those processes which *guide, direct* or *fashion* personal becoming. Education requires an educative agent acting upon the person to be educated. Therefore, fourthly, education is an "*interactive, bipolar process.*" From this it is obvious that this definition of education does not include in it a view of education as a process of unfolding the innate potentialities of a person already present but not apparent.

Pets do help to fashion children's growth as persons. The physical environment of human beings also guides their learning. But the proposed definition of education does not include these as educational agencies. According to it education is restricted to the *direction, by persons*, of personal development. That is to say, the only admissible agencies for education are human beings. Included in such personal agencies is the self. The individual can direct his personal development. This is called *self-education.* It was sated that education is an interactive bipolar process. It is the nature of the self to be bipolar. It has the ability to carry on an internal dialogue. The philosopher or the scientist often does converse with himself. The dialogue may be within one person and if it is both solitary and silent, it becomes *reflection.* All reflective thoughts are inner dialogues. As such, the fifth qualification of the proposed definition is that education is a "*process by persons.*"

Finally, the qualification that completes the definition is that the direction which persons give is "*intentional*" or '*deliberate.*" Friends influence us in many ways; but such influences do not come under education. If a friend deliberately seeks to direct the development of his companion as a person, he becomes an educator. Not all intentional directing of persons can be education. The traffic policeman intentionally directing the automobile driver to slow the speed or take a turn or stop is not education. Such direction does not bring about the growth of the driver as a person. The intent is to get the traffic move smoothly. Only those deliberate processes of directing which are intended to influence personal growth and learning fall within the definition of education.

Thus, the definition of education which has been developed step by step is: "*Education is the process whereby persons intentionally guide the development of persons.*" (Phenix, 1966, p. 13).

This definition of education fits in ell with the theoretical framework of the present Text; and hence it is accepted without any reservation.

Educational Psychology

Psychology is the science of human behaviour and mental processes; and Education is a person-related developmental process, interactive, directional and deliberate. From these two definitions, can we not deduct the *nature and functions* of Educational Psychology?" A student jumped upon his feet and asked: "But how?" The teacher said: "I withhold the answer for the present."

At birth the child brings his biological inheritance with him into the world and comes in contact with an environment. The environment is saturated with social culture. The characteristics of the biological heredity of the child, in themselves are not sufficient to enable him to develop harmoniously in the social culture around him. He has to be helped in acquiring the skills, information, concepts and attitudes concerning his social heritage. Therefore, society provides a variety of educational institutions to stimulate and nourish his development as he grows and learns. The child has to be socialised. Education is a process of socialisation through which he has to be socialised.

"A half century of research has given us a very different picture of the nature of the child from that held in earlier periods. The following brief summary....outlines the essentials of the modern point of view. (1) The child is a growing organism who moves by infinite small changes from a single cell to a complex organisation of structure and function at an adult level....(2) The child is a spatially separated unit that functions as an organised whole in the situations he meets...(3) The child lives in a context, itself neither simple nor unitary, which continuously effects his behaviour and development...(4) The child is engaged in an ongoing process of development that is not reversible." (Carmichael, Ed., 1968, p. 3).

Throughout the history of education, scholars have set forth challenging theories and view points on the problems of growth and learning of the child whose nature is stated above from the modern point of view. The beginnings of educational psychology are to be found within these. A lot of the theoretical frame-work that educational psychology incorporates in it, perhaps originated in the classroom where the teachers were confronted with problems relating to the pupils.

Educational psychology is an applied psychology. It is especially concerned with the application of methods and principles of psychology to human behaviour in educational situations.

"Although educational psychology is a relatively new science, its aims and content have become fairly defined. The aims set forth by a committee into the late 40's are still appropriate today."

"Educational Psychology is concerned primarily with the study of human behaviour as it is changed or directed under the social process of education, and secondarily with those studies of processes that contribute to an increased understanding of how behaviour is changed and directed through education." (Garrison, et al., 1967, p. 5).

Educational psychology is the systematic study of educational growth or development. In the study of educational psychology we try to ascertain the nature of educational growth, to learn its typical features, and the forces which affect it. Educational psychology is an area of knowledge, an application of methods and principles of psychology, and a field for continued study and research.

General psychology and educational psychology are dissimilar in that educational psychology selects and employs certain data from the general field. The major contribution of psychology to education lies in providing a scientific foundation for the art of teaching. The primary aim of educational psychology is to contribute to an understanding of sound educational practices. Its primary concern is to promote the development of professional insights into the principles underlying the teaching art.

"Educational psychology provides the psychological foundations for education in somewhat the same way that physics provides the foundations for structural engineering ....educational psychology contributes to the foundations of education by providing an approach to educational problems, as well as a set of techniques for studying children and the problems that arise in their education. It similarly offers information concerning the developmental, learning and adjustmental processes of children. Educational psychology also provides the skills and techniques required to acquire additional original information, as well as to evaluate and interpret the research findings of others. It consists primarily of a point of view, a body of information, and a group of techniques and procedures." (Sawrey & Telford, 1964, pp. 3-4).

In the passage quoted above, the authors emphasize on an important point, that is educational psychology is chiefly concerned with the development, learning and adjustment of children. Blair, et al., do the same thing when they say: "The teacher who would successfully guide the development, learning and adjustment of children must (1) possess a comprehensive and integrated set of psychological principles which explain human behaviour, (2) possess a technique for studying the individual child in order to determine which principles explain his behaviour in a given situation, and (3) be able to analyse his own teaching and learning procedures." (Blair, et al., 1966, p. 9).

The most acceptable statement of the relationship of psychology to the field of education is that psychology makes it clear that rules don't work in educational practices; what is right in one situation is, as often as not, wrong in the next. And educational psychology is oriented towards the application of the principles and techniques of psychology to the solution of the problems of the classroom. "Kelly has analysed the task of educational psychology into nine different purposes which may be condensed as follows: (1) to give a knowledge of the nature of the child; (2) to give an understanding of the nature, aims and purposes of education; (3) to give an understanding of the scientific methods and procedures which have been used in arriving at the facts and principles of educational psychology; (4) to present the principles and techniques of learning and of teaching; (5) to give training in the methods of measuring abilities and achievement in school subjects; (6) to give a knowledge of the growth and development of children; (7) to assist in the better adjustment of children and to help to prevent their maladjustment; (8) to study the educational significance and the control of the emotions; and (9) to give an understanding of the principles and techniques of character training" (Ellis, 1966, p. 7).

To summarise the discussions carried on so far in the words of G. Lester Anderson:

"(1) Educational Psychology is focused upon the human behaviour. (2) It is a body of facts or information that has resulted from observation and investigation. (3) This body of knowledge can be summarised or generalised into principles or theories. (4) Educational psychology has developed a methodology by which investigations are made, information is discovered, hypotheses are tested and theories are derived. (5) This methodology is useful in arriving at the solution of educational problems as they present themselves. (6) This information, this knowledge, these principles and this methodology constituting the substance of educational psychology, provide a base for educational theory and educational practice."

Educational Psychology draws material from different other branches of psychology, namely, general psychology, experimental psychology, child psychology, clinical psychology, developmental psychology, the psychology of motivation, learning and personality, abnormal psychology, psychological statistics, social psychology and the like, and employs them in solving educational problems. It helps the teachers make wise decisions in their search for solutions to different problems both inside and outside the school. Wide scale research is conducted in the teaching of different school subjects, measurement and evaluation of pupil qualities and characteristics, special education for exceptional children, guidance practices, remedial programmes and social psychology of the classroom. Educational psychology has contributed as much to general psychology as it has had occasion to borrow.

Educational psychology as an applied science is not directly concerned with educational goals. However, in atleast three ways it helps the teacher and school better handle the objectives provided by educational philosophy and society. (1) It helps define these objectives operationally, that is, to translate them into terms of implied action and measurement. (2) It provides experimental methods and evidence yielded thereform as to how objectives may be achieved. (3) It gives various means whereby the attainment of aims can be measured.

"The role of educational psychology in education may be summarised as follows: (1) to evaluate educational theories; (2) to study and evaluate contemporary practices in education; (3) to evaluate different methods of teaching in the light of established principles of learning and motivation; (4) to help teachers solve their personal problems; and (5) to furnish methods to help those engaged in the scientific study of problems in the general area of education psychology." From the discussions carried on so far, it is obvious that the teacher who has a good grounding in the field of educational psychology finds a rationale for the problems he faces and for the decisions he must make.

Teachers Help of Psychology

All other educational problems revolve around the main three—development, learning and adjustment of children. In order to guide these three successfully, the teacher must know children individually, know a set of well formulated psychological principles and know where and how to use these principles. The teacher's position is similar to that of the medical practitioner who must first study his patient before prescribing for him; and a correct diagnosis is needed for a correct prescription. The most important single factor underlying the success of a teacher is his personality and ability to relate it to the class. The best reminder he should take with him into his classroom is that learning is effective to the extent that it involves the goals and purposes of individual children. The teacher's major contribution to the maximum self-realisation of the child is best effected through sensitivity to pupils' needs, goals and purposes. Educational psychology assists the teacher to develop competence in studying children, in utilizing psychological principles, and in evaluating his own teaching methods.

Within the school, there are three main tasks of the teacher to perform. The teacher's task can be described under three broad categories.

Before he enters into the class to teach, or outside the class to help the children under his care, the teacher first has to *select and organise the material to be learned*, "Material to be learned" may include learning a date in history, reading a lesson in language, map reading in geography, typing or riding a bicycle, even learning attitudes, interests or a system of values. Certain material or experience will be presented by the teacher to the pupil at a particular time in the pupils' school life and in a certain order. This is not a simple task. The teacher has to ask hundreds of questions and answer them himself, and make wise decisions, before he takes any step in this direction. An English master asks the question: What English should I present to the beginners? How must grammar can they learn? A Mathematics teacher asks the question: Can a student of Class X master set algebra? A Science master asks the question : Is it wise to present the principle of Archimedes to children of class IV? A Geography teacher asks the question: Should I teach physical geography before I go to regional geography or vice versa? This process of selecting and organising material we call "*building the curriculum.*"

If they are to do their work to the satisfaction of all and build up the curriculum, teachers must ask hundreds of such questions and find out answers for them. The answers should be based on specific information. Educational psychologists have gathered at least a part of such specific information and set down as general principles of child growth and learning. To accomplish his task successfully, the teacher should be aware of this body of knowledge and utilize it judiciously, as it becomes an indispensable part of his professional equipment. Without this body of knowledge educational psychology provides, he would fail in his professional judgements essential in selecting and organising the material that pupils are to learn.

Education is possible because humans can learn. While defining "Education" it was stated that education is a directed and deliberate process. The teacher plans and guides or directs the learning experiences of his pupils in harmony with stated educational objectives. An '*Objective*' is a stated desirable outcome of education. The teacher guides or directs the learning of his pupils. This is a difficult task he has to perform. He should be conscious of the fact that children "learn" while they "grow", and grow while they learn. He should know how children learn and decide before-hand the activities he is to engage his pupils in to bring about behavioural changes in the desired direction. He should have good knowledge of the techniques of motivation of learning in general and classroom motivation in particular. He must be aware of individual differences in learning ability, judicious use of reward and punishment to promote learning and the extent to which learning in one situation gets carried over to another situation.

The major concern of educational psychology is learning. Most of the information available concerning the problems of how children learn, the things that motivate learning, and the many factors that facilitate or retard learning are of use to the teacher. Educational psychologists have formulated principles about the use of rewards and punishment. They can tell us something about the teaching aids we should use while presenting different lessons on different subjects to the children and what can be done to minimise forgetting. All these items of information and more are relevant to the teacher's task as one who guides the learning of others.

(Pupil Qualities and Characteristics

In addition to finding out how far the educational objectives provided by the Nation, the Society and the School have been realised, the teacher should know how well he has performed his task as a teacher. Also he wants to know how well his pupils have learned the material he has presented to them. The pupils want to know their progress; and the parents want to know how well their sons and daughters are doing at school. The college the pupils desire to enter in want to know what they have learned up to date. The employers want to know how well the candidate has done in the school, if the pupil seeks a job. Ultimately, the public demand to be informed about the qualitative aspect of their schools. Therefore, the teacher must test his pupils and evaluate not only their achievement but other qualities and characteristics.

"*Evaluation*" means, first measuring a particular quality or characteristic of the pupils and next attaching a value judgement to the measurement. For measuring the achievement of his pupils or some other quality, either the teacher has to design and construct his own test or select and use tests designed and constructed by others. If he desires to use tests made by others, he should know where they are available. He should know how to administer the test, score it and interpret the results. Also he should have some knowledge of the validity ad reliability of the test. Validity refers to the degree to which a test is capable of achieving certain aims; and Reliability can be defined as the degree of consistency between two measures of the same thing. He has to make reports to students and parents. He has to prepare records which help to decide who should be admitted to college and who should not.

The educational psychologists have investigated these matters. They have developed techniques for increasing the accuracy of general observation of children. They have studied how to measure the qualities and characteristics of people and have made available for use a wide array of formal and informal tests of aptitudes, achievement attitudes, interests, personality and adjustment. They have devised techniques for recording information gathered and for interpreting it. They also use scientific methodology in increasing knowledge in educationally significant areas. The teacher must study the psychologists, findings to equip himself to perform this task of evaluation with professional skill.

Promoting the Personal and Social Adjustment of Pupils

In addition to directing "learning" one other very important task of the teacher is to promote personal and social adjustment of children. The majority of children behave normally and are well adjusted in life situations. But there are a few who deviate from normal course of behaviour and are maladjusted in different degrees. Some of these children misbehave with the teacher and show off in the class. Some others steal or cheat, are lazy or unsocial and withdrawing. And still some others are truants or deface the walls, use foul language and break the light posts. These are *problem children.* These children need sympathetic help from the teacher. The causes at the root of such deviations in behaviour have to be found out and removed. Most of these behaviourism result on account of the child feeling frustrated in personal and social relationships. Teachers should assist these children to set realistic goals which can be achieved. The need for keeping discipline will diminish when children are happy and are busily engaged in activities that appear to them as being of real worth.

Teachers would find a lot of material in Educational Psychology on the basic processes of adjustment. Educational psychologists have borrowed a large amount of material concerning children with problems which handicap them in learning, from the field of mental hygiene, clinical psychology and social psychology. Educational psychology is also concerned with those family, community and cultural influences that affect learning and adjustment. A teacher who seeks the help of educational psychology in solving problems in learning and adjustment shall find that information from these fields has thrown considerable light on the social dynamics of the school and the classroom. Educational psychology furnishes the teacher with the necessary facts and techniques for analysing behaviour—both this own and that of others—to the end that normal adjustment may be facilitated and growth in personality effected.

Evaluation of pupil qualities and characteristics using

educational and psychological tests helps the teacher in *effective guidance and counselling.* For instance, if the achievement test is used sufficiently early, difficulties can be determined and remedial work undertaken to help the student. The test results, presented in the form of a profile chart, help the student determine his strengths and weaknesses, thereby furnishing him with useful and dependable data for making educational and vocational decisions. "Guidance of all kinds has a common purpose—to assist the individual to make wise choices, adjustments, and interpretations in connection with critical situations in his life. This is done in general, through (1) information that he is helped to secure, (2) habits, techniques, attitudes, ideals and interests that he is helped to develop, and (3) wise counsel by which direct assistance is given him to make the choices, adjustments and interpretations." (Jones, 1951, p. 97) Guidance and counseling go hand in hand though the former is more general and the latter more specific. Individual counselling is a vital part of the guidance programme of the school. Students have difficulty with educational problems involving learning and decision making. They have problems that are primarily emotional in nature and problems that are primarily vocational in nature. The teacher has to help them solve these problems. He has to act as their "friend, philosopher and guide."

"Individual counselling is communication between counsellor and counsellee relative to the situation of the latter. Such communication has as its primary purposes the enabling of the counsellee better to cope with his immediate and specific difficulties and to develop his capacity for self - direction and self understanding in order to meet more effectively the problems of living in the future." (Sawoey & Telford. 1964, p. 517) As was state earlier, the teacher's position is similar to that of the medical practitioner who must first study his patient before prescribing for him. For this purpose, the teacher should have a good knowledge of evaluation procedures and use of evaluation results, which he is not likely to have without a sound knowledge of educational psychology. A vital part of educational psychology is

"Measurement and Evaluation in Teaching," which would help the teacher in using the results of evaluation procedures for guidance and counselling. "Assisting a pupil with educational and vocational decisions, guiding him in the selection of curricular and extracurricular activities, and helping him solve personal and social adjustment problems, all require an objective knowledge of the pupil's abilities, interests, attitudes and other personal characteristics. The more comprehensive the picture of the pupil's strengths and limitations in various areas, the greater the likelihood of effective guidance and counseling." (Groulund, 1976, p. 14).

Educational psychology has something significant to say about the conflicting roles, adjustment problems and mental hygiene problems of the teacher himself. It can help teachers solve personal and emotional problems. Teachers, although relatively stable when compared with other professional groups, need assistance in improving their mental health. This need takes on added importance when the undesirable effects upon pupils of teacher maladjustment are considered.

The teacher is a *professional person.* Unless he is in possession of a body of basic knowledge, basic principles and basic laws that are the products of scientific research and scholarly activity in educational psychology, he cannot operate with professional skill and exercise professional judgement. In the teaching enterprise, besides the teacher, there are *educational administrators.* To these administrators, the values of educational psychology *belong to* in one way or another just as they do to the teacher. In many ways they have to make wise decisions that influence the pupils, school and community. They should be able to judge the extent to which the objectives of the school are being achieved, to identify strengths and weaknesses in the curriculum, and to appraise special programmes in the schools. They should have the required information on which to base administrative decisions concerning the placement, grouping and placement of pupils. They should collect objective data to be used in explaining to the community the goals and accomplishments of the school. Learning how to make judgements and to take decisive action, plantfully and carefully, require the administrators and teachers to understand themselves, their pupils and the processes of learning and intellectual development. These understandings are important parts of educational psychology.

Limitations of Educational Psychology

Educational Psychology arise from the nature of "Teaching", the nature of "Science", and the nature of "Psychology" itself. Teaching is more an art than an applied science. Therefore, books and lectures and other media of information render us relatively little help. The only choice left to us is to depend upon the natural aptitude and experience of the teacher. Between two engineers, one old and the other young, you may choose the young engineer on the ground that he is well versed in the modern techniques of engineering. But in so far as music is concerned, that particular musician who sings the song you desire to listen to is needed.

Very often science is indispensable in the solution of a problem. Yet, there are problems which no scientific information in the world can help us to solve. These problems are related to philosophical, ethical and religious values. To make any decision, we have to consult them.

Educational psychology has all the limitations of science. It has a good many limitations on its own account too, that some other sciences do not have. Psychology is not as yet a highly integrated science. It possesses a vast number of facts like most of the other sciences. But unlike many of the other sciences, it has not yet been able to integrate this body of facts into any closely knit pattern. "Thus, whereas the student of applied physics learns relatively a few general laws from which a myriad of specific facts may be deduced, the student of applied psychology must be prepared to get the answer to his problem by consulting spefcific investigations bearing on these problems."

The possible limitations should not discourage us. If teaching is an art, teachers with a natural aptitude, and experience, and capable of personal supervision should be preferred to teachers who possess a body of information only.

REFERENCES

Bhadury, J. et. al. "Some Negative Correlates ofAnti-Social behaviour", *Indian Journal ofCriminology*, Vo. 15, No. 1, January,1987.

Badami, M.D. *Psychological Study of Factors of Juvenile Delinquency.* Unpublished Ph.D. thesis, M.s. University, Baroda, 1961.

Jeyasina, V.J. "Juvenile Recidivism: Socio-Psycological View" *Indian Journal of Criminology & Criminalistics*, Vol. I, No. 4, December 1981.

Mukherjee, K., Basu, M. *An Assessment of Delinquency: An Examination of Personality and Event Interaction*, New Delhi. Wiley Eastern Ltd., 1979.

5

Significant Functions and Behaviouristic Approaches Schools Psychology

Theories of Psychology discussed in this chapter have played an important part in human thought. At present they are of great concern to those who would like to know the why's and wherefore's of human behaviour. As teachers, we have the greatest concern for this phenomena of human behaviour. The Schools of Psychology provide an insight into the major and most fundamental approaches to modern psychology. Theoretical issues make practical research more meaningful and reasonable. In absence of specific data, we try to see if the more general theories may suggest a course of action. Theory makes teaching more interesting and flexible. It gives the teachers a perspective and a feeling of understanding what he is about.

The Structuralistic Approach

Edward Bradford Titchener (1867-1927) was the exponent of "Structuralism" in Psychology. He relate Psychology to science in general. The biologist studies living forms. The physicist deals with non-living forms. The psychologist is concerned with the study of *conscious human experiences*, Conscious experience is dependant upon the experiencing person.

Conscious experience, then, is the subject matter of psychology. But conscious experience is a private affair. It can only be observed by the experiencing person. Therefore, a specialised technique is needed for psychological observation. The method is *introspection.*

Introspection, as Titchener employed the process, is a highly specialised form of self-observation. In this process, the psychologist tries to study his own consciousness scientifically. In the process of introspection, the observed and the observer are, in a sense, one and the same. It you are angry at something or somebody, you are to study how it feels like to be angry. Anger is your own experience. It is the observed and you are the observer. Therefore, the introspectionist requires considerable laboratory training in this special method of observation.

The aim of psychology, Titchener believes, is to answer "what", "how", and "why", of experience. The question of "what"is to be answered by systematic introspective analysis of the mental processes. When the various elements of consciousness have been discovered through introspective analysis, the next question is to find out "how" they are combined into compounds. Titchener, then, considers the problem of "why". He argues that the answer to "why" is not to be sought in the mental processes themselves. Perhaps, he suggests, we ought to look to the nervous system for the cause of consciousness. All the same, he maintains that consciousness parallels nervous processes in the brain; but one is not the cause of the other. This is psychophysical parallelism. Mental science, he says, explains by reference to those nervous processes which correspond with the mental processes that are under observation. For him, ideas are formed under the condition of certain processes in the nervous system.

Titchener and his associates analysed consciousness into its elements. These were found to be sensation, images and affective states, Each of these is an element with attributes such as quality, intensity and duration. From these three building blocks all the complex and varied higher mental processes are derived. In spite of their differences, the several elements nevertheless are all related to a "*common mental ancestor*". This ancestor appeared to be sensation –the basic "*element*" of mind. Titchener devotes half of his text to the sensory processes. Ten he takes up the affective states, attention, perception, memory and thought. He treats memory and retention as manifestations of the mental image.

Titchener tries to solve the problems that result from the special method of introspection.

(1) Introspection as a method is mainly subjective. How can there be an objective, "scientific" psychology if the very process under observation is also doing the observing? To this Titchener answers that the introspectionist needs considerable laboratory experience under supervision before he can qualify as a psychologist. He must study his own consciousness in a detached, objective and systematic manner. For this he must develop an objective attitude. For example, he must describe the hue, brightness and spatial characteristics in his own consciousness when an apple is under observation. This would be valid introspection.

(2) The second problem arises when one is attempting to observe an emotional consciousness. In this case, the calm, scientific attitude which is necessary for laboratory work destroys the very process under observation. Titchener suggests that in such instances the psychologist should allow the emotional experience to go on uninterrupted and then describe his conscious memory of the experience when it is completed.

(3) The third problem is how the psychologist can study the conscious processes of children, animals and mentally disturbed individuals. To this, Titchener's answer is "introspection by analogy". After carefully observing the behaviour of the subject, the psychologist

must put himself in the subjects' place and try to interpret what the individual under consideration is experiencing. Introspection by analogy is quite unsatisfactory and the weakest spot in the work of Titchener.

Though consistent and tightly knit, Titchener's system remained too narrow as it confined only to introspective analysis of consciousness. Consequently, structuralism weakened and ultimately collapsed. However, structuralism as a movement, had brought science to psychology and established psychology as a science. This alone was a great contribution though its method and scope proved too narrow to contain psychology.

Functionalistic Approach

A number of prominent American psychologists whose primary interest was the study of mind as it functions in adapting the organism to its environment, were the exponents of "Functionalism" as a system of psychology. The roots of this point of view extend back to the evolutionary biology of Charles Darwin (1809-1882) and the pragmatic philosophy of William James (1842-1910). The most important psychologists who belonged to this school of psychology were John Dewey (1859-1952), James Rowland Angell (1869-1949) and Harvey Carr (1873-1954).

It has been said that American psychology today is functionalistic because of its emphasis on learning, testing, perception and other such "functional" processes. Functionalism is a less sharply defined system than Structuralism. It is unfair to select anyone psychologists' work as a definitive statement of functionalism. However, to present the system in a coherent form, Harvey A Carr's 1925 exposition has to be chosen since it represents functionalism at its maturity and in its most definitive form. But for appreciation of Carr's system better, the chief contributions of his predecessors, William James, James Dewey and Angell have to be outlined briefly.

William James was a physiologist, psychologist and philosopher. He was a versatile genius. He analysed and criticised the structuralistic psychology originating in Germany in the hands of Wilhelm Wundt (1832-1920) and transplanted to the United States by his disciple, Titchener. James made it clear that his was a functional psychology worse aim was not to reduce mind into elements but to study consciousness as an ongoing process or stream. Mind as it is revealed in habits, knowledge and perception, is constantly engaged in active give-and-take relations with the environment. Mind is not a collection of static conscious states it is highly personal. It cannot be subjected to the objective and scientific analysis favoured by structuralists if it is done, the personal flavour shall get destroyed.

John Dewey is credited with sparking functionalism as a definite movement in psychology. This occurred with the publication of an article on the *reflex are concept.* Reflex action is a relatively simple response largely under the control of a specific stimulus, occurring rather mechanically, such as the papillary response to light or the Knee-Jerk from a tap on the tendon below the knee. Other examples of reflex action are sneezing, perspiring and the beating of the heart. In this article, Dewey argued that the behavioural act involved in a reflex response can not be reduced to the sensory-motor elements of its and still remain a meaningful act. He went on to argue that reflexes and other forms of behaviour ought to be interpreted in terms of their significance for adaptation and not treated as artificial scientific constructs, in this manner he attacked psychological molecularism and reductionism of the structuralists. In short, Dewey believed that the study of the organism *as a whole functioning in its environment* was the proper subject matter for psychology.

James Rowland Angell moulded the functionalistic movement into a working school. This scholarly heritage was taken over by Harvey A. Carr, Angell's successor.

Carr defines psychology as the "study of mental activity". Mental activity, in turn, "is concerned with the acquisition, fixation, retention, organisation and evaluation of experiences and their subsequent utilisation in the guidance of conduct". In the wording of this definition, there is heavy emphasis on learning, a highly functional process. Carr also specifically states that the functionalist is interested in how the mental processes are utilised in conduct. Also he points out that mind is concerned with "attaining a more effective adjustment to the world".

Then he deals with the mind body problem. He admits that these two aspects of the individual must be taken into account in any analysis of behaviour. All mental activity is psychological in the sense that both mind and body are involved in any given task.

In so far as the problem of methodology is concerned, Carr recognises the necessity for introspection, to get at the conscious side of mind, but gives more emphasis to objective observation. Therefore, in course of time, objective methods of observation became the favoured techniques of the functionalists.

With regard to scope, Carr's psychology is much broader than Titchener's. Carr believes, functional psychology and physiology are closely allied, since both disciplines study the human organism. However, psychology must draw material from such disciplines as sociology, neurology, education, anthropology and related sciences for facts and methodological contributions. In turn, psychology should contribute freely, whenever possible, to other disciplines. Thus, Carr opens the door to the possibility of an applied psychology in this way. Next, Carr presents a survey of the nervous system and sense organs as a basis for understanding the higher mental processes.

In the fourth chapter of his 1925 text, Carr's functionalistic position is most clearly developed. In that chapter entitled "Principles of Organic Behaviour", Carr discusses the nature of an adoptive act. Such an act results from motivating conditions arising either in the individual as drives or in the environment as stimuli (Drive is a condition or state of the organism which activates and directs his behaviour and stimulus is some property of the environment). The stimulation from such conditions persists until the individual responds in such a way as to achieve satisfaction. Consequently behaviour is adaptive in the sense that the individual's responses result in a better adjustment to the environment. Carr's analysis of adaptive behaviour is very similar to that found in most present day text books on the psychology of adjustment. A need is a state of tension forcing the organism to activity. All behaviour is caused by a need and is oriented towards the attainment of a goal. When the goal is reached, the need gets satisfied and the tension gets released. When the tension is released the organism returns to a state of equilibrium. This is how the present day texts analyse an adjustive act.

Carr considers "Learning" a central problem in psychology. He treats learning as a "perceptual—motor process. When confronted with a problem for which there is no habitual or immediate solution, the organism engages in a persistent and varied attack on the situation. This problem solving behaviour is neither blind nor random, but utilises previous experience and thus demonstrates that the learner perceives the relevant relationships in the elements making up the problem. When a solution is found, it is fixated and becomes a part of the organism's accumulated experience.

In two additional ways, the strongly functionalistic nature of Carr's psychology is revealed. First, he argues that adaptive acts involve two stages; a preparatory stage of attentive adjustment, making for more efficient perception by excluding irrelevant and distracting stimuli, and a response stage, which is the adaptive act itself. Therefore, attention in Carr's system is considered in terms of its functional utility in dealing with the environment. Second, his functionalistic bias is revealed by his interest in perception. For Carr, perception is a basic process in adjustment, since how we perceive our environment and its challenges largely determines how we respond to it. Carr's writings echo Gestalt Psychology, dealt in some detail in this chapter.

In "classical" functionalism, processes of mind such as learning, attention, perception and intelligence received the major emphasis in both theory and research. Today a large segment of contemporary functionalists are pursuing research in human learning. The mental testing movement and its success is ample testimony to the functionalistic flavour of American Psychology. It may not be out of place to state here that the pragmatism of William James and John Dewey's Pragmatism, experimentalism and instrumentalism much influenced the functionalistic approach to psychology in the United States. Ultimately, functionalism was absorbed into contemporary psychology. This proves its overwhelming success.

The Behaviouristic Approach

John B. Watson (1878—1958) rose in revolt against Structuralism and Functionalism as systems of psychology. He was a staunch *behaviourist.* His strong bias in favour of animal psychology led him to embrace the position of a strict behaviourist. He strongly opposed the analysis of consciousness by introspection as a suitable aim for a scientific psychology, and in its place emphasized the study of behaviour by objective and experimental procedures. His two most important books are "Behaviour, an Introduction to comparative Psychology," (1914), and "Psychology from the stand point of a Behaviourist" (1919). The following summary of Watson's behaviourism is drawn primarily from these two books mentioned. His third book, "Behaviourism" was published in 1925.

Watson found the state of psychology in 1914, quite unsatisfactory for several reasons. They are. (1) A psychology whose method is introspection excludes for all practical purposes, contributions from the animal laboratory collection of data from comparative studies by analogous introspection is absurd. (2) Mentalistic concepts such as "mind", "consciousness", and "image" have no place in a scientific, objective science. (3) The introspective study of conscious processes such as sensations, affective states, and imagery had resulted in disagreement and confusion. (4) The structuralists had failed to resolve such a fundamental problem as how many independent attributes are associated with the elements of consciousness—sensation, images and affective states. (5) Where introspectionists failed to obtain reliable results, the blame was misplaced on the observer. Watson refuses to accept as valid such excuses as "faulty training" or "poor observation", offered by the structuralists to account for these difficulties. In reality, he asserts, the fault was with the method. These difficulties would not occur if introspection were abolished in favour of objective experimental observation.

Watson does not spare the Functionalists. The functionalists too employ terms that are "elusive', such as "emotions", "volition" and "process", he observes. They too are guilty of using introspection, already discredited by him. Therefore, Watson declared: "the behaviourists reached the conclusion that they could no longer be content to work with intangibles and unapproachables. They decided either to give up psychology or else make it a natural science." (Woodworth, 1952, p. 69).

In Watson's "behaviourist manifesto", the following points are clearly made, as Woodworth states.

(1) Psychology is to be the science, not of consciousness, but of behaviour (*definition*).

(2) It is to cover both human and animal behaviour. The simpler animal behaviour is more fundamental than the more complex behaviour of human beings (*scope*).

(3) It is to rely wholly on objective data, introspection being discarded (*method*).

(4) It is to avoid "mentalistic" concepts such as sensation, perception, and emotion, and employ only behaviour concepts such as stimulus and response, learning and habit (*Concepts*).

(5) A scientific basis is to be provided for the practical control of behaviour, that is, "behaviour problems" as they appear in a guidance or psychiatric clinic. (*application*).

(6) The old mind body problem disappears as mind

> disappears and body remains. There is no mystery in the relation of body and behaviour. Behaviourism must not give excessive attention to brain foolishly but must keep its eye on sense organism, muscles and glands. Only objectively observable facts are admissible. (*philosophy*) (Woodworth, 1952, p. 71).

Thus, for Watson, psychology is "the science of behaviour," Behavioural acts are to be described objectively in terms of "stimulus and response, habit formation, habit integration and the like". The aim of behaviourism is straight forward and objective given the stimulus to be able to predict the response and given the response to be able to predict the antecedent stimulus. For Watson, psychology is the science of S--R, where S represents he stimulus and R, a response.

In explaining his views further, Watson said that behaviour was complex and capable of analysis intosimple stimulus-response units which he called reflexes. In explaining whathemeans by *response*, he starts wit the knee jerk and the other reflexes but advances to acts such as taking food, unlocking a door, writign a letter and even building a house. evidently, he is thinking of a response not as composed of muscular elements but as accomplishing certain results in the environemnt. In the same way his examples of a stimulus start with rays of light thrown into the eyes, sounds enteringthe ears, and go on to objects in the environment and to total situations. Watson's real interest is in what the individual will do in a given situation. Forexample, the stimulus is a stick of candy dangled in front of a baby and the response, say, of an eight-month-old, reaching out and grasping the candy and putting it into the month.

The methods proposed by Watson for the behaviourists' research programmes are four in number (Chaplin & Krawice 1974, p. 57).

They are: (1) Observation, with and without instrumental control.

(2) the conditioned reflex method.

(3) the verbal report method.

(4) testing methods.

Of the four methods stated above, numbers 2 and 3 require further comment. Before the advent of behaviourism, conditioning was in use in psychology. Conditioned response was taken over from Pavlov but Watson was responsible for its widespread usage in America. Of all the psychologists who have sought to explain human learning in conditioning theory, Watson went to extremes. He says, "Give me a dozen of healthy infants....and I will guarantee to take any one at random and train him to become any type of specialist I might select", This statement reveals not only his extreme behaviourism but also his environmentalism. It leaves very little room for heredity as an explanatory concept in human behaviour.

In so far as the verbal report method is concerned, Watson makes it clear that the verbal report is entirely different from introspection. In introspection the psychologist and the subject are one and the same. In the use of verbal reports, the psychologist does not report on his own behaviour or mental processes but utilises subjects whose reports become data for the psychologist.

In the system of psychology developed by Watson, behaviour is a sensorimotor activity. In his view, behaviour is an activity of the whole organism in which the brain serves to connect the sensory with the motor nerves and so link the sense organs with the muscles. He treats emotions and feelings as behaviour patterns or reactions, predominantly visceral and largely acquired through conditioning during childhood. Watson suggested that pleasantness was a true sensorimotor affair, the sensori impulses coming in from erogenous zones and the motor impulses going out to muscles and arousing incipient movements of approach. Emotion consists in "profound changes of the bodily mechanism as a whole, but particularly of the visceral and glandular systems", each separate emotion being a particular pattern of such changes. Watson upholds the conditioned response theory of learning. He believes, conditioned response affords the key of all habit formation. Watson's reduction of thinking to implicit motor behaviour is the most famous and distinctive of his theories. It seemed to him that implicit speech movements were the most likely behaviour for thinking. He reduces thought to "laryngeal habits". We talk to ourselves while thinking. Thought is our inner speech.

Watson was favourably inclined towards applied psychology. He was concerned with the practical problem of handling children and contributed a great deal of fundamental research in the area of child psychology. He felt that a behaviouristic psychology had much to offer to such fields as law, industry and education. Such professions would be ideal testing grounds for a psychology interested in discovering the principles involved in prediction and control of behaviour.

Now, to cast a backward glance: Watson solved the dilemma of the relationship between mind and body by disposing of mind altogether. Watson reflected the spirit of the times when he advocated the study of human behaviour with a "*deterministic.*" "*mechanistic*" and strongly "*scientific*" attitude. The early 20th century was wrapped in mechanistic determinism in the field of science in general. Science seemed to have found or to be able to find the answer to everything. Literature, art and philosophy turned to realistic and material themes Idealism began to give way to realism. Therefore, some observers believe that Watsons' crusade for an objective behaviourism did American psychology a service at that time by shifting the emphasis form the study of consciousness to the study of behaviour. Finally, the behaviouristic point of view has remained a strong force in contemporary psychology.

Gestaltists' Approach

For students of psychology, 1912 is one of the most significant years. This is the year of Watson's first promulgation of behaviourism. Several other important developments took place at just about that time. The debate between structuralists and functionalists had begun to die down a little. The modern associationism of Thorndike and of Pavlov was very muchon th eupswing. Thorndike made the full statement of his views in 1911 and 1913. The psychological significance of Pavlov's conditioned reflex was just beginning to be appreciated. The year 1912 was a turning point in the history of Psychoanalysis. This was the time when a split between Freud and two of his early adherents, Adler and Jung took a definite shape, forcing Freud to revise his earlier views and shift over to his quite different later theory. Mc Dougall's purposivism received its full formulation in 1912. Finally, the year 1912, saw the first announcement of the important school of Gestalt Psychology.

Three young German psychologists, Max Wertheimer (1880-1943), Wolfgang Kohler (1887-1967) and Kurt Koffka (1886-1941) were the founders of the school of Gestalt Psychology. Kurt Lewin (1890-1947) may be counted either as an early adherent of Gestalt psychology or as the founder of a closely related school. He was an early ally of this group who later developed a novel approach of his own, referred to as *topological psychology* or even as *vector psychology*. Very often authors call these as "*Field Theories*" and "*Cognitive Psychology*."

These German psychologists took up arms against structuralism as well as behaviourism, grouped under associationism. In essence, the new school was against *reductionalistic analysis*, whether such analysis was structuralistic or behaviouristic. The structuralists reduce consciousness into its elements, namely, sensation, images and affective states by introspective analysis. Similarly, the behaviourists reduced behaviour to conditioned or natural reflexes, resulting in "S—R psychology". Therefore, the *Gestaltists* rose in revolt against the *associationistic theories* of psychology. They called structuralism as "brick and mortar" psychology, meaning elements ("bricks") bound by association ("mortar"). Behaviourism is treated as an extreme form of Connectionism and Connectionism is treated as modern associationism. The associationists suggest the connection or bond formation between stimulus and response to explain behaviour, reducing behaviour to conditioned or natural reflexes.

The Gestalt psychologists emphasize the phenomena of perception. The problems of perception have proved most interesting to them. They have been greatly concerned with explaining how we become aware of the world. For them it is most important to explain how it is that our experience of a situation can remain relatively constant when he physical events responsible for that experience fluctuate in such wild fashion.

The new movement had its start as a result of Wertheimer's interest in the *stroboscopic motion*, an illusion of movement. One phenomenon occurs is moving pictures. The motion picture camera takes a rapid series of snapshots which are "stills", with short blank intervals of darkness between them. In projection each snapshot stands still on the screen and the light is cut off while the shift is made from each frame to the next. Therefore, what is physically presented to you on the screen is a rapidly exposed series of snapshots separated by intervals of darkness. If the short blank time interval separating two successive exposures is about one fifteenth to one sixteenth of a second, the physiological effect is smooth movement. You see an object in the picture moving smoothly along instead of jerking from one place to another as it actually does in the series of views. Illusory,it is true, but just as "good" as real movement.

Here was a phenomenon for which structuralism had no adequate explanation. The illusion of a single object in motion persists no matter how hard one tries to introspect the separate exposures. Here was a case where analysis failed and a fundamental Gestalt principle was strikingly illustrated, namely, that the whole is different from the sum of its parts. An object seen in motion is not merely seen in a series of positions. You see the object's movement as a dynamic whole. Seen movement was important to the Gestalt psychologist as a clear example of the dynamic whole, the whole which dominates its parts. Another clear case was the shape of an object. "Shape" in German is Gestalt. Thus, the word "Gestalt" means a shape, form, figure, pattern, configuration or whole. A 'gestalt' is a whole 'the behaviour of which is not determined by that of its individual elements but where the part processes are themselves determined by the intrinsic nature of the while'. In the eyes of the Gestalt psychologists this relatively simple discovery seemed to challenge the traditional empirical—associationistic—structuralistic psychology which had dominated the field for so many years.

The Gestalt psychologists were quick to seize upon other perceptual phenomenon such as perceptual constancies, prevalence and dominance of structure and marked constancy of patterns of experience in support of their theses that introspective analysis of the structuralists and reductionism of the behaviourists often fail to explain experience. The pattern of experience may remain fairly constant even in the face of continuous change in the outside world. One of the most striking illustrations of the constancy of patterns is the constancy of geometric forms. In object constancy, for example, the window in my room remains a window in appearance in spite of wide variations in viewing conditions. Whenever I see the window from a different angle, it casts a somewhat different picture on my eye. None of these pictures, moreover, is likely to be of a rectangular window. The actual picture in my retina is some sort of rhomboid figure with some acute angles and some obtruse angles. But I do not see the window as a series of changing rhomboids. I see it as always the same shape and always as a rectangle. Perceptually it remains a conventionally rectangular window. An example of size constancy is that a desk just in front of us acts on us very differently from a desk 15 feet away. The latter casts a much smaller image on our retinas, say about one eighth the size. Yet the more distant desk is seen as the same size as the closer desk. Such perceptual constancies is scarcely explicable in terms of structuralism for if the elements of perception change, the perception ought to change with them. Similarly, in brightness, the sensory elements may change radically under different viewing conditions, yet the percept keeps its quality of unique wholeness. Transpose a tune into another key, and it is still the same tune even though the elements are all different. Dismantle a chair, and you no longer have a chair but a mere bundle of sticks.

The Gestalt psychologists argue that experiences carry with them a quality of wholeness that cannot be found in the parts. According to them, experience is always structured. Whenever we are aware of something we are aware of it as part of a complex pattern or structure or organisation. We never perceive a mere mass of separate details. Even when the external environment has little in the way of organisation or structure, the observer will tend to experience some organisation. The pattern or structure of experience completely dominates that experience. It dominates experience to such an extent that if the pattern calls for a detail, we will see that detail whether or not it is objectively present. A rough sketch of a triangle in which the corners are imperfectly joined will still be seen as a triangle, and the imperfections may escape our notice. A continuously changing objective situation may act on us by making us see first one relatively unchanging picture followed suddenly by another relatively constant picture. For these reasons the German noun "Gestalt" is appropriate to characterise their system, since it denotes form, figure or configuration and carries with it the connotation that *reductional analysis destroys a figure, or "Gestalt*".

Gestalt Psychology was formulated in reaction against associationistic theories like structuralism and connectionism considered to be *atomistic* in nature, that is, giving too much attention to supposedly isolated details. The *atomistic approach* is sometimes called the *molecular view*—stress on minute detail and component parts. Field theories, by was of contrast, endorse the *molar view*, which maintains that all parts are intimately interrelated and interdependent. Emphasis is placed on the total organisation of the "field", which is made up of (a) the occurance of many stimuli, (b) these stimuli organised into a meaningful pattern, (c) the reaction of the organism which alters both the external situation and the organism and (d) the organism itself. perhaps the best summary of this fundamental aspect of Gestalt Psychology is that it *represents a molar as opposed to molecular point of view.*

The Gestalt psychologists deplored the attempts to seek the physiological foundations of behaviour in a machine like nervous system in which a point-for-point correspondence is asumed to exist betweenthe environmental stimulus and sensory excitation in the *cortex* (outer layer of the cerebrum). This so-called machine view of the nervous system arose in connection with behaviouristic explanation of learning; the explanation being; "Learning consists of the relaying of impulses that start when elements of the external world stimulate the sensitive neurons of an appropriate sense organ. By way of these *efferent neurons* the impulse travels to the brainand then is transmitted through the afferent neurons to the appropriate muscles and glands. This explanation likened the brain to a telephone switch-board, where each new habit is represented by a neural connection between two cortical centres, just as a telephone operator establishes a connection by plugging in circuits. Gestalt studies of transposability provided experimental evidence opposed to this mechanical "being pushed—moving" theory. For examle, a chimpansee can learn to discriminate in favour of the darkerof two shades of gray, X and Y where X is light and Y dark. If a new shade, W, is introduced, whch is darker than Y, and the animal then is tested for his ability to discriminate between Y and W, he readily makes the discrimination in faovur of the darker W; this despite the fact that he had been previously responding to Y as "darker."

The Gestaltists disagreed with the behaviourists' denial of the validity of introspection as a psychological method. Of course, they did not approve the kind of introspection employed by the structuralists. They favoured the study of conscious experience in a *phenomenological* sense, that is, naïve report on conscious experience, as by a child, as contrasted with trained introspection. In other words, they favoured the study of conscious experience unanalysed.

The Gestalt psychologists took a "*dynamic*" or "*field*" view of the nervous system in place of the behaviouristic machine view. While they did not deny a correspondence between cortical processes and outside stimulation, they saw the relationship as "*isomorphic*" * instead of the point by point correspondence implied by the S—R formula. Whereas the Behaviourists prefer the simple mechanical "being—pushed—moving" analogy, the Gestaltists favour the field models. In Gestalt psychology, the whirlpool is a better analogy than is the motion of the piston in an automobile. In the whirlpool, there is a definite pattern which persists in spite of the changing particles of water. The particles of water do not determine the behaviour of the whirlpool. On the contrary, the general field of forces determine the behaviour of each particle. Each particle, no doubt, may contribute to that total field and hence indirectly it may act on another particle. But remember that it works only through the governing total field. It cannot affect the behaviour of its neighbours unless it can influence that total field.

In the area of perception, the Gestalt psychologists made many valuable and original contributions which lent support to their molar viewpoint. Of these, the principles of organisation of perceptual fields is outstanding. Among these principles, the "*figure—ground*" concept stands prominent and fundamental. "Figure—ground" means that in any perception, whether sensory or mental, some aspects of the total scene are predominant and stand out with clarity while others constitute the fringe, background or the setting. A deer standing on a ride in the early morning sunshine is clearly perceived as figure. Typically the figure is clearly outlined, small and well shaped while the ground is vague, relatively massive and having no definite shape or form. In this scene, the dew on the leaves and the lush green trees make up part of the background, the rest of which is distant mountains, topped by thin clouds and sky. It takes the total to make the scene. Yet the shapely outlined deer is the focus of perception.

The other factors of organisation are (a) Peripheral factors, namely, factors of proximity, similarity, continuity and closure, (b) Central factors, namely, familiarity and set and (c) Reinforcing factors, namely, the factors of pregnance and good figure. While these principles of organisation are most obvious in visual perception, they are equally important in other sensory fields and in the "higher" mental processes. Therefore, the Gestalt Psychologists quickly extended their observations and theoretical interpretations into different areas of psychology, such as learning, thinking and problem solving—in fact to the whole of psychology.

According to the Gestalt psychologists to learn is to form or complete a Gestalt—a pattern or configuration which has meaning. The learner responds as a unified and integrated organism to the total situation—a pattern or structure. For the Gestaltists, learning is chiefly a matter of coming to see relations. We have to see, within one compact pattern, both the problem-to-be-solved and the means-of-solving the problem. Thus, "learning consists of acquiring such 'means-goal' Gestalts or patterns. Once the pattern is formed, learning ceases to be a problem" (Stephens, 1960, p. 251). Indeed, among the classical experiments of the Gestalt school is Kohler's work on *insight learning in* apes. Insight is sometimes defined as the sudden perception of the relationship in a total situation , that is, the relationships between the organism, the goal, and the intervening obstacles. When the teacher arranged problems to organise the elements of classroom exercises into meaningful wholes, insight would occur. Once it had been grasped, the principle of a problem would carry over or transfer to other situations. Of course, transfer of learning takes place to the extent that the learner recognises significant relations in two situational patterns. In poetry, for instance, a particular rhythm may be repeated even though the lines differ in length and have no words in common. The Lewinian concept of the life space, with its many psychological forces, is one kind of Gestalt psychology, better known as "*topological psychology*". It is like the classical Gestalt psychology in holding that the overall pattern or field of events determines experience. It is somewhat different from the classical Gestalt psychology, however, in emphasizing behaviour more than experience and in making greater use of motive or drive.

In course of time Gestalt psychology has made its influence felt in ever-widening circles. There have been extensions of the Gestalt point of view into personality, child psychology, motivation and into social psychology. The primary influence of the Gestalt school on contemporary psychology has been in the fields of perception and learning –especially perception. Indeed, it is impossible to find today a chapter on perception in any general or experimental textbook of psychology that does not show the influence of the Gestalt school.

Psychoanalytic Approach

"The term 'Psychoanalysis' has three different meanings. It is, first, a school of psychology that emphasizes the dynamic psychic determinants of human behaviour and the importance of childhood experiences in molding the adult personality Secondly, psychoanalysis refers to a specialised technique for investigating unconscious mental activities. Finally, psychoanalysis is a method of interpreting and treating mental disorders, especially psychoneuroses.".

Psychoanalysis was never a school or systematic theory of psychology. It did not originate in psychology itself. The psychoanalytic movement developed outside academic circles, in medical practice and from the effort to find some cure for the neuroses. The psychoanalysts were not interested in academic psychology. Learning, perception, thinking and other favourite topics of the academic psychologists had very little use for them. As a symbol of their revolt against it, they left academic psychology alone.

Psychoanalysis could be called a "psychology of behaviour" in this sense that its founder was primarily concerned with the dynamic psychic determinants of human behaviour. But psychoanalysis as a theory and practice is removed very far from behaviouristic methods and concepts. Because of its concern with unconscious motives and conflicts moulding human behaviour; psychoanalysis sometimes used the name "*depth psychology*"; and sometimes called itself "*emotion psychology*".

Psychoanalysis "as a theory" is primarily centred on the study of the cause of the disease, development and treatment of mental disorders. And "*as a practice*", it is a non-experimental clinical technique for treating patients suffering from disorders that are psychogenic in origin. The theoretical position of psychoanalysis is limited in this sense that it has a non-experimental and non-academic background. In spite of these limitations it has profoundly influenced all modern psychologists, social scientists, writers, thinkers, philosophers and laymen as well.

Sigmund Freud (1856—1939) was the founder of the psychoanalytic theory. Freud started his career as a practicing physician at Vienna. He specialised in diseases of the nervous system. His medical experience showed him that many of his patients were in reality suffering from mental conflicts and neurotic states that manifested themselves as physical disorders or as complaints of extreme fatigue and the like. He deeply felt that what these patients really needed was psychotherapy rather than physical therapy.

Freud learned about the considerable success of J.M. Charcot (1825-1893) and J. Breuer (1842—1925) with the *hypnotic treatment* of hysterics who were suffering from ailments caused by psychogenic factors. Freud studied the technique of hypnotherapy and for a spell collaborated with Breur in treating patients with this new clinical weapon. But Freud was disillusioned very soon. He found out that the "cure" with hypnotherapy had been superficial and temporary.

Freud recognised at last that the real utility in hyptonic treatments lay in the psychic analysis involved and had nothing to do with the hypnotic trance as such. Therefore, he used two therapeutic techniques for psychoanalytic treatment that rendered hypnosis unnecessary while at the same time made deeper and more complete analysis of the patient's psyche. These two therapeutic techniques were "*free association*" and "*dream interpretation*".

In so far as the method of "*free association*" is concerned, in the analytical session the patient relaxes on a couch. The psychoanalyst sits at the head of the couch in such a position that he can observe the patient without being observed himself.

This enables the analyst to note the emotional reactions of the patient, and prevents the patient from observing the reactions of the analyst. The patient is encouraged to let his toughts wander and report whatever comes to mind regardless of its nature. Through free association, that is, the spontaneous reporting of random thoughts in disconnected form, elusive fringe memories, impulses and phantasies are permitted overt expression. The therapist listens to the patient without interrupting him in any way and observes and records his emotional reactions, signs of distress and resistance to the treatment. In a successful analysis, a child-parent attachment develops between the patient and the analyst. The patient overcomes his resistances and freely confesses and expresses his repressed painful and unpleasant experiences. During such a session, the therapist aiming to cure his patient of the illness, discusses with his patient interpretations of the material.

A second basic tool in the hands of the psychoanalyst for probing the unconscious mental processes is the "*interpretation of dreams.*" Dreams mirror unconscious conflicts, express repressed wishes and have been called by Freud "the royal road to the unconscious." "Sometimes it happened during the process of free association that the patient remembered and reported a dream, and Freud found that the dream made an excellent starting point for free association....Freud believed that the 'manifest dream' which the patient could remember, was a mere disguise for the real or 'latent dream' and that free association would lead from the manifest toward the latent dream. In dreaming, he believed, one is attempting to find some gratification for unfulfilled wishes" (Woodworth, 1952, p. 162). Therefore, dream analysis became an import part of both the therapeutic process and theory of psychoanalysis.

By 1900 Freud had accumulate sufficient clinical evidence to document his theories. He then announced his discoveries and humbly offered them to the world as a new interpretation of human behaviour. Today his writings and teachings are recognised as psychoanalysis. At first, Freud was given a chilly reception and shrugged off as a misguided neurologist overtly concerned with sex. However, the hostility of his colleagues did not dismay the originator of psychoanalysis. He continued to amass clinical evidence. He corrected some of his hypotheses, discarded some and substantiated others. In a few years Freus's ideas began to make impressions in medical circles. He was invited to lecture at the Vienna Psychiatrical Clinic. Many brilliant students, among them Alfred Adler (1870 1937) and Carl Jung (1875—1961), came to Vienna to study the new science of psychoanalysis. In 1902 an association for the development of spychoanalysis was formed. Some of the original leaders in the school continued to support and put up efforts in behalf of Freud's theories. Others dissented from their master's doctrines and promulgated psycho—therapeutic systems of their own. But all the same, all these scholars became famous throughout the world. Of those who broker away from the master, the most outstanding were Adler, founder of "*individual psychology*" and Jung, founder of "*analytical psychology*." While Adler views were diametrically opposed in most respects to Freud's, that of Jung remained much closer to Freud's original position in both theory and practice.

Out of his clinical experience Freud developed a number of concepts important in building up his theories. The brief summary of the psychoanalytic theory that follows is "essentially limited to a review of Freud's basic formulations as they existed at the time of his death in 1939" (Page, 1947, p. 179).

Dynamics of Behaviour

Freud recognised two fundamental motivating forces governing all our activities, indeed, life itself. These two are the constructive life urges and the destructive *death urges*. The former of these psychic drives finds physiological expression in the building-up or anabolic processes of body tissues, and the latter in the catabolic or destructive processes. Freud christened the life urge *Eros* and the death force *Thanatos*. The aim of the death forces is to injure, destroy and kill. The death drives get expressed in hate, aggression, murder and suicide. The life urges were further divided into two groups; the *ego impulses* promote the organic needs of nutrition and the *sex impulses* find expression in pleasurable and affectional pursuits. The energy of the sex drive is called the *libido.* Ego impulses play an in significant role in psychoanalytic theory whereas sex and aggressive drives are of major importance since their development and expression determine to a great extent the happiness and mental health of mankind. Love and hate are not mutually antagonistic. Often the two are inseparably fused conflicting coexisting motives and attitudes of this kind are included under the heading of *ambivalence* in psychoanalysis.

The energy generated by the body is channeled off into the various life urges. These energised drives create tension, experienced as painful and unpleasant feelings. Therefore, these drives motivate behaviour and impel the individual to engage in specific tensior-reducing activities. The tension produced by libido is best released through amorous activity. However, society places many barriers in the path of sex. Hence the libido is frequently denied normal or direct outlet. This creates a tension reservoir. The pent up sex energy has to be released. This can be done through sublimation or other means. Sublimation consists in the directing of the sex energy into socially approved channels. Poetry, music, art and dancing are some of he common and normal methods of sexual sublimation. The normal individual sublimates his hostility or aggression towards his enemies by digging a garden, chopping wood or going hunting.

Certain guiding principles further supplement the Freudian motivational system. The sex drives are dominated in the early years of life particularly, by *Pleasure Principle*, chaterised by a tendency to avoid pain and to seek pleasure, uninhibited. In course of time the Pleasure Principle comes under the control of *Reality Principle*, closely related with the ego drives. Reality Principle encourages the temporary denial of immediate pleasure to avoid subsequent pan. Its goal is to adapt the individual to the physical, social and moral requirements of the external world. The guiding rule of the death drives the Nirvana Principle, aimed at final return of living matter to the inorganic state.

Psychosexual Development

Psychosexuality involves the development and broad biological, social and psychological manifestation of the sex impulses. It forms the nucleus of psychoanalytic theory and treatment. Psychoanalysts recognize these principal stages in the sexual growth of the individual as three in number The first is the period of *infantile Sexuality*, extending from birth to about age six, having three stages—*the oral, the anal and the phallic.* The libido (energy of the sex drive) is fixated in these three *erogenous zones* of the body during this period. The second is the *Latent Period* from age six to age twelve. The third is the *Genital State* that starts with puberty and extends through adolescence to maturity.

The psychosexual theory has far-reaching consequences and significance for the understanding of human behaviour. Freud believed that many character and personality traits of normal individuals are derivatives and manifestations of infantile sexuality. The more technical aspects of psychosexual development shall be considered in greater detail in other chapters, especially, on development, motivation, personality and adjustment, of this text.

Levels of Consciousness

The mind according to Freud consists of three levels, "*the conscious*" "*the subconscious*" and "*the unconscious*". These divisions are not specific anatomical areas but convenient abstractions.

The "*Conscious Mind*" is the seat of our awareness. It is here that we do our thinking, remember past events and plan future activities. It is the well-lighted region of the mind, but a very minute portion of our mental life. The bulk of mental activity consists of unconscious processes. The "*Unconscious Mind*" may be thought of as a great subterranean storehouse, intensely and eternally dark, which exists below the level of awareness. In the unconscious mind lies a great mass of thought, feelings, memories, desires and experiences which we have either forgotten or never know. The unconscious is timeless, chaotic, infantile and primitive. It is the underworld of the personality that is unconcerned with reality or the rights and rules of society. Somewhere between the end zone of the conscious mind and the darkness of the unconscious is a sort of twilight area called the "*Subconscious Mind*". In it are stored forgotten facts and experiences which under proper conditions may be returned to awareness. At one end the subconscious merges into the unconscious causing things we should remember to be lost, not possible to be recovered again. At the other end, the subconscious is linked with conscious mind and by association of concentration we can bring back experiences to the conscious level and use them.

Psychic Forces in Mental Life

Within the three levels of the mind exist psychic forces or energy systems which by their interplay create an inner world of personality. These psychic forces are called the "*Id*", the "*Superego*" and the "*Ego*". They are distributed over the three levels of the mind as a network of energy but exert their greatest influence within certain boundaries of awareness. These three psychic forces form the components of our personality and rule over it as the "*Triumvirate*".

It may be made clear at the outset that the Id, Ego and Superego are not structures or entities. They are simply symbolic terms which are used to describe certain emotional and psychological activities which seems to be operating within one's personality. The *Id* corresponds roughly to the popular conception of the "*beast*" in man. The Superego is more commonly known as "Conscience." The Ego is the "*I*" that thinks, feels, decides, and wills. It is the administrative officer of the personality and one of the most important functions of the Ego is to co-ordinate the antagonistic strivings of the Id and the Superego.

This much about psychoanalysis will do for the present.

The more technical aspects of the Levels of Consciousness as Energy Systems and the components of personality as Psychic Forces in Mental Life will be discussed in greater detail in chapters on motivation, personality and adjustment.

That both psychoanalytic aims and methods are highly specialised techniques for clinical work is an undisputable fact. As a consequence they are not comparable to those of the academic schools. Some scholars are of the opinion that neither Freud's methods nor his aims have appreciably influenced the evolution of experimental psychology. Beyond doubt, they created a revolution in the treatment of mental disorders, but this occurred in psychiatry rather than in academic psychology. On the other hand Freud's systematic theories did profoundly influence *academic psychology* in several ways.

Prior to the development of Freud's system, academicians paid less attention to the psychology of motivation, particularly *unconscious motivation*. Psychoanalysis did much to remedy this deficiency, since Freuds theories heavily emphasised the unconscious processes of mental life. Freud recognised that traditionally man's rational side had been overemphasised in accounting for behaviour. He introduced the id as one of the components of personality. Logic has no place in the Id. The Id is lacking in morals and ethical judgement, and it has no sense of social values some of his critics believe that Freud went too far in the opposite direction of explaining behaviour almost entirely in terms of irrational processes. The hypotheses formulated by Freud have proved difficult or impossible to test. Frequently they are cast in such a form as to make experimental verification impossible. Therefore, it is unwise to give a final evaluation of Freud's system.

Freud is indirectly responsible for a great deal of the contemporary interest in child psychology and child development. His conclusions that neurotic disturbances originate in infantile sexuality have made virtually everyone who has anything to do with the care or training of children extremely child centred. Today parents, academicians and clinicians are more interested on the child's own nature, needs and potentialities. Sincere efforts are made to discover how these characteristics may be developed at the least cost to his individualism and with the least risk of harming him psychologically.

Freud and his associates are also largely held responsible for the radical change that has taken place in the sexual mores; the change has been in the direction of increased freedom in sexual behaviour. Freudian psychology is also used more as a rationalisation than as a true reason for the new sexual ethic. Freudian psychoanalysis has become greatly over simplified in the public mind; even it is abused very often. Freud actually considered sexual repression necessary if civilisation and culture were to survive. But people overlook this fact, and unfortunately, attribute sexual freedom to Freud. As a result there has been a general loosening of sexual restraint in art, literature, media of entertainment, and behaviour in general.

Finally, Psychoanalysis aroused a strong interest in a number of psychologists in the relatively new field of clinical psychology. This branch of psychology has grown rapidly in recent years. The keener awareness on the part of the general public of the desirability of obtaining psychological assistance for adjustment of problems has resulted in a great increase in counselling agencies, both public and private, whose personnel, in part, are clinical psychologists, in most of the countries in Europe and America. The academic training of a clinical psychologist is typically grounded in experimental psychology, psychometry, abnormal psychology, but not indoctrinated against Freudian theory. He is inspired with an eclectic point of view. Not only does this eclectic point of view recognise the worth of various approaches but also its guiding principle is to test the value of any clinical principle or method by experimental techniques whenever necessary.

Free association, dream analysis and psychoanalytic theory and technique of Sigmund Freud have developed outside of the scope of traditional academic and systematic psychology.

Being a highly specialised one, psychoanalytic methodology appears to be irrelevant to experimental psychology. On the other hand Freud's theories of human motivation and psychogenic development have profoundly influenced academic psychology. They have also generated a great deal of research, debates and interest in the areas of personality and adjustment.

By about 1900 Freud announced his discoveries and humbly offered them to the world. In course of time his teachings came to be recognised as the science of psychoanalysis. Today, just eight and a half decades after the birth of psychoanalysis, some outstanding academicians are of the opinion that a great majority of clinicians accept these theories as fundamental bases for interpreting human behaviour. However, one should not forget that Freud's original formulations have been amended by the findings of modern science so that they now have sufficient scientific verify to merit the serious consideration of all who influence the development of personality. Relatively few pure "Freudians" persist in following rigidly the original principles of psychoanalysis. Eighty years of research have so modified Freud's pronouncements that we now refer to this science as "*Psychodynamics*" to distinguish it from the earlier theories, bitterly criticised for a long time.

Approach of the Purposive or Hormic Psychologists

Some authors are of the opinion that in describing general behaviour, there are three main schools or theories. These are the *connectionists*, or *modern associationists* the *Gestalt or field psychologists* and the *purposivists.* Under the third category get included Freudian psychologists and William McDougall and his supporters.

The *purposivists* have objected to any emphasis on intelligence, perception, learning and thinking. They insist that the most important part of psychology has to do with motives, purposes and urges. They emphasize on the study of emotion, motivation and personality. McDougall and his supporters are also called *hormic psychologists.* In Greek, *horme* means "an urge" As the Gestalt Psychologists rose in revolt against the reductionistic analysis of the structuralists and the behaviourists so too the purposivists or hormic psychologists against the S—R psychology of the connectionists. The most militant of these rebels was William McDougall, with his *purposivism or hormism.*

Psychology on the whole had tended to avoid solving the problem of why people do the things they do; the problem of motives, of the sources and springs of action. Science tends to shy off from the question "*Why*?" But in animal activities, and especially in human behaviour, the question *why* certain things are done is so insistently present to common sense that sooner or later it must be observed by science. Thus observed Woodworth when he gave his lectures on *dynamic psychology*, in the Columbia University.

"Woodworth, however, was not the person chiefly responsible for raising this question in contemporary psychology. When he gave his lectures on dynamic psychology, the questions of the springs of action was already in the air. William McDougall had brought it prominently into the foreground in his Introduction to Social Psychology, a book that advocated a theory of instinct which immediately commanded attention" (Heidbreader, 1971, p. 315). However, McDougall does not go without a pungent remark against him. The remark is : "*William McDougall* (1871—1936) formulated his social psychology around instinct theory; and his formulation was treated too kindly by his contemporaries and too harshly by history" (Chaplin & Krawice, 1974, p. 649).

The purposive psychologists start from the fact of "*purpose*". This is because they are impressed by the *Constancy of the result produced*, by the fact that the same result can be obtained by a wide variety of movements. The same person may use different movements to accomplish the same result. At one time he may sound the bell by pressing the button with his left hand and at another time with his right hand. At still another time he may use his thumb or the back of his hand. Yet with each of these diverse movements he accomplishes the same result, that is, sounding the bell, and completes the same behaviour sequence. To explain the dominance of the result to be achieved, the purposivist insists that we must use the concept of "*goal-striving*."

"Purposive behaviour is the same as goal seeking, In a full-fledged purposive act, as we know it, in ourselves, two factors are combined; desire and foresight. We foresee the goal and we desire to reach it. Foresight and desire do not always go together. The aviator in a certain predicament may clearly foresee that he is going to strike a tree—without desiring that result. The hungry infant desires a full stomach –without knowing what he desires. In the primitive kind of goal seeking there is a striving without any clear foresight of the goal. Purposivism asserts the prime role of striving in all behaviour; it emphasizes striving rather than foresight, through inclined to place much emphasis on foresight as well, even in animal behaviour. It is because of its major emphasis on striving that it has adpted the name of hormic psychology" (Woodworth, 1952, pp. 215—216).

And McDougall champions a *Harmic Psychology*. He was one of the first to define psychology as the science of behaviour. Behaviour is the characteristic of living things. The striving to achieve an end is the mark of behaviour. The fundamental appeals or motives that lead to goal-seeking behaviour are the "*instincts*". For McDougall, "*instincts*" are as quoted by Chaplin & Krawice (1974, p. 649): innate or inherited tendencies which are the essential springs or motive powers of all thought and action, whether individual or collective, and are the bases from which the character and will of individuals and nations are gradually developed under the guidance of the intellectual faculties" (McDougall, 1921, p. 20).

An instinct for McDougall was not a mechanical affair like a reflex or a chain of reflexes. If was rather a motive, a striving toward some type of Goal. He regarded an instinct as a complete mental process at the primitive level, capable of analysis into three parts.

For him, an instinct is an innate or inherited mental structure which determines its possessor to perform certain Specific actions in certain Specific situations. Therefore, on the *Cognitive* side or the *receptive* side it is a predisposition to notice significant stimuli—like food odour when one is hungry. The instinctive disposition is organized on its Cognitive side. So that it is stimulated into activity by a specific excitement; and on its *Conative* side or executive side so that one action rather than another is performed. On its *executive* side, it is a predisposition to make certain movements or to approach a certain goal. In between is the *affective* side, the *emotional impulse* or the striving, the core of the whole instinct.

Perhaps, the most distinctive feature of McDougall's argument is his insistence on a specific emotion being the central, essential, unchanging aspect of every instinct. Thus, he says, the emotion of fear is the central aspect of the instinct of escape, anger the invariable can concomitant of combat, tender emotions of parential instinct, and so on. When we are looking for motives in the behaviour of the lower animals we invoke the principle of instinct, but when we do so in man's behaviour we invoke emotion. It is instict which impels a bee to go through its wonderful cycle of activities, but that it is anger or pride or fear that makes a man behave in a certain way. Common sense, then, says that motives in man and the higher animals, are emotions; that in the lower animals they are instincts.

The instinctive tendencies become combined into "sentiments". They become combined by being attached to the same object. In common speech the word '*sentiment'* is not clearly distinguished from "*feeling* and *emotion'* and yet as McDougall points out, a distinction is vaguely recognized. We speak, for example, of a sentient of hatred, but of a feeling or emotion of anger, the difference being that the sentiment is a permanent part of ourselves, while the emotion or the feeling is merely a passing experience. Sentiment is the name we give to a complex at a certain level of development. When a complex acquires a certain degree of stability, when it becomes an important part of the mind, we call it a sentiment.

The typical sentiment involves the funtioning of several of the instincts, these being habitually directed toward its object. Your sentiment for a person is whatthe person means to you emotionally. Your sentiment for any object is what the object means to you emotionally. Love and partriotism are sentiments. The master sentiment is the sentiment of '*Self-regard*. Character is just the Organised self—the organisation of our instincts and emotions and sentiments into the master sentiment. There is no single instinct of love or patriotism. In so far as the sentiment of patriotism is concerned, a man's native land becomes the object of several instincts. His country in danger awakens fear in him. An attack on his country awakens his anger. His country in rivalry with another country awakens his self-assertive tendency. As his home it awakens loving emotions in him. Thus his country becomes the object of his complex sentiment of patriotism which can be a powerful motivating force in his behaviour. The self assertive instinct is an important factor in any sentiment. Ultimately, this results as the sentiment of self-regard or the master sentiment. Human behaviour is motivated by sentiments, said McDougall. Behaviour is not driven by purely rational considerations; but by love and hate, interests, zeals, rivalries and enthusiasms.

From the 'behaviour' definition of psychology, McDougal leads us to a psychology of the social group—a collective mental life. Any group of people—a crowd, a church, a trade union, a nation—possesses a "*group mind*" which is greater than the sum of the individual minds which compose it, because of the interactive effects of individuals upon individuals. The cement that finds the group together is intensification of emotions. In a panic situation a crowd of people behave like a herd of mindless animals. They trample each other to death in a blind attempt to escape danger. Such reactions McDougall attributed to "*primitive passive sympathy*." Sympathy is the feeling or affective aspect of gregarious instinct. Just as we can share the feelings of our fellows, so we can share their thoughts. We may share the thought of others without any known purpose and without understanding. This is "*suggestion*." The person to whom ideas are suggested thinks that they are his own, never dreaning that they come from an outside source. Suggestion may be regarded as the cognitive aspect of the gregarious instinct. The fundamental condition of collective mental life is that the members of the group should act, feel and think together.

The positive reaching of Mc Dougall was his insistence that the instincts are the great driving forces of human conduct. Directly or indirectly the instincts are the prime movers of all human activity, not excluding the intellectual. Only at the life-giving touch of the instincts are the human mechanisms stirred to action. Contain, that is purposive striving toward a goal is in itself not reducible to mechanism; and, for McDougall, it is the fundamental category in psychology.

On the negative side, McDugall's doctrine emphatically denied two notions. The first was the conception of the rational man found in social and political theories. The second was that he did not take into account the findings of the mechanistic psychology, that is, modern associationism, in explaining the problem of the springs of action. In spite of all his efforts in trying to explain mass movements, national characteristics and the structure of permanent social institutions by an extension and application of his instinct theory, the lasting contribution of McDougall is evaluated as minimal. His theory was unable to survive the strong behaviourist reaction set in motion with the ascendance of J.B. Watson and his school. These American psychologists sought to rid his theory of instincts, propensities and other nonobservables though they looked kindly on animal psychology. For the Structuralists, particularly Titchener, psychology is the study of consciousness by the method of introspection. This is for the purpose of answering three questions about mental phenomena. What? How? Why? Titchener relates psychology to science in general. The overall programme for psychology is essentially similar to that of the other natural sciences. When the scientist has decided what aspect of nature he is going to study, he then proceeds to discover its elements, shows how these are compounded into more complex processes, and finally formulates the laws that govern the behaviour of the phenomena under study. Titchener and his associates analysed consciousness into its elements, namely, sensations, images and affective states but found out that all these three stemmed out of a common mental ancestor; and to them this ancestor appeared to be sensation. Though structuralism was the most consistent of all the early systems, the American psychologists were not content with restricting psychology to the introspective analysis of consciousness. Consequently, structuralism weakened and finally collapsed.

The primary interest of the Functionalists was the study of mind as it functions in adapting the organism to its environment. Functonalism ranges over a long period, from the mid 1850 to contemporary times. Broadly Speaking, American psychology today is functionalistic. The exposition of Harvey A. Corr represents functionalism at its maturity and in its mot definitive form. Carr defines psychology as the study of mental activity. Mental activity is concerned with the acquisition, fixation, organisation, and evaluation of experiences, and their subsequent utilisation in the guidance of conduct. This is a functional point of view indeed ! Though Carr recognises the necessity of introspection, he gives more emphasis to objective observation. Carr's psychology is much broader than Titchener's. He believes, functional psychology is closely allied with physiology, but it should raw material from other related sciences for facts and methodological contributions and whenever possible, psychology in turn ought to contribute freely to other disciplines. In this way he opens the door to the possibility of an applied psychology. Carr discusses the nature of an adaptive act and thanks that behaviour is adaptive in the sense that the individual's responses result in a better adjustment to the environment. According to Carr, learning is a perceptual—motor process. He considers attention in terms of its functional ability in dealing with the environment. For him, perception is a basic process in adjustment, how we perceive our environment and how we respond to it. As a systematic point of view, functionalism was an overwhelming success. Finally, it was absorbed into contemporary psychology, which proves its success.

John B. Watson championed the Behaviouristic approach to psychology. He revolted against both the structuralists and the function a lists. For him the structuralists worked with intangibles and unapproachables which he resented. He thought functionalism as a timid, half-hearted, half-way measure, confusing and ineffectual. He strongly opposed the analysis of consciousness by introspection as a suitable aim for a scientific psychology and in its place emphasized the study of behaviour by objective, experimental procedures. The following points are clearly made in the behaviourist manifesto of Watson. (1) Psychology is to be the science not of consciousness, but of behaviour. (2) It is to cover both human and animal behaviour. (3) it is to rely wholly on objective data, introspection being discarded, (4) It is to avoid mentalistc concepts. (5) A scientific basis is to be provided for the practical control of behaviour. (6) Behaviourism must give up mind and brain and keep its eyes fixed on the sense organs, muscles and glands. Thus, Watson aims at Stimulus—Response (S—R) psychology. The methods proposed by Watson for the behaviourists are: (a) Observation with and without instrumental control; (b) the conditioned reflex method; (c) the verbal report method; and (d) the testing method. Watson favours learning by conditioning and stands and environmentalist. For him behaviour is a sensorimotor activity of the whole organism. Emotion are behavioural patterns largely acquired through conditioning. He reduced thought to laryngeal habits. Behaviourism was truly an S—R Psychology. Watson favoured applied psychology and research in child psychology. His approach to psychology was deterministic, mechanistic and scientific.

The Gestalt Psychologists revolted against reductionistic analysis in psychology, whether such analysis was structuralistic or behaviouristic in origin. They called structuralistic and associationistic theories as "brick and mortar psychology". They proved experimentally that the whole is different from the sum of its parts. This is indeed a fundamental Gestalt principle. They emphasised upon the phenomenon of perception in explaining experience. Experiences carry with them a quality of wholeness that cannot be found in the parts. For this reason the German noun "Gestalt" is appropriate to characterize the system of the Gestalitists, since it denotes form, figure or configuration and carries with it the connotation that reductional analysis destroys a figure or "Gestalt". The Gestalt psychologists extended their observations and theoretical interpretations into other areas of psychology such as learning, thinking and problem solving. Gestalt psychology represents a molar as opposed to molecular point of view. They, the Gestalt psychologists, opposed the machine view of the nervous system that arose in connection with behaviouristic explanation of learning, and took a "dynamic" or "field" view o the nervous system. They disagreed with the behaviourrists' denial of the validity of introspection and favoured the study of conscious experience in a phenomenological sense. In the area of perception the Gestalt psychologists made many valuable and original contributions. For the Gestalisis, learning is insightful. For them, to learn is to complete a "Gestalt". Gestalt point of view is today felt everywhere in the whole of psychology.

Psychoanalysis grew outside academic circles under the leadership of Sigmund Freud. The psychoanalytic movement developed in medical practice from the effort to find some cure for the neuroses. The psychoanalysts were primarily concerned with the dynamic—psychic determinants of human behaviour. As a theory, psychoanalysis has a nonacademic and non-experimental background and as a practice, it is a nonexperimental clinical techniques. In spite of these limitations, it has exerted profound influence on modern psychology and other related sciences. Out of his clinical experience Freud developed a number of important concepts as those he used to describe the dynamics of behaviour—the life urge and the death drive, and the components of personality—the ego, id and superego, the levels of consciousness—conscious, subconscious and unconscious and those which he employed in elaborating the various stages of psychosexual devèlopment—infantile sexuality, latent period and the genital stages and so forth. Freud used two therapeutic techniques—free association and dream interpretation, to treat his psychoneurotic patients. Psychoanalytic aims and methods are highly specialised techniques for clinical work. Psychoanalytic theory draws the attention of academic psychologists to unconscious mental processes and motivation.

Freud is indirectly responsible for a great deal of interest in child psychology in the present. Psychoanalytic theory is responsible to some extent in the changed outlook on the sexual ethics. Psychoanalysis is largely responsible for the development and expansion of clinical psychology and a great deal of experiment and research in the area of personality and adjustment. In the present, the term "Psychodynamics" is used instead of "psychoanalysis".

William McDougall was the exponent of Purposivism or Hormic Psychology. McDougall and the other purposivists were, concerned with the urges, purposes and motives of human behaviour. Purposive behaviour is the same as goal striving. For McDougall, the fundamental appeals or motives that lead to goal-seeking behaviour are the "instincts". An instinct is an innate or inherited mental structure which determincs its possessor to perform certain specific actions in certain specific situations. The instincts are the great driving forces of human activity. The primary instincts in human beings are escape, pugnacity, curiosity disgust, parental behaviour, self assertion and self abasement, gregariouness and imitation. Each of the primary instincts is paired with a primary emotion, for example, escape with fear, pugnacity with anger, curiousity with wonder and so forth. There are also sentiments like love, loyalty and patriotism which are complex products of instinct, intellect and emotion, and which derived whatever motive power they possess from their instinctive components. Only at the life giving touch of the instincts are the human mechanisms stirred to action. Any group of people possesses a group mind which is greater than the sum of the individual minds which compose it, because of the interactive effects of individuals upon individuals. Intensified emotions bind the group together.

6

Adolescence in the Psychoanalytic Theory

The subject of adolescence after an interval of twenty years. During this time much has happened in analytic work to throw added light on the problems concerned and to influence the conditions of life for young people, whether normal or abnormal. Nevertheless, in spite of partial advances, the position with regard to the analytic study of adolescence is not a happy one, and especially unsatisfactory when compared with that of early childhood. With the latter period, we feel sure of our ground, and in possession of a wealth of material and information which enables us to assume authority and apply analytic findings to the practical problems of upbringing. When it comes to adolescence, we feel hesitant and, accordingly, cannot satisfy the parents or educational workers who apply for help to us and to our knowledge. One can hear it said frequently that adolescence is a neglected period, a stepchild where analytic thinking is concerned. These complaints, which come from two sides, from the parents as well as from the analytic workers themselves, seem to me to warrant closer study and investigation than they have received so far.

Adolescence in the Psychoanalytic Literature

The psychoanalytic study of adolescence began as it well known, in 1905 with the relevant chapter of the Three

Essays on Sexuality. Here, puberty was described as the time when the changes set in which give infantile sexual life its final shape. Subordination of the erotogenic zones to the primacy of the genital zone; the setting up of new sexual aims, different for males and females; and the finding of new sexual objects outside the family were listed as the main event. While this exposition explained many features of the adolescent process and behaviour which had been unexplained before, the newly developed notion of the existence of an infantile sex life could not but lower the significance of adolescence in the eyes of the investigators. Before the publication of the three essays, adolescence had derived major significance from its role as the beginning of sex lie in the individual; after the discovery of an infantile sex life, the status of adolescence was reduced to that of a period of final transformations, transition and bridge between the diffuse infantile and the genitally centered adult sexuality.

Seventeen years later, in 1922, Ernest Jones, London, published a paper on "some Problems of Adolescence" which dwelt on a "correlation between adolescence and infancy" as its most distinctive point. Following the pronouncement in the Three Essays that the phase of development corresponding to the period between the ages of two and five must be regarded as an important precursor of he subsequent final organisation, he showed in detail how "the individual recapitulates and expands in the second decennium of life the development the passed through during the first five years..." He ascribed the difference in "the circumstances in which the development takes place" but went as far as propounding "the general law...that adolescence recapitulates infancy, and that the precise was in which a given person will pass through the necessary stages of development in adolescence is to a very great extent determined by the form of his infantile development". In short: "these stages are passed through on different planes at the two periods of infancy and adolescence, but in very similar ways in the same individual".

Jones's important but isolated contribution to the problem

coincided with a peak in the publications of Siegfried Bernfeld in Vienna, a true explorer of youth, who combined work as a clinical analyst and teacher of analysis with the unceasing study of adolescence in all its aspects of individual and group behaviour, reaction to social influences, sublimations, etc. His most significant addition to the analytic theory was the description of a specific kind of male adolescent development (1923), the so-called "protracted" type which extends far beyond the time limit normal for adolescent characteristics, and is conspicuous by "tendencies toward productivity whether artistic, literary or scientific, and by a strong bend toward idealistic aims and spiritual values..." As the solid background for his assumptions, Bernfeld published, in cooperation with W. Hoffer, a wealth of material consisting of self-observations of adolescents, their diaries, poetic productions, etc.

While Bernfeld accounted in this manner for the elaborations of the normal adolescent processes by the impact of internal frustrations and external, environmental pressures, August Aichhorn, also in Vienna, approached the problem from the angle of dissocial and criminal development. His work lay with those young people who answer to the same pressures with failure to adapt, faulty superego development and revolt against the community. His book *Wayward Youth* (1925) acquired world renown as the outstanding pioneering attempt to carry psychoanalytic knowledge into the difficult realm of the problems of the young offender.

Based on familiarity with S. Bernfeld's views, and intimately connected with A. Aichhorn's studies, I contributed in 1936 two papers under the titles "The Ego and the Id at Puberty" and "Instinctual Anxiety During Puberty." In my case, interest in the adolescent problems was derived from my concern with the struggles of the ego to master the tensions and pressures arising from the drive derivatives, struggles which lead in the normal case to character formation, in their pathological outcome to the formation of neurotic symptoms. I described this battle between ego and id as terminated by a first truce at the beginning of theatency period and breaking out once more with the first approach to puberty, when the distribution of forces inside the individual is upset by quantitative and qualitative changes in the drives. Threatened with anxiety by the drive development, the ego, as it has been formed in childhood, enters into a struggle for survival in which all the available methods of defense are brought into play and strained to the utmost. The results, that is the personality changes which are achieved, vary. Normally, the organisation of ego and superego alter sufficiently to accommodate the new, mature forms of sexuality. In less favourable instances a rigid, immature ego succeeds in inhibiting ordistorting sexual maturity; in some cases the id impulses succeed in creating utter confusion and chaos in what has been an orderly, socially directed ego during the laterncy period. I made the point that, more than any other time of life, adolescence with its typical conflicts provides the analyst with instructive pictures of the interplay and sequence of internal danger, anxiety, defense activity, transitory or permanent symptom formation, and mental breakdown.

Interest increased in the postwar years and brought a multitude of contributions, especially from the United States. Fortunately for the student of the subject, Leo a. Spiegel published in 1951 a lengthy "Review of contributions to a Psychoanalytic Theory of Adolescence." Although his attempt to construct an integrated theory out of often widely divergent parts could hardly be successful, the paper serves a most useful purpose by abstracting, reviewing and classifying the material. He groped the publications under headings such as:

"Classification of Phenomenology" (Bernfeld, hartmann, Kris, and Loewenstein, Wittels)

"Object Relations" (Bernfeld, Buxbaum, H. Deutsch, Erikson, fenihel, A. Freud, W. Hoffer, Jones, A. Katan-Angel, Landauer)

"Defense Mechanisms" (Bernfeld, H. Deutsch, Fenichel, A. Freud, Greenacre, E. Kris)

"Creativity" (Bernfeld, A. Freud)

"Sexual Activity" (Balint, Bernfeld, Buxbaum, H. deutsch, Federn, Ferneczi, S. Freud, Lampl-de Groot)

"Aspects of Ego Functioning" (Fenichel, a. Feud, Harnik, Hoffer, Landauer)

"Treatment" (Aichhorn, K.R. Eissler, A. Freud, Gitelson, A. Katan, M. Klein, Landauer, A. Reich).

A detailed bibliography attached to the review contained altogether forty-one papers by thirty-fur authors, covering apparently every theoretical, clinical, and technical aspect of the subject.

But in spite of this impressive list of contributors and contributions the dissatisfaction with our knowledge of the field remained unaltered, nor did our own, or the parents', confidence in our analytic skill with adolescent patients increase. There was now much published evidence to the contrary; nevertheless, adolescence remained, as it had been before, a stepchild in psychoanalytic theory.

Difficulties of Fact-Finding Concerning Adolescence

There are, we believe, two different causes, which may, possibly, account for our bewilderment when faced with all he intricacies of the adolescent process.

When, in our capacity as analysts, we investigate mental states, we rely, basically, on two methods: either on the analysis of individuals in whom that particular state of mind is in action at the moment, or on the reconstruction of that state in analytic treatment undertaken at a later date, the results of these two procedures, used either singly, or in combination with each other, have taught us all that we, as analysts, know about the developmental stages of the human mind. (It may be worth while to remind the reader in this connection that our knowledge of the mental processes of infancy has been derived from reconstructions in the analyses of adults and was merely confirmed and enlarged on later by analyses or observations carried out in childhood.)

It happens that these two procedures, which have served us well for all other periods of life, prove less satisfactory and less productive of results when applied to adolescents.

Reconstruction of adolescence in adult analysis.—As regard reconstruction, I am impressed how seldom n the treatment of my adult cases I succeed in reviving their adolescent experiences in full force. By that I do not mean to imply that adult patients have an amnesia for their adolescence which resembles in extent or in depth the amnesia for their early childhood. On the contrary, the memories of the events of the adolescent period are, normally, retained in consciousness and told to the analyst without apparent difficulty. Masturbation in preadolescence and adolescent, the first moves toward intercourse, etc, may even play a dominant part in the patients conscious memories and, as we know well, are made use of to overlay and hide the repressed masturbation conflicts and the buried sexual activities of early childhood. Further, in the analyses of sexually inhibited men who deplore the loss of erective potency, it is fairly easy to recover the memories of the bodily practices carried out in adolescence—frequently very crude and cruel ones—which served them at that time to prevent erections, or to suppress them as soon as they occurred. On the other hand, these memories contain no more than the bare facts, happenings and actions, divorced from the affects which accompanied them at the time. What we fail to recover, as a rule, is the atmosphere in which the adolescent lives, his anxieties, the height of elation o depth of despair, the quickly rising enthusiasms, the utter hopelessness, the burning—or at other times sterile—intellectual and philosophical preoccupations, the yearning for freedom, the sense of loneliness, the feeling of oppression by the parents, the impotent rages or active hates directed against the adult world, the erotic crushes—whether home-sexually or heterosexually directed—the suicidal fantasies, etc. These are elusive mood swings, difficult to revive which, unlike the affective states of infancy and early childhood, seem disinclined to re-emerge and be relived in connection with the person of the analyst.

If this impression, which I gathered from my own cases, should be confirmed by other analysts of adults, such a failure—or partial failure—to reconstruct adolescence might account for some of the gaps in our appraisal of the mental processes during this period.

Analysis during adolescence.—When discussing in his "Review" the contributions dealing with the analytic therapy of adolescents, Spiegel 91951) deployed what seemed to him an undue pessimism on the part of some authors. He pointed to the need of adapting the analytic technique to the adolescent Patients' particular situation and expressed surprise at the absence of explicit discussions of an introductory phase "analogous to the one used with children and delinquents."

Actually, since 1951, some further papers on the subject of technique appeared in print. Two of the dealt with the opening phase,(Fraiberg, 1955; Noshpitz, 1957), a third with the terminal one (Adatto, 1958).

While these authors brought material to highlight the special technical difficulties encountered in the beginning and ending of the therapy, work on adolescents done in our Hampstead child-therapy clinic emphasized special technical difficulties met with in the very center of it, i.e., at the critical moment when preadolescence gives way to adolescence proper, when the revolt against the parents is anticipated in the transference and tends to lead to a break with the analyst, i.e., to abrupt and undesirable termination of treatment from the patient's side.

Thus, according to experience, special difficulties are encountered in he beginning, in the middle, and in connection with the end of treatment. Put in other words, this can only mean that the analytic treatment of adolescents is a hazardous venture from beginning to end, a venture in which the analyst has to meet resistances of unusual strength and variety. This is borne out by the comparison of adolescent with adult cases. In adult analysis we are used to handle the difficult technical situations with certain hysterical patients who cannot bear frustration in the transference and try to force the analyst to enact with them their revived low and hate feelings in an actual personal relationship. We are used to guard against the obsessional patients' technique of isolating words from affect and of tempting us to interpret unconscious content while it is divorced from its emotional cathexis. We attempt to deal with the narcissistic withdrawal of the borderline schizophrenics, the projections of the paranoid patients who turn their analyst into the persecuting enemy, the destructive hopelessness of the depressed who claim disbelief in any positive outcome of the analytic effort; the acting out tendencies and the lack of insight of the delinquent or psychopathic characters. But in the disturbances named above, we meet either the one or the other of these technical difficulties, and we can adapt the analytic technique to the resistance which is specific for the type of mental disorder. Not so in adolescence where the patient may change rapidly from one of these emotional positions to the next, exhibit them all simultaneously, or in quick succession, leaving the analyst little time and scope to marshal his forces and change his handling of the case according to the changing need.

Obstacles in the libido economy. Comparison with the states of mourning and unhappy love.—experience has taught us to take a serious view of such major and repeated in adequacies of the analytic technique. Hey cannot be explained away by individual characteristics of the patients under treatment nor by any accidental or environmental factors which run counter to it. Nor can they be overcome simply by increased effort, skill and tact on the part of the analyst. They have to be taken as indications that something in the inner structure of the disturbances themselves differs markedly from the pattern of those illnesses for which the analytic technique has been devised originally and to which it is most frequently applied (Eissler, (1950). We have to gain insight into these divergences of pathology before we are in a position to revise our technique. Where the analyses of children, of delinquents and of certain borderline states are concerned, this has happened already. What the analytic technique had to provide for in these cases were the immaturity and weakness of the patients' ego; their lower threshold for the toleration of frustration; and the lesser importance of verbalization with increased importance of action (acting out) for their mental economy. It remains to be pointed out what corresponding factors are characteristic for the adolescent disorders, i.e., to what specific inner situation of the patients our technique has to be adjusted to make adolescents more amenable to analytic treatment.

So far as I am concerned, I am impressed by a similarity between the responses of these young patients and those of two other well known types of mental upset, namely the reactions to treatment during unhappy love affairs and during periods of mourning. In both these latter states there is much mental suffering and, as a rule, the urgent wish to be helped; in spite of this, neither state answers well to analytic therapy. Our theoretical explanation of this comparative intractability is the following; being in love as well as mourning are emotional states in which the individual's libido is engaged fully in relation to a real love object of the present, or of the most recent pat, the mental pain being caused by the difficult task to withdraw cathexis and give up a position which holds out no further hop for return of love, that is, for satisfaction. While the individual is engaged in this struggle, insufficient libido is available to cathect the person of the analyst, or to flow back regressively and reinvest former objects and positions. Consequently, neither the transference events nor the past become meaningful enough to yield material for interpretation. The immediate object (of love, or of morning) has to be given up before analytic therapy can become effective.

To my mind the libidinal position of the adolescent has much in common with the two states described above. The adolescent too is engaged in an emotional struggle. And moreover in one of extreme urgent and immediacy, his libido is on the point of detaching itself from the parents and of cathecting new objects. Some mourning for the objects of the past is inevitable; so are the "crushes," i.e., the happy or unhappy love affairs with adults outside the family, or with other adolescents, whether of the opposite or the same sex;

so is, further, a certain amount of narcissistic withdrawal which bridges the gap urging periods when no external object is cathected. Whatever the libidinal solution at a given moment may be, it will always be a preoccupation with the present time and, as described above, with little or no libido left available for investment either in the past or in the analyst.

If this supposition as to the libido distribution in the adolescent personality can be accepted as a correct statement, it can serve to explain some of our young patients' behaviour in treatment, such as: their reluctance to cooperate; their lack of involvement in the therapy or in the relationships to the analyst; their battles for the reduction of weekly sessions; their unpunctuality; their missing of treatment sessions for the sake of outside activities; their sudden breaking off of treatment altogether. We learn here by contrast how much the continuity of the average adult analysis owes to the mere fact of the analyst being a highly cathected object, quite part from the essential role played by the transference in the production of material.

There are, of course, those cases where the analyst himself becomes the new love object of the adolescent, i.e., the object of the "crush," a constellation which will heighten the young patient's keenness to be "treated," But apart from improved attendance and punctuality, this may mean merely that the analyst is brought up against another of the specific difficulties of the analyses of adolescents, namely the urgency of their needs, their intolerance for frustration and their tendency to treat whatever relationship evolves as a vehicle for wish fulfillment and not as a source of insight and enlightenment.

Under these conditions it is not surprising that besides analytic therapy many alternative forms of treatment for adolescents have been evolved and practiced, such as manipulation of the environment, residential treatment, the setting up of therapeutic communities, etc. Valuable as these experimental approaches are from the practical point of view, they can not, of course, be expected to contribute directly to our theoretical insight into the unconscious contents of the adolescent 's mind, the structure of his typical disturbances, or into the details of the mental mechanisms by which these latter are maintained.

Clinical Applications

What follows is an attempt to apply at least some of our hard won insights to three of the most pressing problems concerning adolescence.

The Adolescent Upset Inevitable

There is, first, the ever recurrent question whether the adolescent upheaval is welcome and beneficial as such whether it is necessary and, more than that, inevitable. On this point, psychoanalytic opinion is decisive and unanimous. The people in the child's family and school, who assess his station eh basis of behaviour, may deplore the adolescent upset which, to them, spells the loss of valuable qualities, of character stability and of social adaptation. As analysts, who assess personalities from the structural point of view, we think otherwise. We know that the character structure of a child at the end of the latency period represents the outcome of long drawn-out conflicts between id and ego forces. The inner balance achieved, although characteristic for each individual and precious to him, is preliminary only and precarious. It does not allow for the quantitative increase in drive activity, nor for the changes of drive quality which are both inseparable from puberty. Consequently, it has to be abandoned to allow adult sexuality to be integrated into the individual's personality. The so-called adolescent upheavals are no more than the external indications that such internal adjustments are in progress.

On the other hand, we all known individual children who as late as the ages of fourteen, fifteen or sixteen show no such outer evidence of inner unrest. They remain, as they a have been during the latency period, "good" children, wrapped up in their family relationships, considerate sons of their mothers, submissive to their fathers, in accord with the atmosphere, ideas and ideals of their childhood background, convenient as this may be, it signifies a delay of normal development and is, as such, a sign to be taken seriously. The first impression conveyed by these cases may be that of a quantitative deficiency of drive endowment, a suspicion which will usually prove unfounded. Analytic exploration reveals that this reluctance to "grow up" is derived not from the id but form the ego and superego aspects of the personality. These are children who have built up excessive defenses against their drive activities and are now crippled by the results, which ct as barriers against the normal maturational processes of phase development. They are, perhaps more than any others, in need of therapeutic help to remove the inner restrictions and clear the path for normal development, however "upsetting" the latter may prove to be.

The Adolescent Upset Predictable

A second question which we are asked to answer frequently concerns the problem whether the manner in which a given child will react in adolescence can be predicted from the characteristics of his early infantile or latency behaviour. Apart from the more general affirmative answer given by Ernest Jones (1922), only one among the authors named above has made clear and positive assertions in this respect. Siegfried Bernfeld (1923), when discussing his protracted type of male adolescence and its characteristics, established the links between this form of puberty and a specific type of infantile development based on the following three conditions: (a) that the frustration of infantile sex wishes has been shattering for the child's narcissism; (b) that the incestuous fixations to the parents have been of exceptional strength and have been maintained throughout the latency period; (c) that the superego has been established early, has been delineated sharply from the ego, and that the ideals contained init are invested with narcissistic as well as with object libido.

Other and less precise answers to the same question are scattered through the literature. We find the opinion that, in the majority of cases, the manifestations of the adolescent process are not predictable since they depend almost wholly on quantitative relations, i.e., on the strength and suddenness of drive increase, the corresponding increase in anxiety causing all the rest of the upheaval.

I suggested in another place (1936) that adolescence brings about occasionally something in the nature of a spontaneous cure. This happens in children whose pregenital activities and characteristics remained dominant throughout latency until the increase in genital libido produces a welcome decrease in pregenitality. This latter occurrence, on the other hand, can be matched by a corresponding one which produces the opposite effect: where phallic characteristics have remained dominant during latency, the increase in genital libido produces the effect of an exaggerated and threatening aggressive masculinity.

It seems to be generally accepted that a strong fixation to the mother, dating not only from the oedipal but from the preoedipal attachment to her, renders adolescence especially difficult. This latter assertion, on the other hand, has to be correlated with two recent findings of a different nature which we owe to work done in our Hampstead Child-Therapy clinic. One of these findings is derived from the study of orphaned children who were deprived of the relationship to a stable mother figure in their first years. This lack of a mother fixation, far from making adolescence easier, constitutes a real danger to the whole inner coherence of the personality during that period. In these cases adolescence is preceded frequently by a frantic search for a mother image; the internal possession and cathexis of such an image seems to be essential for the ensuing normal process of detaching libido from it for transfer to new objects, i.e., to sexual partners.

The second finding mentioned above is derived from the analyses of adolescent twins, in one case children whose twin relationship in infancy had been observed and recorded in minute detail (Burlingham, 1952). In their treatments it transpired that the "adolescent revolt" against the love objects of infancy demands the breaking of the tie to the twin in no lesser degree than the breaking of the tie to the mother. Since this libidinal (narcissistic as well as object-directed) cathexis of the twin is rooted in the same deep layer of the personality as the early attachment to the mother, its withdrawal is accompanied by an equal amount of structural upheaval, emotional upset, and result symptom formation. Where, on the other hand, the twin relationship survives the adolescent phase, we may expect to see a delay in the onset of maturity or a restrictive hardening of the character of the latency period similar to the instances mentioned above in which the childhood love for the parents withstands the onslaught of the adolescent phase.

To return to the initial question: it seems that we are able to foretell the adolescent reactions in certain specific and typical constellations but certainly not for all the individual variations of infantile personality structure. Our insight in to typical developments will increase with the number of adolescents who undergo analysis.

Pathology n Adolescence

This leaves us with a third problem which, to my mind, out weight the preceding ones so far as clinical and theoretical significance are concerned. I refer to the difficulty in adolescent cases to draw the line between normality and pathology. As described above, adolescence constitutes by definition an interruption of peaceful growth which resembles in appearance a variety of other emotional upsets and structural upheavals. (Adolescence, of course, is not the only time in life when alterations of a physiological nature cause disturbances of mental equilibrium. The same happens in later years in the climacterium; and recently, Grete L. Bibring (1959) has given a convincing description of similar damager to the equilibrium of mental forces during pregnancy.) The adolescent manifestations come close to symptom formation of the neurotic, psychotic or dissocial order and merge almost imperceptibly into borderline states, initial, frustrated or fully fledged forms o almost all the mental illnesses. Consequently, the differential diagnosis between the adolescent upsets and true pathology becomes a difficult task.

For the discussion of this diagnostic problem leave most other authors in the field to speak for themselves and summarise my own impressions based on past and present clinical experience.

In 1936, when I approached the same subject from the aspect of the defenses, I was concerned with the similarity between the adolescent and other emotional disturbances rather than with the differences between them. I described that adolescent upset take on the appearance of a neurosis if the initial, pathogenic danger situation is located in the superego with the resulting anxiety being felt as guilt; that they resemble psychotic disturbances if the danger lies in the increased power of the id itself. Which threatens the ego in its existence or integrity. Whether such as adolescent individual impresses us, then, as obsessional, phobic, hysterical, ascetic, schizoid, paranoid, suicidal, etc., will depend on the one hand on the quality and quantity of the id contents which beset the ego, on the other hand on the selection of defense mechanisms which the latter employs. Since, in adolescence impulses from all pregenital phases rise to the surface and defense mechanisms from all levels or crudity or complexity come into use, the pathological results—although identical in structure—are more varied and less stabilized than at other times of life.

Today it seems to me that this structural description needs to be amplified, not in the direction of the similarity of the adolescent to other disorders but in that of their specific nature. There is in their etiology at least one additional element which may be regarded as exclusive to this period and characteristic for it; namely that the danger is felt to be located not only in the id impulses and fantasies but in the very existence of the love objects of the individual's oedipal and preoedipal past. The libidinal cathexis to them has been carried forward from the infantile phases, merely toned down or inhibited in aim during latency. Therefore the reawakened pregenital urges, or—worse still—the newly acquired genital ones, are in danger of making contact with them, lending a new and threatening reality to fantasies which had seemed extinct but are, in fact, merely under repression. (An important clinical instance of this can be found in adolescent girls with anorexia nervosa. Here the infantile fantasies of oral impregnation receive added impetus from the new real possibilities of motherhood opened up by genital development. Consequently, the phobic measures adopted against the intake of food on the one hand and identification with the mother on the other hand are overemphasized to a degree which my lead to starvation.) The anxieties which arise on these rounds are directed toward eliminating the infantile objects, i.e.., toward breaking the tie with them. Anny katan (1937) has discussed this type of defense, which aims above all at changing the persons and the scene of conflict, under the term of "removal." Such an attempt may succeed or fail, partially or totally. In any case, I agree with Anny Katan that its outcome will be decisive for the success or failure of the other, more familiar line of defensive measures which are directed against the impulses themselves.

A number of illustrations will serve to clarify the meaning of this assumption.

Defense Against the infantile Object Ties

Defense by displacement of libido.—there are many adolescents who deal with the anxiety around by eh attachment to their infantile objects by the simple means of flight. Instead of permitting a process of gradual detachment from the parents to take place, they withdraw their libido from them suddenly and altogether. This leaves them with a passionate longing for partnership which they succeed in transferring to the environment outside the family. Here they adopt varying solutions: Libido may be transferred, more or less unchanged inform, to parent substitutes, provided that these new figures are diametrically opposed in every aspect (Personal, social, cultural) to the original ones. Or the attachment may be made to so-called "leaders'," usually persons in age between the adolescent's and the parents' generation, who represent ideas. Equally frequent are the passionate new ties to contemporaries, either of the same or of the opposite sex (.e., homosexual or heterosexual friendships) and the attachments to adolescent groups (or "gangs"). Whichever of these typical solutions is chosen, the result makes the adolescent feel "free,' and revel in a new precious sense of independence form the parents who are treated, then, within difference bordering on callousness.

Although the direction taken by the libido in these instances is, in itself, on lines of normality, the suddenness of the change, the carefully observed contrast in object selection, and the overemphasis on the new allegiances mark it as defensive. It represents an all too hasty anticipation of normal growth rater than a normal developmental process. It makes little further difference to the emotional situation whether the libidinal flight is followed by actual flight, i.e., whether the adolescent also "removes" himself bodily from his family. If not, he remains in the home in the attitude of a boarder, usually a very inconsiderate one so far as the older and younger family members are concerned.

On the other hand, the withdrawal of cathexis from the parents has most decisive consequences for the rest of the defensive processes. Once the infantile objects are stripped of their importance, the pregenital and genital impulses cease to be threatening to the same degree. Consequently, guilt and anxiety decrease and the ego becomes more tolerant. Formerly repressed sexual and aggressive wishes rise to the surface and are acted on, the actions being taken outside the family in the wider environment. Whether this acting out will be on harmless, or idealistic, ordissocial, or even criminal lines will depend essentially on the new objects to which the adolescent has attached himself. Usually the ideals of the leader, of the adolescent group, or of the gang, are taken over wholeheartedly and without criticism.

Adolescents of this type may be sent for treatment after their actions have brought them into conflict with their schools, their employers, or the law. As far as psychoanalytic therapy is concerned, they seem to offer little chance for the therapeutic alliance between analyst and patient without which the analytic technique cannot proceed. Any relationship to the analyst and, above all, the transference to him would revive the infantile attachments which have been discarded; therefore the adolescent remains unresponsive. Also, the escape from these attachments has suspended the feeling of internal conflict, at least temporarily; consequently, eh adolescent does not feel in need of psychological help. A. Aichhorn had these points in mind when he maintained that adolescents of this is social and criminal type needed a long period of preparation and inner rearrangement before they could become amenable to analytic treatment. He maintained that the latter would be successful only if, during this preparation in a residential setting, the adolescent made a new transference of object love, reawakened his infantile attachments, internlised his conflicts once more, in short, became neurotic.

To try and analyse adolescent in his phase of successful detachment from the past seems to be adventure doomed to failure.

Defense by reversal of affect.—A second typical reaction to the same danger situation is, although less conspicuous outwardly, more ominous in nature inwardly.

Instead of displacing libido from the parents—or, more likely, after failing to do so—the adolescent ego may defend itself by turning the emotions felt toward them into their opposites.

This changes love into hate, dependence into revolt, respect and admiration into contempt and derision. On the basis of such reversal of affect the adolescent remains himself to be "free' but, unluckily for his peace of mind and sense of conflict, this conviction does not reach further than the conscious surface layer of his mind. For all deeper intents and purposes he remains as securely tied to the parental figures as he has been before; acting out remains within the family; and any alterations achieved by the defense turn out to his disadvantage. There are no positive pleasures to be derived from the reversed relationships, only suffering, felt as well as inflicted. There is no room for independence of action, or of growth; compulsive opposition to the parents proves as crippling in this respect as compulsive obedience to them can prove to be. (Ferenczi has pointed to this effect of "compulsive disobedience" many years ago.) Since anxiety and guilt remain undiminished, constant reinforcement of defense is necessary. This is provided in the first place by two methods: denial (of positive feeling) and reactions formations (churlish, unsympathetic, contemptuous attitudes). The behavioural picture that emerges at this stage is that of an uncooperative and hostile adolescent.

Further pathological developments of this state of affairs are worth watching. The hostility and aggressiveness, which serve as a defense against object love in the beginning, soon become intolerable to the ego, are felt as threats, and are warded off in their own right. This may happen by means of projection; in that case the aggression is ascribed to the parents who, consequently, become the adolescent's main oppressors and persecutors. In the clinical picture this appears first as the adolescent's suspiciousness and, when the projections increase, as paranoid behaviour.

Conversely, the full hostility and aggression may be turned away from the objects and employed inwardly against the self. In these cases, the adolescents display intense depression, tendencies of self-abasement and self-injury, and develop, or ever carry out, suicidal wishes.

During all stages of this process, personal suffering is great and the desire to be helped intense. This, in itself, is no guarantee that the adolescent in question will submit to analytic therapy. He will certainly not do so if treatment is urged and initiated by the parents. Whenever this happens, he will consider analysis as their tool, extend his hostility or his suspicions to include the person of the analyst and refuse cooperation. The chances are better if the adolescent himself decides to seek help and turns to analysis, as it were in opposition to the parents' wishes. Even so, the alliance with the analyst may not be of long duration. As soon as a true transference develops and the positive infantile fantasies come into consciousness, the same reversal of affect tends to be repeated in the analytic setting. Rather than relive the whole turmoil of feelings with the analyst, many adolescent patients run away. They escape from their positive feelings, although it appears to the analyst that they break off treatment in an overwhelmingly strong negative transference.

Defense by withdrawal of libido to the self.—to proceed in the direction of increasing pathology:

Withdrawal of libido from the parents, as it has been described above, does not, in itself, decide about its further use, or fate. If anxieties and inhibitions block the way toward new objects outside the family, the libido remains within the self. There, it may be employed to cathect the ego and superego, thereby inflating them. Clinically this means that ideas of grandeur will appear, fantasies of unlimited power over other human beings, or of major achievement and championship in one or more fields. Or, the suffering and persecuted ego of the adolescent may assume Christ-like proportions with corresponding fantasies of saving the world.

On the other hand, the cathexis may become attached to the adolescent's body only and give rise there to the hypochondriacal sensations and feeling of psychotic illness.

In either case analytic therapy is indicated as well as urgent. Treatment will dispel the appearance of severe abnormality if it reopens a path for the libido, either to flow backwards and recathect the original infantile objects, or to flow forward, in the direction described above, to cathect less frightening substitutes in the environment.

What taxes the analyst's technical skill in these cases is the withdrawn state of the patient, i.e., the problem of establishing an initial relationship and transference. One this is accomplished, the return from narcissistic withdrawal to object cathexis will relieve the patient, at least temporarily.

I believe, there are many cases where the analyst would

be wise to be content with this partial success without urging further treatment. A further, and deeper, involvement in the transference may well arouse all the anxieties described above and, again, lead to abrupt termination of the analysis due to the adolescent's flight reaction.

Defense by regression.—The greater the anxiety aroused by the object ties, the more elementary and primitive is the defense activity employed by the adolescent ego to escape them. Thus, at the extreme height of anxiety, the relations with the object world may be reduced to the emotional state known as "primary identification' with the objects. This solution with which we are familiar from psychotic illnesses implies regressive changes in all parts o the personality, i.e., in the ego organisation as well as in eh libido. The ego boundaries are widened to embrace parts of the object together with the self. This creates in the adolescent surprising changes of qualities, attitudes and even outward appearance. His allegiance to persons outside himself betrays itself in these alterations of his own personality (.e., his identifications) rather than in an outflow of libido. Projections, together with these identifications, dominate the scene and create a give-and-take between the self and object which has repercussions on important ego functions. For example, the distinction between the external and internal world (i.e., reality testing) becomes temporarily negligible, a lapse in ego functioning which manifests itself in the clinical picture as a state of confusion.

Regression of this kind may bring transitory relief to the ego by emptying the oedipal (and many of the preoedipal) fantasies of their libidinal cathexis. But this lessening of anxiety will not be long lived. Another and deeper anxiety will soon take its place which I have characterized on a former occasion (1951) as the fear of emotional surrender, with the accompanying fear of loss of identity.

Defense Against Impulses

Where the defenses against the oedipal and preoedipal object ties fail to achieve their aim, clinical pictures emerge which come nearest to the borderline toward psychotic illness.

The "ascetic" adolescent.—One of these, the "ascetic" adolescent, I have described before as fight in all his impulses, preoedipal and oedipal, sexual and aggressive, extending the defense even to the fulfillment of the physiological needs for food, sleep, and body comfort. This, to me, seems the characteristic reaction of an ego, driven by the blind fear of over whelming id quantities, an anxiety which leaves no room for the finer distinctions between vital or merely pleasant satisfactions, the healthy or the morbid, the morally permitted or forbidden pleasures. Total war is waged against the pursuit of pleasure as such. Accordingly, most of the normal processes of instinct and need satisfaction are interfered with an become paralyzed. According to clinical observation, adolescent ascerticism is, with luck, a transitory phenomenon. For the analytic observerit provides precious proof of he power of defense, i.e., of the extent to which the normal, healthy drive derivative are open to crippling interference by the ego.

On the whole, analytic treatment of the ascetic typedoes not presnt as many technical difficulties as one would expect. Perhaps, in these individuals, defense against the impulses is so massive, that they can permit themselves some object relationship to the analyst and, thus, enter into transference.

The "uncompromising" adolescent.—Another, equally abnormal adolescent, is described best as the "uncompromising" type. The term, in this instance, does refer to more than the well-known conscious, unrelenting position adopted by many young people who stand up for their ideas, refuse to make concessions to the more practical and reality-adapted attitudes of their elders, and take pride in their moral or aesthetic principles. "Compromise," with these adolescents, includes processes which are as essential for life as, for example, the cooperation between impulses, the blending of opposite strivings, the mitigation of id strivings by interference from the side of the ego. One adolescent whom I observed in analysis did his utmost, in pursuit of this impossible aim, to prevent any interference of his mind with his body, of his activity with his passivity, his loves wit his hates, his realities with his fantiatises, the external demands with his internal ones, in short, of hi ego with his id.

IN treatment this defense was represented as a strong resistance against and "cure," the idea of which he despised in spite of intense suffering. He understood correctly that mental health is based in the last resort on harmony, i.e., on the every compromise formations which he was trying to avoid.

The Concept of Normality in Adolescence

Where adolescence is concerned, it seems easier to describe its pathologicalmanifestatios thanthe normal processes. Nevertheless, there are in the above exposition at least two pronouncements which there are in the above exposition at lesttwo pronouncements which may prove useful for theconcept: (1) that adolescence is by its nature an intrruption of peaceful growth, and (2) that the upholding of a steady eqilibrium during the adolescent process is in itself abnormal. Once we accept for adolescence disharmony within the psychic sructure as our basic fact, understanding becomes easier. We beginto see the upsetting battles which are raging between id and ego as beneficient attempts to restore peace and harmony. The defensive methods which are employed either against the impulses, or against the object cathexis, bein to apper legitimate and normal. If they produce pathological results, this happens not because of any malignancy in their nature, but because they are overused, over stressed, orused in isolation. Actually, each of the abnormal types of adolescent development, as it is described above, represnts also a potentially useful way of regaining mental stability, normal if combined with other defenses, and if used in moderation.

To explains last statement in greater detail: I take it that it is normal for an adolescent to behave for a considerable length of time in an inconsistent and unpredictable manner; to fight his impulses and to accept them; to ward them off successfully and to be overturn by them; to love his parents and to hate them; to revolt against them and to be dependent on them; to be deeply ashamed to acknowledge his mother before others and, unexpectedly, to desire heart-to-hart talks with her; to thrive on imitation of and identification with others while searching unceasingly for his own identity; to be more idealistic, artistic, generous and unselfish than he will ever be again, but also the opposite; self-centered, egoistic, calculating. Such fluctuations between extreme opposites would be deemed highly abnormal at any other time of life. At this time they may signify no more than that an adult structure of personality takes a long time to emerge, that there go of the individual in question does not cease to experiment and is in no hurry to close down on possibilities. If the temporary solutions seem abnormal to the onlooker, they are less so, nevertheless, than the hasty decisions made in other cases for one-sided suppression, or revolt, or flight, or withdrawal, or regression, or asceticism, which are responsible for the truly pathological developments described above.

While an adolescent remains inconsistent and unpredictable in his behaviour, he may suffer, but he does not seem to me to be in need of treatment. I think that he should be given time and scope to work out his own solution. Rather, it may be his parents who need help and guidance so as to be able to bear with him.

REFERENCES

Adatto, C.P. (1958), Ego Reintegration Observed in analysis of Late Adolescents, Int, J. Psa.

Bibring, G.L. (1959), Some considerations of the psychological processes in Pregnancy. *The Psychoanalytic Study of the Child*, XIV, New York: International Universities Press.

Deutsch, H. (1944), *The Psychology of Women*, I, New York: Grune & Stratton.

Eissler, K.R. (1950), Ego-Psychological Implications of the Psychoanalytic treatment of Delinquents, *The Psychoanalytic Study of the Child*, V. New York: International Universities Press.

Geleerd, E.r, (1957), Some Aspects of Psychoanalytic Technique in Adolescents. *The Psychoanalytic Study of the child*, xii, New

York: International Universities Press.

Harnik, J. (1923), The Various developments Undergone by Narcissism in Men and Mewn, *Int. J. Psa.*, V. 1924.

Katan, M. (1950), Structural Aspects of a Case of Schizophrenia. *The Psychoanalytic Study of the Child*, V. New York International Universities Press.

Maenchen, A. (19460, A Case of Superego Disintegration. *The psychoanalytic Study of the Child*, II, New York: International Universities Press.

Spiegel, L.A. (1951), A Review of Contributions to a Psychoanalytic Theory of Adolescence. *The Psychoanalytic Study of the Child*, VI, New York, International Universities Press.

7

The Child Guidance Clinic as a Centre of Prophylaxis and Enlightenment

The content of this chapter is based on material collected in the Hampstead Child therapy clinic with the aid of grants by the Field Foundation, Inc, New York.

Child Analysis before the child Guidance Era begin with my personal recollections about the development of these relationships, recollections which make me fele that analysts and child analysts owe the child guidance clinics a debt of gratitude. Before such clinics existed, we analysts felt that we were in possession of much solid analytic knowledge potentially useful for the upbringing of children, their teaching, and the treatment of their problems. But there were no recognized channels of communication, neither with parents nor with the professional workers within he children's services. All that the analysts could rely on in this respect were chance contacts: parents while or after undergoing a therapeutic analysis themselves could not help but apply some of their newly acquired insight to the handling of their children; teachers who for personal reasons, underwent analysis were expected to carry back to the teaching profession some analytic findings concerning child development It was a thrilling occasion when in Vienna (approximately in 1930) an inspector of nursery schools invited us to conduct a seminar for a small group of nursery school teachers to discuss their problem children; or when an inspector of municipal play centres invited me to give a series of introductory lectures to his workers. Actually, one of the first schools to make systematic use of analytic child psychology was the Walden School in New York, a fact which Dr. S. Ferenczi learned on one of his early visits to the States and reported on most enthusiastically after his return. But these hopeful sins of possible cooperation between analysis and work with children remained few and far between.

There was another side to the same picture which was no less frustrating, We knew that there was a large amount of child material near at hand from which we, as child analysts, could have profited greatly. There were all the initial states of mental disturbance, as they show up in childhood, the many transitional stages between health and illness, the common developmental difficulties of all young children, their relationships to the more circumscribed syndromes of the infantile neuroses—all this was potentially available in our environment and, still, we were denied access to it. The children brought to us in private practice or within the hospital services were those where mental illness had passed the initial phase of behaviour disorder or symptom formation and had become ingrained in the personality in a massive way, causing severe breakdowns or permanent deviations of character. Again, there was little or nothing that we could do to alter the position.

But it is precisely this situation which has changed with the advent of the child guidance clinics. Since they have come into being they have opened up a two-way traffic between parents and professional workers with children on the one hand and child analysis or child psychiatry on the other hand. It is the child guidance clinics which act at present as mediators between the two fields and serve as clearing house between them: they receive material from the public to pass on to the child analysts and child psychiatrists, and conversely they receive information from child psychiatry (or analysis) to hand out to the public. This is an important and formidable assignment, and it seems worth while to me to investigate how far the child guidance clinics of our knowledge have been able and equipped to fulfill this double task.

The Child Guidance Clinic as a Clearing House

As regards the first side of the assignment, the collection of available case material, there is no doubt tat the existing clinics are eminently successful. Probably on the basis of their status as public institutions they have done what they private child analyst had been unable to achieve: namely, to gain the confidence of the public. (It was August Aichhorn who remarked first on this difference between private and public work with parents. When praised for the hold he hand on parents and the amount of information he gathered from them, he would answer: "don't forget what I represent for the parents. As official advisor, appointed by the authorities, I am backed up by the whole Municipality.") As director of a child guidance clinic, or when talking to one of directors, you will find that collecting the material presents no difficulty. If anything, trouble arises in the opposite direction; there is too much material. Clinics are swamped with the cases sent in to them by the parents themselves, by teachers, youth workers, general practitioners and pediatricians, almoners of hospitals, probation officers from the courts, child welfare organisers, etc. There is everything from the most common difficulties of management with which parents used to deal on their own (such as the early sleeping, feeding, and toileting troubles), to the severe retardations, borderline and autistic and atypical states. There is, indeed, more than the diagnostic skill o the child psychiatrist or child analyst can cope with at present. The bewildering variety of pathological, or seemingly pathological manifestations, seems to call for new diagnostic categories based not on symptomatology but on developmental considerations. But, however this may be, the case material is there to be looked at by the analyst, studied, sorted out for therapy, understood, and, perhaps, in the future, to be newly classified.

There is, as said before, no lack of confidence in the clinic on the part of the public; again, if anything, thee is too much. With many people, the concept of treatment in a clinic has acquired a magical connotation. Little difference is made between children who suffer from environmental neglect, unsuitable parents, tragic bereavements, and those cases where something has gone wrong in the development and personality structure for internal reasons. In both instances to know that a child is in treatment seems to spell safety to parents, welfare agencies or public authorities, as if ever non-organic disturbance were automatically suitable for psychological treatment, and as if treatment guaranteed a cure in all cases. Paradoxically enough, it will soon be necessary on the part of the clinics to disabuse the public, i.e., to induce people to lower their expectations of therapy to a level more justified by the conditions and limitations imposed by reality.

The Application of Analytic Knowledge

The clinics have been less successful where the receiving and application of analytic knowledge is concerned. At lest, there is in this respect a wide gap between the "analytic" clinics as they exist in some of the big European and American centres, usually in close collaboration with a local psychoanalytic society and training institute, and the ordinary, although frequently "analytically oriented" child guidance clinics as they exist in larger or smaller numbers allover the countries. The analytic clinic usually has a fully trained analyst as psychiatrist-in-charge with several younger staff members in analytic training. The analytically oriented clinic may base its whole connection with psychoanalysis on some contact with analysis which a senior staff member has had at one period of his career. What has been brought back from such contacts are often no more than single pieces of analytic findings which bear the hallmark of a certain phase of analytic thinking. I name as such the following; emphasson the pathogenic role of repression of infantile sexuality (resulting in therapeutic emphasis on sex enlightenment, dealing with guilt arising from oedipal fantasies, masturbation conflicts, etc.): emphasis on the pathogenic repression of aggression (with therapeutic emphasis laid on the discharge of the child's aggressive and destructive tendencies); emphasis on the mother-infant unity in the earliest years (treatment being directed toward the aftereffects of traumatic separations); emphasis on the pathogenic role of the mother's abnormal personality, emotional withdrawnness, severely neurotic or psychotic traits (with consequent inclusion of the mother in the child's treatment). Not that these findings do not represent all-important parts of the analytic knowledge of child development as it stands at present, but they have to be pieced together and fitted into the framework of analytic child psychology before their clinical application can be wholly useful. When they are used in isolation, the diagnostic as well as the therapeutic issues become distorted, a frequent occurrence for which psychoanalysis has had to take much blame. Perhaps in future our distinction between analytic child guidance clinics and others should be based less on the therapeutic time available for each patent (one weekly versus daily treatment) but on the fact whether the whole analytic knowledge of children is available for application or merely selected portions of it.

We are left with the question where to place the responsibility for this, to the analyst, unsatisfactory state of affairs and where to look for remedies. The fault may lie mainly with us analysts who are notoriously bad at public relations and known to publicize findings all too often in unsuitable language or with exaggerated emphasis on the most recent discoveries. On the other hand, the fault may lie with the clinics where people fail to sift, weight, and integrate data before applying hem to therapy and guidance work. The necessity for such discrimination in this field is not so different, after all, from the corresponding one in the medical field where knowledge of new findings, new methods or new drugs has to be pursued constantly and integrated with former knowledge before application.

The Distribution of Analytic Knowledge

For discussing the distribution of knowledge I turn

once more to the experience of those clinics where a considerable fund of reliable and comprehensive analytic data is available for use. The points of contact with the public open to them are of various kinds.

Diagnostic Assessment

Thee are, for one, the constant demands for the assessment of children, as they are made on all child guidance clinics for purposes of the juvenile courts, or placement for adoption, with foster parents, in residential institutions, for selection of school, etc. Where the assessment is made not in terms of symptomatology but from the wider point of view of personality structure and development (as mentioned above), and where the language is non-technical, more than the immediate practical purpose can be served. Here is a legitimate channel of communication which can be used to acquaint the referring agencies with the clinical (and theoretical) aspects on which the clinic's understanding of the child is based. In time these case histories will illustrate many of the main issues of analytic child psychology, such as the interdependence of environmental and internal factors, of body and mind, of emotional and intellectual capacities; the overding importance of drive activity and its position in the personality structure; the role of anxiety and of defense activity leading to inhibition of function or to symptom formation; the developmental aspects of social or dissocial development, etc. (In the East London child-Guidance Clinic Dr. Augusta Donnard has carried out valuable work of this kind of or a number of years, She has done an effective teaching job with the school and welfare authorities in her area through answering their requests for diagnostic assessment by means of elaborate and enlightening developmental pictures of the children referred to her.)

Instruction of Professional Workers

A second and more direct channel of communication is opened up by the constant demands for instruction which arrive from the professional workers in the field, such as pediatricians, nurses, or teachers. It is true that many of us feel that the teaching role of the clinic is a very temporary one with regard to these. By rights, instruction in child development should be an integral part of the medical or nursing courses as well as of the teachers' training colleges. But while developments in these institutions have to be waited for, there is a gap to fill, and it may be worth while to discuss how to do this constructively, avoiding past mistakes. (The next speaker in the Symposium, Dr. Grete Bibring, will report on the manner in which the nalytic theory of child development is taught today already to pediatricians and other residents in the Beth Israel hospital, Boston, Mass, Another participant in the Convention. Dr. Anny Katan, might tell us about the way in which such knowledge is integrated with the medical course form the first year onward in Western Reserve University, Cleveland, Ohio.)

So long as the general knowledge of child development has to be introduced as an afterthought to the majority of the members of the medical, nursing, and teaching professions, the success or failure of such ventures will depend on three factors: 910 the selection of the right teaching method: (2) the selection of the right facts; (3) some over-all considerations which provide a framework.

To take the lat point first: when working with doctors, nurses, or teachers, it is essential to remember that not all the psychological data which we can offer are suitable for immediate application, since the condition under which they work are different from ours. It is only a short time ago that teachers learned that the child's intellect does not function divorced from his feelings and that, therefore, some connection with their pupils' emotional life is indispensable for teaching. For the medical world it is a similarly recent discovery that the child's body is not divorced from his mind and that, therefore, physical and mental matters are interrelated sufficiently to influence and interfere with each other. But schools and hospitals as institutions have antedated all these new findings. The application of the latter, therefore, implies a whole host of changes which range from the free entry of parents to schools and hospitals to the rota of changing nursing personnel and the very arrangements of school room or ward, changes which especially for nurses and doctors may mean a more or less complete upheaval in the established conditions of their work.

As regards teaching methods, many of us agree that formal courses in child development remain effective before links have been established between the data offered in them and those contained in formal professional training on physical matters. On the other hand, openings are provided by those patients or pupils how remain "problems" in medical practice or school room, i.e., where the physical or intellectual data fail to explain the picture. Teaching "on the case" has been found satisfactory by many analysts for these reasons.

As for the selection of facts for teaching, I emphasize, as before, that few analytic data are beneficial if applied out of context. Schools, for example, may profit greatly from applying the analytic concept of sublimation to the teachers' work. By deflecting libidinal energy from its original sources and harnessing it to school subjects much drudgery in school can be changed into activities pleasurable almost as play. On the other hand, progressive schools will come to grief if they base their schedules too consistently on this single piece of analytic knowledge. Psychoanalytic theory also has much to say about the essential differences between play and work, the first being governed by the pleasure principle, the latter by the reality principle. It is one of the main tasks of education to lead each individual child from the earlier to the later mode of functioning. Only the integration of the knowledge of sublimation with the ore intricate knowledge of mental functioning on the various stages of development will be of real benefit to the psychological orientation of the modern schools.

Pediatricians might be similarly misled if they meet the present psychoanalytic campaign against hospitalization of small children unconnected with other facts. It is true that a first early separation form home for purposes of medical or surgical intervention may prove traumatic to the individual child and that the psychological damage done by it may go as far as out weighting the physical benefit in health. On the other hand, doctors should not be impressed exclusively with the fact, or the effects, of separation. It is equally necessary for them to learn what part physical illness as such even when undergone at home plays in the mental development of children. Again, it is only the combination and integration of both these lines of inquiry which will lead benefit application.

Work with Parents

This leads us to the third and lat channel of communication with the pubic, the work with parents which will remain the Clinic's domain, whatever the developments.

There is at present the widespread belief, held by all clinic personnel, that work with parents (or in the case of young children with their mothers) is effective only if directed toward changes in their personalities. Consensus on this point has been reached, I believe, on the rebound from earlier and outmoded attitudes toward the parents, attitudes which included much teaching of facts on a purely intellectual basis, advising in an authoritative manner or, at worst, preaching and exhorting. Our analytic discoveries have laid bare the intricate emotional relationships between child and parent, the role of internalization of the parents' personalities, and identification with their qualities, the consequences of love and hate, the subtle or crude forms of seduction the overriding importance of any one of the developmental phases, whether libidinal or aggressive, being acceptable or repulsive to the parent. Once the parent-child relationship is seen in this light, work wit a parent ceases to imply a teacher-pupil attitude and takes on the aspect of a therapeutic relationship.

Most analysts subscribe to these arguments, which are, after all, derived from their work, although with the provide that experience in analytic practice also teachers to be modest in the expectation of personality changes through any but the most intensive therapy.

For my own person, I remain a heretic in some of these

respects. I am far from denying the effect on a child from a beneficial change in he parents' attitudes. Still, I cannot help believing that this therapeutic approach to the parents is not more than one among a whole series of possible approaches, all of them serving the same ultimate purposes of beneficial change, prevention, and enlightenment. In what follows I shall try to justify this rather unpopular view of mine by outlining a number of these possibilities as I have learned to see them.

The therapeutic approach

Those instances where we have no hesitation and no reservation in joining the popular demand for therapeutic dealings with the parents. There are the cases, by now known to most clinics, where the mother's and the child's pathology are completely intertwined. We believe that very young children have some primitive pathway of communication with their mothers' unconscious which render them sensitive and vulnerable for the letter's unconscious libidinal or aggressive impulses and fantasies. A young child may merely act out the mother's fantasy in play, or may defend himself against it in some complicated way, or may build a complex pathological structure of his own on the basis of the mother's secret or manifest disturbance. In the most extreme instances the mental disorder of mother and child will be fitted together as if they were pieces in a jug saw puzzle or—to compare it with adult disorders—as in a *folie-adeux*.

In our Hampstead Clinic we have studied a number of such mother-child couples over the years by analyzing both partners simultaneously under different therapists and analysts and coordinating the results. Our aim is to determine the limits of dependence and independence in their disturbances and to assess the therapeutic chances for those other cases where only the child, i.e., the more passive factor in the partnership, is taken into treatment. On the basis of several of these investigations we have concluded that there is some hope in a altering the condition by the child's analysis alone so long as the pathogenic agents from the mother's side remain in the realm of thought and fantasy; but that nothing except simultaneous treatment will alter the position where these mental influences are reinforced by actions of the mother which tie the child to her as a result of pleasurable or painful actual excitations.

The therapeutic approach to the mother is equally vital in those cases where young children show the various signs of deprivation of mothering, though in the mothers presence. This may be caused by a depression of the mother, or period of actual mourning which causes withdrawal of feeling from the object world, including the child. Her incapacity to fulfill the task of mothering may be caused, equally, by the consequences of a pathogenic masculinity complex, etc. Again, nothing except therapy will have a chance of altering the position. But, since the therapeutic results are slow to come, we have seen repeatedly that the change in the mother comes too late for the child on whose handling he deficiency became apparent and that it is the next born infant who benefits from the preventive measure. (Mrs. Kata Levy, London is responsible for drawing our Clinic's attention to the difference between the mother's disturbance being (a) a direct agent in the child's pathology through identification and excitation; (b) an indirect agent through incapacitating the mother for her task of mothering.)

The Semitherapeutic Approach: Guiding the Parents through the Child's Analysis.—The close interdependence of mother and child t the beginning of life, and the exaggeration of this factor in some abnormal cases, should not make us ignore the fact that children are growing personalities in their own right with a wide range of possible disturbances and conflicts within their structure. But while they need treatment in their own right, their mother will be severely affected by this procedure and will need to be helped and guided through the period. To safeguard the child's future in the family after conclusion of treatment, the parents, and especially the mother, should be allowed or even urgent to accompany the analytic process to some degree. This implies facing their own adult resistances against the repressed remnants of infantile sexually and the cruder forms of infantile aggression, all the more so since the child's impulses are directed against their persons and become increased temporarily during treatment as a rule. The child's treatment acts as a threat to the defenses of the mother, quite apart form the violent feelings of jealousy and competition with the child analyst which are aroused by the young patient's positive attachment to the latter's person. Much human tact plus therapeutic skill on the part of the clinic's representative (whether therapist, psychiatrist, or psychiatric social worker) will be needed to handle these difficulties of the parents and to safeguard treatments.

The therapeutic-Guiding Approach; Dealings with the Mothers of Handicapped Children—the approach is different again where the mothers of abnormal children are concerned, i.e., those who are either born physically or mentally defective (blind, deal spastic, deformed, Mongol, etc.) or have acquired such abnormalities in early life, or undergo some unusual experience or fate (traumatic separations, deprivations, adoption, fostering, mother, or dietary restrictions). There is no reason to expect that mothers are equipped automatically for the specialised as of bringing up such a child in a manner calculated to minimize the handicap. On the contrary, the mother's natural hurt and despair concerning her child's defect, the injury to her pride and pleasure in the child, will all work toward estranging her from the task of mothering thereby increasing the initial damage. There is her ea specially difficult therapeutic task with the mothers which has been tackled in few places. But there is, besides it, also the need for expert advice, based on knowledge of the abnormalities concerned, such as the following: how to ensure with the blind infant that contact with the object world by sight is substituted for through other channels; how to provide motor outlet for the blind toddler, thereby preventing many of the abnormalities following on motor restriction; how to prevent necessary dietary restrictions from being understood by the child as punishments and experienced as intolerable deprivations; how to minimize the effect of inevitable separations from the mother; how to prepare for operations and meet their equally inevitable aftereffects, etc., etc. There are a whole host of emergency situations of this kind in which the normal mother will feel helpless without guidance.

The Guiding approach; Treatment of the Young Child by the Mother.—A number of analytic clinics, besides ours, have devised a procedure recently in which an intuitive and willing mother, free from severe pathology herself, is helped to guide hr own child through the phases of an average developmental disturbance or infantile neutosis. Such work implies close contact with the mother usually through weekly sessions, in which the child's difficulties, his tantrums, his behaviour, his play or whatever other material has been elicited are discussed, assessed, and elucidated for the mother who then bases her next handling of the child on her understanding. Inevitably this implies also much reassurance of the mother, so far as the severity of the pathology, the comparison with other children, the confidence in her own ability as a mother are concerned. I have reported elsewhere personal experience with two cases of this kind, one a case of soiling in a two-and-a-half-ear-old boy, the other an incipient but violent school phobia in a six-year-old girl. In both instances satisfactory results were achieved, n spite of the therapeutic aspects of the work being concentrated on the child alone. That the mother's attitudes during the cooperation have to be met with understanding, patience, and sympathy goes without saying. Also, the mothers suitable for this type of cooperation have to be selected carefully; but there are more than a few who will be able to respond positively to the appeal to their reason, common sense, and good will, who will cope with their own resistances and succeed in the task, helped by the satisfaction that their child need not be handed over to a stranger for therapy.

The Indirect Approach by Way of Public Opinion—It is not only on the basis of the foregoing considerations that I refuse to believe that mothers need to change their personalities before they can change the handling of their child. Assertions of this kind, I find, are not based on facts, above all not on historical facts. Even in the last 30 to 40 years during which was able to observe the methods of upbringing, changes have been remarkably great. Beast feeding, for example, has been adopted, given up, is being adopted again, and may be on the way out once more. Feeding schedules have been extremely strictly observed for two or three decades (with some disastrous results for the later feeding disturbances), have given way to feeding on demand (with other disturbing results), and show some indication at present of returning with more moderation. Toilet training before the war in England began with official hospital approval soon after birth, was delayed in the postwar period until the end of the first year, and is postponed now by man mothers until the second or even third year. To widen the picture we need think only of the question of sexual enlightment now accepted as a must by almost al parents; of the immensely increased freedom given to the child's aggression, even if directly expressed toward the parents; of the altered attitude to corporal punishment as a recognized tool of education, etc. Far-reaching developments of this kind are not due directly to personality changes in the individual mothers but indirectly to a alterations in the social atmosphere to which the mothers cannot help but respond. My contention is, therefore, that in rearing their children mothers are not only guided by instinct and misled by distorting personal influences, but they are to an even larger degree dependent on tradition and public opinion, both of which are open to change.

For the child guidance clinic this opens up the possibility of playing a part in the setting up of new traditions. As described above, they have gained the confidence of the public already where the treatment of problem children is concerned. T should not be difficult for them to establish a similar position of trust with regard to the handling of normal children during the all-important first four or five years of life, very much in the manner in which the well-baby clinics have established their traditions with regard to the healthy infants' physical needs. This will be slow work, supplanting gradually what is left of religious, national, and class traditions, but it will e no less effective so far as influence on the mothers is concerned. Further role for the child guidance clinics. At present all the workers in the children's services, whether in schools, hospitals, courts, clinics, suffer from the effects of specialized training and lack of coordination and integration in the field. It is as rare for a teacher to deal with a sick child as it is for a hospital nurse to handle a healthy one, or a pediatrician to come in contact with the juvenile courts. This limits each specialists' outlook on childhood of which the various tasks show no more than a single aspect.

REFERENCES

Burligham, d. (1932), Child Analysis and the Mother. *Psa.* Quart, IV, 1935.

Freud, A. (1954), In: Problems of Infantile Neurosis: A Discussion. *The Psychoanalytic Study of the Child,* IX, New York: International Universities Press.

Freud, A. (1958), Child Observation and Prediction of development: a Memorial Lecture in Honor of Ernst Kris. *The Psychoanalytic Study of the Child,* XIII, New York: International Universities Press, pp. 100-102.

Goldberger, A., Lussier, A. (1955), simultaneous Analysis of Mother and child. *The Psychoanalytic Study of the Child,* X, New York: International Universities Press.

8

Problems of Diagnosis and Selection

During at lest the ten years that we have been here, here, we have never been able to meet the demands of the community for child psychiatric services. Since cannot possibly do all the things relating to child psychiatry that need to be done, we probably meet only a small fraction of the need. We know that it is unlikely that we will be able to do so in the foreseeable future. What needs shall we meet? To what extent and how? This is our problem. We hoped to make order out of the choas that existed when the clinic was operated by responding to pressures for service. I was only the realization of the hopelessness of trying to be governed by pressure for services that led to the discarding of that method and taking the reins in our own hands. In this procedure the first thing that had to be decided was how to handle the pressures on the clinic so that we could effectively work in peace.

In this chapter deal only with that phase of the program which deals with the problem of diagnosis and selection for treatment which is vital to the whole plan. There existed a long waiting list for treatment, and the cases that survived the waiting list were usually the most serious and least hopeful ones, requiring long term treatment. The clinic was at the same time loaded down with long, almost interminable cases; hence, the longer the system continued, the less new cases we were able to take on. The most serious cases are the ones with the greatest emotional appeal to the staff so that this also meant they were most likely to be accepted. These cases also were not necessarily the most treatable kind, and we felt that in the long run we were not using our staff time as efficiently was we could by letting the cases select themselves wither by pressure, survival of the waiting list by the continuation of crises, or by playing on our feelings where we felt too guilty to reject distressing cases.

We began with a policy of not accepting more than 10 per cent long-term cases of dubious prognosis. The policy was fine, but seemed unenforcible. Either the cases were misdiagnosed of each staff member presenting a case for admission found special reasons why an exemption should be made in each instance. The reasons were valid, but so was the need to balance the case load of the clinic. We found that we could not get the staff to say no to a parent when there was urgent need for treatment regardless of the treatability of the case or the over-all needs of the community.

We next grappled with this problem and felt that it was impossible to teach staff members involved with needy parent or children to deny them treatment unless we could come up with an answer as to how to handle the pressure coming from outside of the clinic and the pressure of the guilt feelings of the staff members. The former was easily dealt with by a directive from the director, but the latter did not so readily respond to directives. Another answer had to be found and that was to develop another kind of service which could be of some help to those in great need of help, though it may be far from sufficient to satisfy our own standards and our own drives to rescue everyone that comes to us for help. Furthermore, the staff had to be developed in their diagnostic thinking so as to gain information regarding treatability during the diagnostic process.

In the diagnostic process or, as the caseworkers choose to call it, intake process, it has always been assumed that each case will be a treatment case unless proven otherwise. This was changed to the opposite thinking; that each case will be seen only for diagnostic and consultation service, and only when treatment time is available for a given type of case will treatment be considered.

It became all the more important to pay attention to the diagnostic function of the clinic and to define more precisely what is to be accomplished in the initial intake and diagnostic phase of contacts with families. We have set up the following requirements of accomplishments during this phase.

1. To obtain a reasonably clear picture of the manner in which the family operates. If that picture could not be determined, the obstacles to that goal must be visualized.

2. A general picture of the psychodynamics of each member of the family.

3. An assessment of the strengths and weaknesses of the patient an those upon whom we are dependent for reality support in treatment, thus indicating what strengths we can ally with in treatment.

4. Indications as to what motivates the patient to come in for treatment, both consciously and unconsciously, and whether these can be used or changed so that they can be utilized to help the patient.

5. Indications that the demands upon the patients in the treatment process are explained to the patient and that he really accepts them or can be helped to accept them.

6. The ability of the patient to get involved into a treatment relationship such as is demanded by the type of treatment to be used.

The initial interviewing is assigned only to the most experienced staff members, whose diagnostic acumen is more mature. In contrast to earlier practices of being careful to not get patients involved, we deliberately attempt to involve the patient in a treatment relationship from the very onset in the hope that whatever information is given is given in a meaningful, feeling-full manner to which the interviewer can respond in a like manner with indications of acceptance, understanding, and possibly clarification.

This procedure serves several purposes: (1) It tests the patients' ability to relate and accept help as we need it. (2) It indicates to the patient that here is someone who not only demands information but who can also give understanding and through it help. (3) It allows quicker accessibility to the inner feelings which hasten the diagnostic process. It allows quicker accessibility to the inner feelings which hasten the diagnostic process. IT also has its disadvantages in that the staff members feel more obligated to continue or promise treatment and experience greater guilt in separating from the patient when they successfully involve the patient in a therapeutic relationship. Unless very skillfully handled, the patient also may be traumatized by either being refused treatment or upon reassignment for treatment to someone other than the original interviewer.

During the interviewing process the interviewer is constantly alert to determine the primary core of the problem both as to person and as within the person. For instance, who in this family most urgently needs treatment that would be of greatest benefit to the whole family? This person is not necessarily the sickest one, for the latter may be untreatable or too difficult to treat—it ma, in fact, be the health stone, for her presents the potentiality for pulling himself up and carrying the rest of the family with him. In a given individual what changes need to be made to obtain desired results? It the ideal result cannot be achieved which factor that is most amenable to brief treatment would most benefit him or preferably might so help to redirect the persons' thinking and feeling that further maturation can be expected?

It is expected that in many cases these questions can be answered fairly early, and indications of these answers are given to the patient also as a test of his ability to accept them., develop insight, and utilize them. This also serves to given the patient something that he often can very constructively utilize in his or the family's interest if further treatment is not available. The results in some of these cases that have had only from one to ten interviews is often quite astounding and demonstrate how they were able to carry on once their eyes were opened to some understanding of even only one facet of their struggle.

Through this change in he intake and diagnostic procedure, the latter has become a like, meaningful, highly responsible task instead of the routine presentation of information for an intake conference, and we do obtain much more useful information for the decision of selection of cases, and the patients are much better prepared for treatment once assignments are made.

In considering the selection of cases for treatment, we must first consider the basic function of the clinic. We basically exist to treat, to train, and to carryon research. Fortunately, the latter two functions serve materially to carryon the primary aim of treatment, but influence the selection of cases in that direction. It is inevitable that for each trainee a balanced case load of required variety be selected, and that certain types of cases be avoided at given times for a specific trainee or that he be assigned certain kinds of cases that would be specifically helpful in working out certain problems in the individual's training. We have tried repeatedly to define the kind of cases we would like trainees in the different disciplines to start out with, but have never been successful in meeting our criteria. Somehow the cases we considered ideal to begin training with are rarely available at the right time for the right person. We do, however, make every effort really to get acquainted with the new trainee before assignment are made so as not to overwhelm him at the outset by the assignment of cases which might activate serious conflicts within the trainee. Too often, we learn of the trainees difficulties only after the cases are assigned, with unfavourable reactions for all concerned.

Each research project needs specific case material, and selection therefore is simply determined by whether the cases meet the needs of the specific project being carried out. It is vital, of course, that it be determined beforehand that the staff participating in each project be competent to handle such case in treatment.

The selection of cases for treatment is furthermore complicated by the varied degrees of training and varied personalities of the staff of the clinic. It might be ideal to have a clinic with a fully developed, mature, psychoanalyzed staff that could take on any case, but in most clinics such as ours, most of the staff members are in various phases of training and experience, each one with their own limiting personalities which makes it essential that we not only know our cases well, but also that we thoroughly know the strength and weaknesses of each staff member prior to the selection of cases for treatment. In addition, we are also dealing with three different disciplines of varied training which again poses the problem of what skills may do best in a given case, or frequently the question must be raised whether the given staff person with the given skill and limitations will do at all.

These are practical realistic factors that must be dealt with before each cases can be considered on its own merits.

In a public clinic, what criteria should one use in the selection for treatment? Or course, we have to determine that the case is treatable, or can be made so, but we have to turn way every many treatable cases. Shall we accept only cases, as he director of one clinic expressed himself, who have parent with healthy egos? We see some such cases in private practice, but very few come into the clinic. What a wonderful way of cutting our budget to a fraction of its present size. Shall we given preference to behaviour conduct disorders where there is no organized neurosis yet? Theoretically this can be justified, but in reality some of these, because they are tied to neurotic family members, may be less amenable to treatment then some neurotic family members, may be less amenable to treatment than some of the organised neuroses.

We select by certain symptoms either because of their importance or because they are most amenable to treatment.

But where is the case with just one symptom? A mother, for instance, may bring a child in because of enurisis. This is the presenting symptom so far as the mother and child are concerned, but is that all that concerns us? We must then dilineate what kind of enuresis and what goes with it, so that we may have to set up impossible algebraic or geometric formulae as guides.

So far as symptoms being amenable to treatment are concerned, we have all had experiences of unsuccessful cases, for instance, where the presenting symptom were given up after the first visit, and quite successful cases where the symptom may till persist by the time successful treatment is terminated.

If we try to set up criteria for selection on a genetic level, we are again in trouble, because as important as it is for us to know the level of functioning of our patient and level of genesis of his symptoms, this does not provide a clear line of cleavage which can serve as the sole basis for selection. The genetic considerations are vital in determining the method of treatment to be employed, though taken by themselves they are not nearly as much so in children as in adults; particularly is this so in the younger children.

Various devices have been employed by different clinics to limit selection of cases. This is relatively easy in cities where there are many clinics or the special purpose clinics that have no obligations to the community beyond what they wish to make it. For instance, the captive type of clinic within a school or hospitals of necessity limited in its cases, but the problem of selection for treatment nevertheless arises because of the time consuming aspect of our work. Age limitations are in common use, but within each age there are still a great variety of cases.

One clinic in this region has set up a system of grading cases from I to III on he basis of estimated treatment time needed, and balancing the case load with preference being given to the group with the least length of time required for treatment. We tried this system and have met with complete lack of success, in that we still tend to remain overloaded with long-term cases of dubious progrnosis; particularly, since this system requires turning away the group III cases (the group with the longest treatment time and the poorest prognosis) which the staff finds rather difficult to do.

In our long struggle with this problem of selection, we gradually evolved a scheme which I hope will work ultimately an thus far, as it has been applied, gives promise of doing so. In this scheme we have set down six simple criteria for the selection of cases for treatment, regardless of the diagnosis, symptoms, or ho good or bad the prognosis. The criteria to be met are:

1. The patient must be accessible to treatment.
2. There must be sufficient inner resources that can be utilized in treatment.
3. There must be sufficient environmental resources to support treatment.
4. A reasonable goal can be attainment in treatment in a reasonable, foreseeable time.
5. The goal chosen must be sufficiently important to the individual in our judgment and of sufficient help to be worth while for the patient.
6. There is good likelihood that the patient can maintain the gains to be aimed for after treatment is terminated.

This plan allows for a great deal of flexibility in case selection but also demands a realistic approach. It does not allow too rigid exclusion, nor the catering to impossible aims. It eliminates neither long-term nor short-term treatment. Its only demands that whatever is done be worth while to the individual; and if it is not so, that neither the patient's nor the staff's time and hopes be wasted by trying to do the impossible or not getting enough return in the time and effort.

For instance, most clinics turn away th intellectually

borderline and mentally deficient. Why? Just because we cannot raise their intellectual level to normal? Quite often with the expenditure of a relatively small amount of time with the child and family, either in a short period of treatment, or in guidance over a prolonged period, or both, treatment may make a tremendous difference to that child, his family, as well as the community. Because we cannot make them top-notch citizens, should we not at least accept a lesser goal if it is attainable within a reasonable expenditure of time and effort? The same question must be raised in regard to some of the physically handicapped children. If a psychotic child can be helped to make some adjustment and hold on to a marginal function, should we not try? Under this scheme the answer would be yes only if we have the requirements for treatment, and that these goals can be achieved in sufficient time really to be of lasting value. The answer would be definitely no if it appears that at the end of a long treatment period the patient might be changed but no better off. We can decide to take on one case for long-term treatment because the goal thereby attainable is worthwhile, but in another case not. For instance, I recall a little twelve-year-old girl with a disturbance in which she would rock back and forth. This was embarrassing to her and the family. While this was a relatively mild symptom, I felt its roots were such as to require years of treatment and I did not feel this to be a worth-while undertaking. She did invest a year or more in treatment at another clinic without any gains. In contrast to this, I recall accepting for treatment a psychotic girl, though thee were great odds against treatment and though I anticipated that she would probably be withdrawn from treatment. I felt that there was a possibility even in a short time to reach her an help her to get a grip on reality which could possibly sustain her. We have a tendency in clinics to refuse to treat children when the parents are uncooperative and when we cannot hope to gain their full cooperation. Need we be so exclusive? Sometime, but not always. There are situations where despite all odds, sufficient help can be given to do a sufficiently worth-while amount of good. We do have to be sure that we are offering the patient a reasonably seaworthy raft, that he can hold on to, that will not be taken away from him, and that with it he can reach shore. We must not waste resources building for him a yacht or battleship he cannot get into, cannot use. We might be able to teach him to swim we might even have to carry him ashore, or we might just need to show the way to the shore. However, if he cannot swim, or we have o raft, he can not take the direction or could not last long if he should reach shore – why then make a demonstration of heroism when there are others who can be rescued in the meantime? Why appease our conscience by offering him a useless straw to hold on to?

Of course, it is very pertinent to this scheme of criteria for selection for treatment tat we be realistic in setting attainable goals and not chase after rainbows. It means that often, particularly in the long-term cases of dubious prognosis and the otherwise handicapped, we must be satisfied when a reasonable goal is reached.

9

Nursery School as a Diagnostic help to the Child Guidance Clinic

The Nursery school referred to in this chapter is part of the Department of Psychiatry of the Western Reserve School of Medicine. The School has a capacity for fifteen children of preschool age who are suffering from various kinds of emotional disorders. Depending on the diagnosis, the children either receive treatment themselves (psychoanalysis or psychotherapy) or are helped via the mother, with whom the child therapist does a certain type of guidance work. This work ha been described by Mrs. Erna Furman in her article "Treatment of Under-Fives by Way of Parents"

This viewpoint makes present-day diagnosis consist of a meta psychological evaluation of the total personality. It seems to me that this new formulation is of the greatest importance for the evaluation of the conflicts of the child under five. The child under five gives us the opportunity to study two types of conflict, namely, the one existing between the infantile ego and the environment, and the other type in which the conflict has already become internalized. This diagnostic distinction between two groups, in which either the external or the internal conflict prevails, leads, as will presently discuss, to the decision whether guidance of the mother can be expected to be of sufficient help or whether direct treatment of the child will be necessary. Where the conflict is still an external one, that is, between the ego and objects in the environment, there of course we have to include in our evaluation all the parties concerned. It will not be sufficient to study the conflict only from the side of the child, but it will also be necessary to take into our consideration the attitudes of the objects, attitudes which are of course based upon the personality structure. Thus we have focus our attention upon the interplay between the child and his environment. With this group of children, a change brought about in the object may be sufficient to produce a favourable change in the development of the child.

It is evident that in those cases in which the conflict is already internalized, a change in the object will no longer be sufficient to solve the internal conflict.

Since, upon the admission of children, the mothers stay with them in the nursery for as long a period as we consider necessary, our nursery school setup in Cleveland offers an excellent opportunity to observe and to evaluate the interplay between mother and child.

For instance, one of the most frequent problems for which mothers seek help is separation anxiety. The origin of this problem can lie in traumatic events, in separations, such as the hospitalization of either mother or child, or the child might have a problem concerning aggression and therefore have the need to be with mother constantly, to reassure himself that mother I all right. On the other hand, it may be the mother who is anxious about her child and cannot let the child separate from her. Often the mother is not conscious of this, nor can she tell us about it, for this anxiety can be rooted in deep-seated conflicts within herself. Such a separation anxiety of the mother will of course induce insecurity and fears in the small child, and this situation often cannot be cleared up in observations of short duration. For instance, a single diagnostic interview that we would have with mother and child would not suffice.

Mothers bring children to us, seeking help consciously for a certain problem that may not seem of too great importance. It then often happens that our diagnostic study and observation in the nursery school reveal more serious problems which the mother has to deny, and she therefore displaces her worry to some minor difficulties. IF a mother uses denial as a defense against recognition of certain difficulties in the child, we can be sure that the child has taken over this same denial, and we have to rely on the objective observation in the nursery to recognize the real trouble.

Case Studies

Catherine was three years old when she was admitted to the nursery school because she seemed to her mother to have an acute reaction to the birth of a bay sister, now four months old. In the mother's interview with Mrs. Benkendorf, the mother said that her relationship with Catherine had become very saying about routine matters such as getting dressed, etc. Catherine had never been a very good sleeper, but she now refused to go to bed, would wake up during the night screaming, could not be alone any time during the day or night, could not bear to be separated from mother. At this point in the interview Mrs. Benkendorf asked the mother under what circumstances she had left to go to the hospital to have the baby, and it turned out she had left in the middle of then night without saying good-by to Catherine. The child had also gone back to wetting and soiling, although bowel and bladder control had been easily achieved at the age of two and had seemed well established. Catherine also needed her bottle very much again, although she used a cup when she went visiting.

The mother was very perceive of her child's unhappiness, tried very hard to be as giving as possible and reassuring of her love, but was puzzled by the child's steadfast refusal to grow up and to talk. This interview with the mother seemed to show beyond any doubt that the child's separation anxiety was due to the trauma of mother's sudden hospitalization, and her regressive behaviour was due to jealousy because of mother's attentiveness to the bay sister.

Let us now see the report of the teacher after Catherine had attend the nursery school six days: The child's adjustment to school has been a slow, arduous process, and although she has seen in school six days now, she cannot even stay through records yet.

It has been very difficult for the mother to allow Catherine to become interested in being part of the school or in doing things for herself. Mother hovered about Catherine for several days, pouring juice for her, telling her what to say and then saying it for her, helping her with her things in the bathroom, telling her when to go to the bathroom, etc. She could not keep away from Catherine, although he teacher continually requested that she stay out in the office.

A report on part of Tuesday morning will show how things went:

She began her morning in the waste room today. The first thing she had to do was to go to the toilet. She said she wanted to go alone. She crept into the bathroom and closed the door. After a while the door opened and she asked for her mommy. Her mother rushed in to help her immediately. When Catherine cam out, she thought she might like to blow bubbles, and she smiled just slightly once when I showed her how to blow to blow one.

After the bubbles, and she smiled just slightly once when I showed her how to blow one.

After the bubbles, which she just barely touched, she worked at the ironing board a long time (about ten minutes) with obvious enjoyment and contentment. When she finished, she ran to her mother for a hug, and her mother asked, "you'd like a drink of water, wouldn't you?" Catherine nodded. Mother said. "Then go get a drink. As soon as Catherine reached the fountain, mother asked, "Catherine, do you have to go to the toilet?" Catherine nodded again. Mother said, "Well, hurry, hurry," Catherine smiled, and it looked s though she were wetting her pants right then and there. She looked at her mother, and her mother said, "You want me to help you" (statement). They went to the bathroom together, and mother emerged with the wet pants. She did not seem at all surprised that the child had wet, although Catherine had been to the toilet fifteen minutes before.

At juice time it was suggested that mother sit in the office and that Catherine come and go as she pleased. Catherine ate and drank nothing and refused to answer when the teacher asked whether she was through.

At music, Catherine said she could come upstairs without the teacher. She poked her head in, and when I said, "Come in, join us," she became frightened or angrily resistant and started to sob. We took her down stirs where she became involved with her mother again. Mother could not stay in the office but found excuses to follow Catherine outdoors. Mother improved at lunch and stayed in the office throughout lunch.

The teacher became very direct with the mother and told her that the separation problem was hers and not Catherine's, and that it would be necessary for her to remaining the office if she expected Catherine to learn to stay at nursery school. Since then the mother has been doing a little better, but it is still very difficult for her to allow the teacher to do things for Catherine when she needs help.

Usually Catherine speaks only a word if she wants to make a point very badly, and this word seems to come out of her with terrific reluctance, Sometimes she will make only a grunting-moan kind of sound and expect you to understand her. On a few rare occasions she hands carried on what might be called a conversation—several words and phrases linked together and spoken with some animation and a bit less hastily. One subject with which she was able to do this was her daddy. She told me that she and mommy were going shopping for a birthday present for her daddy and that he would have a cake. This, of course, was not all told in one sentence but sort of coaxed out of her. However, her eyes were bright and her voice had some animation and lightness in it—something we do not often hear. Also, she laughs occasionally and smiles, which changes her whole personality. This seems to be about the only part left of her that is really Catherine and has not been superimposed.

Catherine wet herself purposely whenever she feels the urge. It can be fifteen minutes after having gone to the toilet, and it can take place while she is in the bathroom washing her hands or playing at the bowl. She stands still, a smile comes across her face, and then you know she is wet. For the first few days her mother had to help her almost completely in the bathroom, because she wanted to and because Catherine wanted her to want to. After mother began to remain in the office more consistently, Catherine began to expect as much from the teachers as she was used to from the mother. I have Catherine a little chair to sit on in the bathroom, and in two minutes the wet pants and overalls were off and the clean ones on. It was very apparent at that time that Catherine is willing to help herself and would quickly learn to do so if her mother could allow it. However mother also stresses the toilet a great deal, mentions and reminds her very often to make a pee-pee, and is generally very involved with toileting the child and changing her. Sometimes when Catherine has wet herself and we want her to change herself, she sys, "see, Mommy," and we know she is angry with us because, after all, her mommy will do it all for her, whereas we expect something of her.

The first time Catherine stayed for lunch, she at first refused to come to the table but sat in the office with mommy. The teacher asked her to pass some biscuits to her mommy and then to put one on her own plate. Catherine finally came to the table, and while everyone else was finishing desert or listening to records in the other room. Catherine ate helping after helping of peas, and nothing but peas. The next day Catherine ate a fairly good lunch of wieners, toast, and tomato, with no fuss at all. With the third lunch, however, e began pattern that she has followed ever since; she took a bite of egg-salad sandwich and held this bite in her mouth for at least fifteen minutes, although the teacher explained that she did not have to eat anything she did not want and could spit it out at any time. Catherine seemed to expect the teacher to reach into her mouth and take it out for her, but when she understood that this would not happen, she spirit out herself.

The mother had been watching this lunch process from the boot, and when she emerged from the booth her face was very smug and satisfied-looking as if to say, "See, they can't handle may child here as well as I do!" It is evident that mother is glad when the teachers fail with her child in situations where she succeeds, and she definitely has a need to prove that she can handle her child the best. Whether it is getting Catherine to go to the toilet (a feat on which she puts a high premium) or to eat her lunch or whatever, this feeling prevails.

Although we have felt that Catherine's adjustment to school has been very rough-going, we may be accomplishing a little bit, as evidenced by Catherine's behaviour toward her mother on one occasion. After lunch one day she was getting ready to go home and began to comb her hair. Mother took the comb from her and said, "I'll do it for you," Catherine aid, "why?" The when they were ready to go, mother said, "Okay, Bugs Bunny, let's go," Catherine said very firmly, "I Catherine," and turned to me and said, "I Catherine"

After this report, our assessment of Catherine' separation difficulties will be a different one.

It was obvious that this mother had difficult in separating from the child or in letting the child become active and independent. And it was finally the child who had to tell and shown mother that she wanted to do things for herself and not be kept little.

10

Environment as Bases of Behaviour

Educational psychology uses the methods of science as its primary "tools" of investigation. It has certain things in common with all the sciences to the extent that educational psychology uses scientific methodology. The latter is certainly the more crucial aspect since it not only permits the discovery of knowledge but also affords us the means for accelerated scientific progress. Therefore, Kendler (1975, p. 3) states: "Science is a method designed to discover and interpret knowledge based on rules of evidence and logic." However, the *basic aim of science is theory*. The basic aim of science is to explain phenomena, natural or man-made. Such *explanations* are called *theories*. Instead of trying to explain each and every separate behaviour of children, the scientific psychologist seeks general explanations that encompass and link together many different behaviours. The teacher may not go on explaining children's methods of solving problems in mathematics. He may seek general explanations of the all kinds of problem-solving. He might call such a general explanation a theory of problem—solving.

It is the job of scientific enquiry to discover those conditions or factors that bring about, determine or cause a particular event. Science can be said to have four purposes: (a) to *describe*, (2) to *predict*, (3) to *control*, and (4) to *explain*.

All sciences have as a goal the accurate description of

some aspect of the natural universe—description of some natural or even man-made phenomenon. The psychologist, of course, has chosen the behaviour of man and other animals as his sector of the universe. Behaviour is what organisms do: how they act and what they experience. Descriptive investigations also involve the discovery of new phenomena. Many important scientific discoveries have been made in the process of describing events or structures. The descriptive function of science depends upon instrumentation for measurement and observation; for example, the use of electron microscope by the biologist and the standardized tests of intelligence by the psychologist are quite essential for description of phenomena of interest to these scientists. Advancement of science is not possible without identification and accurate description of objects, events, persons and situations.

Description provides the basic knowledge hat is necessary for realizing the other purposes of science. One of these purposes is prediction, which is the ability to predict phenomenon X from phenomenon Y. For example, the next stage of an embroy's development can be predicted very accurately from knowledge of the embroy's current stage. A student's achievement in school can be predicted fairly accurately by an aptitude test administered a year or two earlier. To make a scientific prediction we must first identify consistent relationship between persons, events, situations, and conditions. The ability to predict is an important step toward explaining phenomena. Observations of association between phenomenon X and phenomenon Y may arouse the curiosity of the scientist about why the association occurred. This will load to the development of a theory or an urge to collect further data about the phenomena.

The third purpose of science is to gain *control* over the phenomena being studied. Scientific experiments are designed to achieve this purpose. In an experiment, phenomenon X is manipulated to determine whether it exerts control over phenomenon Y. The control purpose of science is closely related to its predictive purpose. The major difference is in whether phenomenon X is manipulated by the scientist. In predictive enquiry the scientist studies naturally occurring associations between phenomena. In experiments, the scientist manipulates phenomena to determine whether he can control the condition of some other phenomenon. Experimental manipulation leads to more powerful statements about associations between phenomena than does predictive enquiry. Experimental results do permit conclusions about cause and effect relationships which predictive associations between phenomena necessarily do not. In the field of psychology during the past few decades, the ability to plan and direct many aspects of human behaviour has increased considerably. In the area of vocational guidance, for example, psychologists have been able to determine how success and satisfaction in a particular occupation are related to specific patterns of abilities, interest sand other measurable human characteristics. Utilizing this knowledge, the vocational counselor is able, through personal interview data and psychological test scores, to offer advice as to the vocational fields that are most likely to offer success and happiness for a particular client. Such control is used widely by the armed forces of U.S.A. and other European countries in classifying men for special training.

The fourth purpose of science –*explanation*—is considered to be its ultimate goal. If scientists are able to explain a set of phenomena, it means that they can describe, predict and control the phenomena with a high level of certainty and accuracy. Scientists have always been eager to understand the phenomena they investigate. Scientific understanding of an even occurs when the event is explained. The function of Science is to discover those factors which determine the occurance of an event. This is essentially what an explanation is –the specification of those factors or conditions related to the occurance of an event. Higher order explanations consist of general statements that apply to many different events having some feature or features in common. Everybody observed that apples fell, that stones tossed high up ultimately came down, and that the waters of the seas periodically rose and fell, and also that planets followed certain paths in their trip around the sun. Galileo and Newton saw a basic similarity among these events. The theory of gravitation, that is, the attraction that masses of matter have for each other, was formulated to apply to all of these formerly "isolated" events. Thus, a theory is a statement or a group of statements the purpose of which is to explain a group of events. The theory of gravitation, like all scientific theories serves two major functions. In the first place, it *integrates* existing data, and t\in the second place, it predicts new events. To conclude scientific *explanation* takes the form of a theory about the phenomena being investigated.

Scientific Theories and Language of Research: To repeat: Scientific explanation takes the form of a theory about the phenomena being investigated. Scientific theory is defined as "a system for explaining a set of phenomena by specifying constructs and the laws that related these constructs to each other" (Brog & Gal, 1983, p. 22). And also as: "*A theory is a set of interrelated constructs (concepts), definitions and propositions that present a systematic view of phenomena by specifying relations among variables, with the purpose of explaining and predicting the phenomena* (Kerlinger, 1973, p. 9).

The definition of scientific theory by Kerlinger says three things. "One, a theory is set of propositions consisting of defined and interrelated constructs. Two, a theory sets out the interrelations among a set of variables (constructs) and in so doing, presents a systematic view of the phenomena described by the variables. Finally a theory explains phenomena. It does so by specifying what variables are related to what variables and how they are related, thus enabling the researcher to predict from certain variables to certain other variables" "Ibid, p. 9).

An educational psychologist might have a theory of school achievement in mathematics. His variables might be intelligence, socio-economic status, personality adjustment, motivation and spatial relationships and numerical aptitudes. The phenomenon to be explained is school achievement in mathematics. School achievement in mathematics is explained by specified relations between each of the six variables and school achievement in mathematics, or by combinations of the six variables and school achievement in mathematics. The educational psychologist successfully using these set of constructs, the "*understands*" school achievement in mathematics. He is able to "*explain*" and to some extent at least, "*predict*" it.

In this section, rather in the discussion carried on so far in this chapter, certain terms that are quite new for you have been used. Any scientific discipline has need for a specific language for describing and sumarising the observations in that area. Scientists need terms at the empirical level in order to describe particular observations. Also they need terms at the theoretical level for referring to hypothetical processes. The scientists use terms that are labels for concepts and constructs, both at the descriptive and theoretical levels. The following are some of the general terms used in educational and psychological research.

(a) Concepts and Constructs: A concept is a class of stimuli which have common characteristics. These stimuli are objects, events or persons. We ordinarily designate a concept by its name, such as book, tree, liquid or war student or dedicated teachers. A concept is a word that represents the similarities or common aspects of objects or events that are otherwise quite different from one another. Words such as 'tree' and 'liquid' represent common aspects of otherwise diverse things. The purpose of a concept is to simplify thinking by including a number of events under one general heading. Some concepts are quite close to the events they represent. Thus, for example, the meaning of the concept 'tree' can easily be illustrated by pointing to specific trees. The concept is an abstraction of the characteristics that all trees have in common—characteristics that are directly observable.

Constructs are created to summarize observations and to provide explanations. Terms such as '*motivation*' or 'problem-solving ability' cannot be easily illustrated, by pointing to specific objects, events or persons. These are higher level abstractions referred to as constructs. From the concepts, scientists have constructed these complex abstractions. Constructs are created by combining concepts and less complex constructs in purposeful patterns. As a scientific construct, "motivation" means both more and less than it may mean as a concept. As a construct, it can be used in two ways. One, it enters into theoretical schemes and is related in various ways to other constructs. For example, we may say, "*school achievement* is in part a function of intelligence and motivation." Two, "motivation" is so defined and specified that it can be observed and measured. We can observe the motivation of children by administering a properly designed test on them or we may ask the teachers to tell us the relative degrees of motivation of their pupils. We can combine concepts such as '*visual acuity*,' 'symbol discrimination,' 'listening ability,' and others, in a purposeful pattern to produce the construct "reading readiness." Constructs are useful in interpreting experimental data and in building theory. They are used to account for observed regularities and relationships.

Concepts and constructs should be defined in abstract terms, which give the general meaning they are supposed to have and in terms of the operations by which they can be measured in the particular study. The former type of definition is called the *constitutive* definition and the latter is known as the *operational* definition.

(b) Constitute and operational Definitions: A constitutive definition refers to a more formal type of definition in which a construct is defined by using other constructs. For example, "*intelligence*" may be defined as "the ability to think abstractly." In this definition we have substituted one concept for another. This type of definition helps to convey the general nature of the phenomenon in which the investigator is interested as well as to show its relation to other theories and studies using similar concepts. A constitutive definition elucidates a concept or construct and perhaps, gives some insight into the phenomenon described by the term. "All constructs, in order to be scientifically useful, must possess constitutive meaning", says Torgerson. (Torgerson, 1958, p. 5 and referred to by Kerlinger, 1973, p. 31). This means that they must be

capable of being used in theories.

An Operational definition is one which assigns meaning to a concept or construct by specifying the operations that must be performed in order to measure that concept, construct or variable. This type of definition is essential in research since data must be collected in terms of observable events. Constructs like 'anxiety or 'achievement' must represent some kind of observable events for any empirical study. To define a term operationally, scientists must choose discriminable events as indicators of the concepts and devise operations to obtain data relevant to them.

Intelligence can operationally be defined as the scores on X intelligence test, or intelligence is what X intelligence test measures. An operational definition of creativity may refer to scores made on the Minnesota Test of Creativity. An operational definition is a sort of manual of instructions to the investigator. Operational definitions permit the researcher to find a relationship between two sets of observable and measurable data that were selected to represent the concepts, constructs or variables. For example, an investigation of the relation of constructs—creativity and intelligence—in practice will relate scores on an X intelligence test to scores on an X measure of creativity.

(c) Variables: A variable is a attribute. It reflects or expresses some concept for construct. A variable takes in different values. It varies in the same individual from onetime to another; and it varies between the individuals at the same time and between averages for groups. Intelligence, Achievement, Sex and social class are all variables, While height and weight are physical variables, intelligence and anxiety are psychological variables. Educational psychologists are concerned in determining how such variables are related to one another. The concepts and constructs that are of interest in a study become variables.

Some variables are antecedent to other variables. For example, to be able to read, one must have some degree of intelligence. Here, the variable intelligence is antecedent to the variable reading ability and to some extent, the latter is a consequence of the former. The level of reading ability is dependent on the level of intelligence. In research, Variables that are consequences of or dependent upon antecedent variables are called dependent variables and the variables that are antecedent to dependent variables are called independent variables. Independent variables predict the dependent variables. In experimental research, a change in the dependent variable brings about a corresponding change in the dependent variable under study.

Jut as the teacher does in working through an immediate practical problem in the classroom, the scientists, even on the highest level, observes, generalizes, makes inferences, observes further and then accepts, revises ore rejects his generalization. In other words, scientific method is a "problem-solving activity" and especially, "a hypothesis generating and testing sequence." The teacher may use the essence of the scientific method in dealing with a problem in the classroom. A student, say, 'R' entered the eighth class a month ago. The teacher notices that 'R' obtained the lowest score in the last arithmetic test, in the class. (This is the initial observation of the teacher.) He then checks back and discovers that 'R' has completed his homework in arithmetic only twice during the past month, has obtained falling scores on both tests given, and has not answered to oral questions during this time. (For the teacher, these are the observed regularities) then the teacher conjectures : "Perhaps, 'R' is mentally retarded." (This is the hypothesis.) If so, 'R' must be doing poorly in other subjects. (This is the further inference or deduction.) the teacher checks the records and finds that 'R' is doing better than average work in geography and science and is only slightly below average in everything else, except translation work. (These further observations discredit the hypothesis which is then discarded.) Can 'R' be emotionally disturbed and fearful in the new school? (Thus, the teacher formulates a new hypothesis.) If so, it should show up in all school subjects (new inference). The records have already shown that this is not so (hypothesis discarded). Perhaps "R" has a specific disability in arithmetic (third hypothesis). If so, a diagnostic test should be helpful (deduction). A standardized diagnostic arithmetic test showed that 'R' was unable to do any sum on 'fractions', but could do almost all other arithmetic processes fairly well (hypothesis supported). If the trouble of "R' is of this specific type, teaching him the 'fraction' processes should bring about improvement (further deductions from the hypothesis). Providing remedial work and following up on the consequences willlead to either acceptance, rejection, or modification of this hypothesis. And, this is a "hypothesis generating and testing sequence."

Methods of Study

Each method contributes in its own way to the final solution. In planning a study, the scientist attempts to select the method or methods most appropriate to the particular problem under consideration. The scientist has to collect empirical data to test the hypothesis he has formulated. On the basis of the research evidence, the scientist accepts or rejects the hypothesis. Kerlinger tries to include all the methods of investigation under his caption. "Observation-Test-Experiment." We shall now consider some of the methods y means of which the educational psychologists obtain their data. The five chief methods that the psychologists use are the experimental methods, the observational method, the survey method, the text method and the case study method. These methods are not mutually exclusive and a variety of observational and measurement techniques are used in each.

Experimental Method

The essense of the experimental method is simple. The experimenter (1) changes or varies something, (2) keeps other conditions constant, and (3) looks for an effect of the change or variation upon the system he has under observation. Since educational psychology is the science of human behaviour in educational situations, the experimenter looks for an effect of the changes he has made upon behaviour of the subject or subjects. This is simple enough, but becomes more and more complicated as we consider the experimental method is greater detail.

The experimental method can be used outside the laboratory as well as inside. The distinguishing characteristic of a laboratory is that it is a place where the experimenter can carefully control conditions and take measurements in order to discover orderly relationships among variables. The ability to exercise precise control over variables distinguishes the experimental method from other methods of observation. In every experiment we must have at least one independent variable and one dependent variable. In simple experiments, such as the one described below as an example, there is only one variable of each kind. But it is possible with appropriate experimental design to have several independent variables and several dependent variables in the same experiment.

A teacher (the experimenter) seeks to discover whether learning ability depends on the amount of sleep a pupil has had. The teacher can control the amount of sleep by arranging to have several groups of subjects spend the night in the school laboratory. One group might be allowed to go to sleep at 11-00 P.M., another rat 1.00 A.M., and the third group might be kept awake until 4-00 A.M. By waking all the subject s at the same time and giving each the same learning task, the teacher-experimenter can determine whether the subjects with more sleep master the task more quickly than those with less sleep. In this study the different amounts of sleep are the antecedent conditions, the learning performances are the result of these conditions. Thus, in this study the amount of sleep is the independent variable It is independent of what the subject doe and the teacher can manipulate this variable learning ability in this experiment is the dependent variable. It is affected by charges in the antecedent conditions or the independent variable. The dependent variable is a measure of the subject's behaviour which the experimenter does not manipulate. The experiment described here can be clearly and simply expressed by the formula: $Y = f(x)$. In this formula y represents the dependent variable or the learning performances of the subjects; f frepresents the phrase "is a function of " in the sense of "is causally dependent upon"; while x represents the independent variable, the antecedent condition, that is, the different amount s of sleep, upon which the occurance of y depends. Thus, for the experiment under consideration we could say that the subject's ability to master a learning task is a function of the amount of sleep he has had.

A very important characteristic of the experimental method is control. In an experiment it is important that only the variables be allowed to change. Factors other than the independent variable which might affect the dependent variable must be held constant. It would do not good to study the effects of varying an independent variable if other factors, unknown to the experimenter, changed also. In an experiment we must control conditions which will give misleading results. Because of the greater difficulties in controlling experimental conditions in the behavioural sciences of which educational psychology is one, and also education is included, experimental research is very difficult to apply to certain, kinds of educational problems. The typical experimental design, often called the before-and-after experimental design, used in educational research involves: (1) the selection of a sample of subjects; (2) random assignment of these subjects to experimental and control groups; (3) the exposure of the experimental group to a treatment that is withheld from the control group; (4) and, finally, the evaluation of the two groups on the dependent variable, that is the variable the teacher-experimenter is attempting to change. A simple experimental study described below shall clarify these steps.

Suppose, we want to prove the efficacy of Problem-Development method over all other methods of teaching Geography. The first step we should take is to select a sample of 200 pupils from a particular class and randomly assign 100 pupils to the experimental group and 100 pupils to the control group, after administering on the subjects an achievement test in Geography as a pretest. The next step for us is to teach Geography using the Problem-development method to the experimental group and to the control group any traditional method. This process continues for about one year. At the end of one year, as our next step in experimental research, we administer an achievement test in Geography on both the experimental and control groups, as the post-test. Now we have the required data on hand for statistical computation to determine whether the subjects who had been exposed to the treatment, that is, taught Geography by the Problem-Development Method, have obtained more favourable scores on he achievement test given as the post-test, than those students who comprised the control group. If the subjects of the experimental group scored higher than that of the control group, it would prove the efficacy of the Problem-Development Method over other methods, to some extent. This is also called the pretest-posttest experimental design.

Observational Method

The most basic technique in psychology, as in any other science, is observation, But incidental observation of naturalistic behaviour is neither scientific nor psychological. Of course, the early stages of a science necessitate exploration to become familiar with the relationship that will later become the object of more precise study: but, incidental observation of naturalistic behaviour is seldom a useful source of data or inference. Incidental observations are typified by the anecdotal accounts of the behaviour of one's pet dog or cat or of one's own children. Reports of the behaviour of wild animals by naive and untrained observers are also included in this class.

Because psychology is the science of behaviour and mental processes, some scholars areof the opinion that there are two kinds of observations which have been employed in psychological research – *introspection* and *objective observation.* It has already been mentioned in Chapter II of this text that Wundt, Titchener and their followers used the technique of *introspection* to analyse conscious experience. The psychologist himself, being a trained introspectionist, observed his own mental processes and furnished information in the form of verbal reports. The behaviourists doubted the validity of this method. It could not be employed to analyze the conscious activities of animals and children. However it gets employed in the form of verbal reports in an objective manner uptill how. Hilgard et al., (1979, p. 18) have referred to Masters and Johnson who in their extensive study of the physiological aspects of human sexuality, developed appropriate methods for observing and recording the responses of the subjects in the laboratory. The data included (1) observations of behaviour, (2) recording of bodily changes, and (3) responses to questions asked about the subject's sensations before, during and after sexual stimulation, which means that the subjects made a verbal report of their conscious experiences in so far as their sexual response was concerned.

The second major technique psychologists use to obtain facts about behaviour is *objective observation*. Here the experimenter notes what his subject does—not what he feels or thinks. The environmental conditions under which a response occurs, as well as the response itsel fare systematically described. Systematic and objective observations of people, usually children, under natural conditions can be very informative Objective observation is mainly concerned with what goes on in the external world. However, the psychologists of this age have many instruments for observing what goes on inside the organism. Among these are devices for studying the electrical currents of the brain and the changes in conductivity of th eskin durgn emotions. Introspection is aimed at describing inner experience and objective observation at describing aspects of behaviour observable to others. Thus, some psychologists think, they supplement each other, and then they are used in combination. An example of this combined technique is an experiment conducted to investigate the ability of blind people to orient themselves in space.

In educational research, observational method is given a very important place. It is treated as basically a measurement technique of gathering data about the subjects involved in a study. Of course, the techniques employed in observational methods are different to a very great extent form other measurement techniques. Observational methods permit the collection of direct information about human behaviour tat can be collected only indirectly measurement techniques such as paper and pencil tests.

Observational methods help the investigator to study in detail specific areas of human behaviour. For example: (a) how do preschool children respond to a television programme that contains a high number of violent acts? (b) What specific counseling procedures are most highly related to realistic vocational decisions by high school students?

The tools generally used in observational research are: (1) Standard Observational Schedules, (2) Audiotape and videotape Recorders, (3) rating scales, (4) Audiotape and Videotape recorders, (3) Rating scales, (4) Sociometric techniques (50 Anecdotal Records and the like. Observational methods to be successful, observation of behaviour must be made by trained observer or observers; observational information should be properly recorded; the observed behaviour should be objectively defined and the data collected should be analysed as completely and as quantitatively as possible.

Survey Method

Some problems are very often difficult to study by direct observation. Also very often it is not feasible or desirable to spend a long period of time in the field or to obtain data about all the individuals in a group. In such circumstances, much information, useful and valuable, army be obtained conducting a survey. In this method the investigator, by using written questionnaires or oral interviews, obtains data from a selected group. It is important that he chooses carefully so that it will constitute a *representative sample* of the larger group or *universe*: in which he is interested. A representative sample is one drawn in such a way that every person in the universe from which it is drawn has an equal chance of being selected. If the sample is not representative, the data collected will be of little value. Therefore this method is known as "*Sample Survey Method.*" The best known type of survey are the "opinion poll," and "census."

Survey research in education typically employs questionnaires and interviews to determine the opinions, attitudes, preferences, and perceptions of persons of interest to the investigator. Survey studies that deal with sensitive topics such as "premarital sex relations" frequently use interviews. Surveys in education can be used to explore a very wide range of topics such as the extent to which open classrooms are being used at the elementary school level and the perception of teachers and principals about the effectiveness of such classrooms; and procedures currently used to help handicapped children adjust to regular classrooms problems encountered by first year elementary school teachers also can be taken for survey study.

The Method

The tests and scales are important research instruments in contemporary education and psychology. They are used to measure all kinds of variables—achievement, intelligence, aptitude, interest, attitude, and other kinds of abilities and accomplishments. Tests and scales are measuring instruments. However, while tests are scales, scales are not necessarily tests. Scales do not ordinarily have the meanings of competition and success or failure that tests do. Significantly, we say "achievement tests" and scales can be divided into the following classes: intelligence and aptitude tests, achievement tests, personality measures. Tests enable the investigator to obtain large quantities of data from people without elaborate laboratory equipment. A test essentially presents a uniform situation to a group of people who vary in aspects relevant to the situation. An analysis of the results then relates variations in test scores to variations among people.

A coefficient of correlation is alternative to experimentation. Suppose, a teacher wishes to find out the extent to which "intelligence" affects the "achievement" of pupils. His hypothesis is "intelligence influences Achievement." He wants to test this hypothesis. Treating "intelligence" as the independent or predictor or X variable and "achievement" as the dependent or criterion or V variable, he administers an intelligence and an achievement test on a sample of pupils drawn from the population. The, he scores both the tests and computes a coefficient of correlation between the two sets of scores. He then proceeds to estimate the regression of X on Y and the regression of Y on X. With the help of these regression coefficients the teacher is able to tell us the extent to which "intelligence" affects or predicts "achievement," that is, statistically put, if values of Y variable are predictable from values of X variable.

Tests and Scales are indispensable for educational research, particularly in causal-comparative method or export facto research, correlation a studies and evaluation research. The study of relationships between educational variables is extremely important. The causal comparative method is one approach for exploring relationships between variables. The correlation method provides another approach for exploring relationships. Like causal—comparative approach, the distinguishing characteristic of correlational studies is the way in which the relational data are analysed. "Educational evaluation is the process of making judgement about the merit, value, or worth of educational programmes, projects, materials and techniques". (Brog & Gall, 1983, p. 733)

The causal comparative method is often used instead of the experimental method because many of the cause and effect relationships that we wish to studying education do not permit experimental manipulation. It should be emphasized again that Tests and scales are very essential for all these types of research. However, test construction and use are no simple mattes. They involve many steps in item construction, item analysis, scaling, establishing norms and so on and so forth. Later chapters may explore the problems of testing in a very brief manner.

The Case- Study Approach

Some authors call the case-study approach as life-History

Method. In the case study approach, the investigator studies the conditions in people's lives which have led to their becoming whatever they are, be they physicians, teachers, politicians, alcohol edicts or even criminals. The investigator wishes to find out the causes of a specific form of behaviour by studying the antecedents. But according to some authors, the case study in its simplest form, involves an investigator who makes a detailed examination of a single subject or group or phenomenon.

Including only the clinical method under case-study approach, Sawrey and Telford (1964, p. 14) proceed to say" "The clinical method is not primarily a research method, it is rather a set of procedures for the diagnosis and treatment of people with behaviour problems," Including case-study approach under observational research, Borg and Gall (1983, p. 489) write: "Several kinds of case studies can be found in behavioural science literature. These include: (1) Historical case studies of Organisations....(2) Observational case studies...(3) Oral histories.... (2) Observational case studies...(3) Oral histories...(4) Situational analysis ...(5) oral histories...(4) Situational analysis...(5) Clinical case study". "The tree basic life-history methods are the daybook method, the clinical method and the biographical method'. States Ruch (1970, p. 24). This text follows Ruch.

The daybook method is often used in child study. The child's development is carefully observed and recorded day by day. Accumulated records of this kind provide us standards by which we are able to judge the normality of the development of individual children.

The starting point of a clinical investigation is an individual who needs and/or seeks help and the procedure ideally terminates with the better adjustment of the individual. Thus, the clinical method is ordinarily used when and only when people come to the psychologist with personal problems. Not all clinical problems require thorough study. But when they do, the psychologist usually begins by getting a detailed account of the past life history and present life situation of a person in an effort to discover the cause of and salution to some emotional or social adjustment problem. This information is usually gained by interviewing the person and his associates. The clinical study to be most effective needs three professional functions. A physician examines the individual for signs of physical illness; a specially trained social worker examines the patient's home conditions, social background and environment; and a psychometrician administers and scores various tests of aptitude and personality. The clinical investigator may seek the help of these professionals to obtain the required data. When a full record has been, obtained of the past and present influences in the patients' life, the information is put together, discussed and steps are taken to diagnose the problem, treat or remedy the difficulty. The tests, the diagnosis and the remedy, of course, will differ from case to case.

The biographical method is simply an attempt to obtain psychological understanding from an analysis of the records of men's likes as set down by themselves or others. Scientific biographies are important sources of data for psychologists studying individuals. "Most case histories are prepared by reconstructing he biography of a person according to remembered events and records. Reconstruction is necessary because the person's earlier history often does not become a matter of interest until he develops some sort of problem at such time understanding of the past is thought to be important to comprehension of present behaviour.

Environment as Bases of Behaviour

Man is a multi-cellular organism He grows by increase in cell size and division of his constituent cells. Each human child begins life as a one-celled organism—a fertilized egg cell or Zygote, which is formed from the fusion of the male germ-cell or the sperm of the father and the female germ-cell or the ovum of the mother. The germ-cells of the parents unite and then divide. The Zygote grows by a process of cell division and specialization. Ultimately it gives rise to a new multicellular individual. The information needed to reproduce a complex multicellular individual is thus transmitted through a single cell, and each dividing cell in turn must contain the information required to reproduce itself. The elements of heredity belong to the cell.

Every cell capable of reproduction has a nucleus. During cell division, the nucleaus divides by an elaborate mechanism (mitosis) that leads to the reproduction of an exact copy of each constituent chromosome. It is the chromosomes in the nucleus that carry the material basis of heredity. Chromosomes are hereditary elements. They are long strings of thread like substances and are composed chiefly, of three types of chemical substances: *proteins, deoxyribo-nucleic acid* (DNA), which is translated as "an acid, in the nuclei of cells made of deoxidized sugar," and *ribenucleic acid* (RNA). Chromosomes mean "Coloured bodies." They are observable under a powerful microsope. Each human cell neuleus contains approximately forty-six chromosomes with the exception of egg and spermcell, which contain half as many. Hen the sperm and ovum cells combine in the fertilized egg, the Zygote, the normal cell complement of chromosomes is reached. This means, the father contributes 23 chromosomes and the mother as many; and hence, in the fertilized egg again e find 23 pairs of chromosomes.

Each chromosome contains genes—the seeds of inheritance—of which there are believed to be thousands in the human body. The genes themselves are complex chemical packets. "Since te mother and the father contribute an approximately equal number of genes for a new life, the number of possible combinations is staggering. Genes are passed directly from parents to children and have been so assed since man first appeared on earth. Thus in every cell in our bodies we have bits of matter that are directly descended from Dawn man. "Our ancestors", says a doctor at the Rockefeller institute, "are present in our chromosomes and reach down to influence the chemistry of every cell in our bodies". (Ratcliff & Platt, 1964, p. 31).

It was stated tat one of the chemicals the chromosomes

contain is the DNA or deoxyribonucleic acid. "This single molecule is the marvelous inheritance machine. But it is more than that. DNA is life itself." (Ibid, p. 34) Your personal DNA carries the full information about you. DNA makes every living thing different from dogs and gods different from birds. "The coded direction in your DNA were compiled by chance selection from those of your mother and father at the conception of your egg cell. That first cell was a complete you, your first person singular. Its DNA was prepared to generate on a prearranged schedule. Your heart, lungs and kidneys, your eleven pints of blood, twenty-five feet of intestines—all of you. It help advance reservations for all the body functions of your life span, bestowed all the equipments and talents you will ever have". (Ibid, p. 35).

(a) Principles of Inheritance: Like Begets Like: "Like tends to beget like " is the general principle of inheritance. Human beings tend to be alike rather than different. This is called the principle of Conformity. When interpreted, this principle means that bright parents tend to have bright children; average parents tend to have average children; and dull parents tend to have dull children. But a child in the true sense is not the offspring of its parents. A long line of ancestors have preceded the child's parents. Thus, a child inherits all those potentialities that are common in the human race in general and common to the family of which he is a member I particular. The school and the teachers should be aware of this principle of inheritance for successful guidance of learning. On the average, the children tend to be like the parents; but there are many exceptions to the rule. This fact leads to the second principle of inheritance.

(b) The Principle of Variation

Children are not carbon copies of their parents. Children of the same parents tend to be alike yet no two of them, excepting the "identical wins," resemble each other completely. The principle of variation explains why children in the same family differ in intellect, physical structure or behaviour characteristics. The reason is that the children are a product of the combinations of the genes in the parents' germ cells. At the same time they may possess characteristics that can be traced through parents to members of earlier generations of the families represented by the parents themselves. Though they differ, brothers and sisters tend to be more alike than do unrelated children. Teachers should be well acquainted with this principle of inheritance too. The younger child of a particular family may not possess characteristics similar to those of the older child. The two children. therefore, should not be expected o display the same behaviour traits. One may be brilliant in academic pursuits while the other in games or other psychomotor skills. Therefore, a wise teacher should treat each of the children separately and individually, even though they have come from the same family.

(c) The Principle of Regression: Children of bright parents tend to be less bright than their parents. Children of very inferior parents tend to be less inferior than their parents. This tendency is known as the principle of regression. There is a tendency for the children to regress towards or to move towards the average, for any trait. For instance, children of tall parents tend to be taller than the average but not as tall as their parents. The children of a very gifted father or mother are not so gifted as the parents. Similarly, the children of less able parents may exceed parental ability. There are various reasons for the principle of regression.

Mr X is a gifted man. He possesses certain traits for which he is treated as gifted. A most fortunate combination of the genes contained in the germ-cells of his parents resulted in his inheritance of this giftedness. But the germ cells he himself carries are, on the average. Inferior to the particular fortunate combination from which he himself developed. Mr X, the gifted ma, marries a lady who is not supposed to be as gifted as the man whom she married. The germ-cells she carries may not be as good as the ones that combined, out of which she was conceived. Hence, the children of Mr X and his wife will tend to be decidedly above the average, but not as gifted as their father.

Similarly, the germ-cells of two less able presents are probably better tan the combination from which they developed. Therefore, the children of such parents would tend to be better able than their parents. Occasionally, a child of two feeble-minded parents has average intellectual ability. Sometimes, there are children who are stupid, but not as stupid as their parents.

The principles of inheritance—conformity, variation and regression—are useful in trying to understand human characteristics. These principles account for individual differences in human beings to a great extent.

The Human Organism

During the prenatal period, that is from the time of its conception till the time of this birth, which is about 280 days, the human organism passes through three stages of growth—germinal, embryonic and fetal. The germinal stage refers the egg like organization that lasts for about two weeks after the Zygote is formed. From the third to the eighth week, the human organism is in the embryonic stage of growth. During this period of development, the structure of the organism definitely shows human characteristics. The fetal stage of growth lasts from the ninth week to birth of the human baby. During this period, the new life continues to develop into full human structure. The bodily organs grow in shape and size. After approximately 280 days from the time of its conception the human organism reaches a stage of growth which does not necessitate it to remaining the womb of the mother any further. It emerges into the world outsides as a fully grown human baby and is called a neonate.

The neonate or new-born baby is equipped with physical functions such as respiration, blood circulation, digestion, evacuation and glandular function, it is equipped with receptive organs, the eyes, ears, nose, tongue and the skin, that is, the sense organs. Also it is equipped with effective organs for making movements. The effective organs are the muscles, the glands and the limbs. It is equipped with an integrating system—the nervous system. Without these equipments, the human child cannot grow and develop any further. It cannot behave.

The Needs We Are Born With

The physical structure we inherit, warrants certain physiological functions in us. The heart beats; the lungs breath; the glands secrete: the muscles stretch and contract; and the anabolic, or building-up, and the catabolic: Or destructive, processes of body-tissues go on continuously. The demands of the body-tissues go on continuously. The demands of the body-tissues must be fulfilled for the survival of the human organism. Therefore, we are also born with certain needs. A need is best conceived as a state of tension forcing the organism to activity. The needs we are born with are called *Biological Needs* or *Biogenic Needs.* They are also called physical, physiological and organic needs. The needs we are born with are physiological in nature and inherited as a part of our body structure.

We need food, air, liquid, chemicals and vitamins to satisfy our hunger, thirst and anabolic process—to sustain life. There is a need for proper temperature. Regulation of bodily temperature is a must. We need to dress warmly when it is cold and shed clothes when it is hot. A rhythm of activity and rest seems to be a biological essential in the development of the human beings. We should exercise to maintain muscle tonus and rest when fatigued. Regular and adequate elimination of the waste materials (urination, defecation and seating) or products of the body is another important biological need. Unless this basic need is satisfied, it would cause both physical and mental harm. Man also seeks sensory pleasure. He derives pleasure our of the stimulation of the genitals, even of the mouth and the process of evacuation. In the second chapter of this book we have red that the psychologist. Sigmund Freud and others of the psychoanalytic school have held that frustration of this basic need, the sex drive, is a chief cause of personality maladjustments and nervous disorders. Avoidance of pain and injury another basic need present in all the human beings.

These bodily or tissue needs create a state of restlessness or tension in he organism which is reduced only when the appropriate goal or satisfier is reached. The biological needs or rives of the individual sere as potent motivators of behaivour. Behaviour is goal-oriented. A child whose basic physical and physiological needs are severally frustrated will not develop or behave normally. There shall be no motivation of learning at all as we shall see in the later chapters of this text. For the present it is sufficient to say that motivation is the process n which the energy generated by the needs gets expended in the direction of the goals. Children whose basic needs get frustrated, very often become problem children.

The Effects of the Glands upon Behaviour

"Three mysterious substances, in minute quantities, control the chemistry of the human body. Some of the most important facts about them have been discovered only within recent years. These substances are the hormones, those powerful chemicals secreted in the body by the endocrine glands; the enzymes, which turn one chemical substance into another; and the vitamins. These magic chemicals maintain an extraordinary balance among force so powerful that any of hem could be destructive if unchecked—Bruce Bliven". (Ratcliff, 1964, p. 294).

In the human body there are two types of glands—the duct glands or glands of external secretion and the ductless glands or *endocrine glands*. The duct glands throw their secretion through tubes or ducts to some opening on the surface of the body or the mucous lining. Some of the important duct glands are the salivary, gastric and tear glands. These glands serve in the digestion of food, excrete waste products from the body, condition the body and help regulate bodily temperature, lubricate the eyes and serve in reproduction.

The ductless glands or endocrine glands are the glands

of internal secretion. They have no special ducts or outlets. They discharge their secretion directly into the blood stream which carries the products to all the tissues of the body. These glands are responsible for the normality or abnormality o human behaivour. They influence the behaviour of individuals according to their balanced or imbalanced functioning. The endocrine glands secrete drug-like substances known as hormones. Over secretion or under secretion of hormones by any of these glands may exert a tremendous influence upon an individual's development and consequently upon his personality. "Hormones circulating in your blood-steam are much like miniature hydrogen bombs—powerful almost beyond belief". (Ibid, p. 294). They are; the pituitary, the pineal, the thyroid, the parathyroid, the thymus, the liver (in part), the adrenal, the sex (in part), and the pancreas (in part). The thyroid gland. The Thyroid Gland consists of two lobes which are situated in the neck on either side of the windpipe. It secretes a hormone called thyroxin. The functioning of the thyroid gland has a great effect upon the growth of intelligence, the rate of metabolism and upon behaviour in general. "The thyroid gland in the neck produces no more than a teaspoonful of hormone in a year. But if the teaspoon is partially filled, a new-born baby can develop into a creation—a malformed idiot". (Ibid, p. 294) Under functioning of the thyroid gland turns school children and adults as well, sluggish, sleepy, too fat, with decreased rate of metabolism. If the thyroid is too active, the result is wolfish appetite, pounding heart, high blood pressure, tremor, sweating and heat intolerance and so on. Children whose thyroid gland is too active, would continuously whisper and disturbe others in the class or move about restlessly without any reason, would talk in a loud voice and become irritated for nothing. When teachers come across children whose thyroid gland underfunctions or overfunctions, they should advise the parents to consult a doctor for treatment. Many individuals suffering from a shortage of thyroxin, including cretins, have been brought up to normal or near normal as a consequence of feeding the individuals thyroid tissues or extracts. Interacting children whose thyroid gland is too active, the usual method is to remove part of the thyroid gland by surgery or destroy a portion of it by means of X-ray or radium or radioactive iodine treatment, which can exert a calming influence and decrease the amount o glandular secretion that is pouring into the bloodstream.

The pituitary gland. "The pituitary is perhaps the most remarkable component of the human body. Because of its influence on other glands it has been compared to the conductor of a great symphony—the symphony of life" (Ibid, p. 296). It is located in the centre of the head in a small bony pocket and is about the size of a large pea. Malfunctioning of the pituitary gland in a child frequently creates conditions which may have important effects upon his personality and behaviour. One of the most fascinating of pituitary chemicals is the growth hormone. Undersecretion of this hormone leaves the child short, and physically and sexually underdeveloped. Oversecretion of this hormone may result in gigantism and precocious sexual maturity. Marked physical daviations just discussed affect the personal-social adjustment of children. Lack of size, excessive height or weight and other physical deviations greatly disturb the adolescents and elementary school children as well. "Anmalies o physical development explain many a problem child" (Pressey et al – 1959, p. p. 9). As the result of medical treatment involving the pituitary gland, the course of physical growth and development may be altered, and that personality changes may be brought about.

The adrenal glands. "The adrenal glands produce only a teaspoonful of hormone in a lifetime. But let their hair line balance be upset and we are prey to a host of crippling and disabling diseases. Or let them go on strike for any reason and life unreels at a dizzy pace: in months, a vigorous young male can become a doddering old man...Most endocrinologists rank the adrenals next in importance to the pituitary. Like little tricorn hats, these yellowish brown glands sit on top of the kidneys," (Ratcliff. 1964, pp. 294- 297) Each gland consists of two parts – a central portion known as the medulla and a surrounding outer portion known as the cortez. Adrenal cortical deficiency result in fatigue, lethary, weak heart action, low blood pressure and general interference with the growth process. Over activity of the adrena cortext leads to adrenal virilism. This disorder is characterized by recocious growth and sexual maturity. The medulla secretes as substance known as "*adrenin,*" which prepares a person to meet emergency conditions. Therefore, the adrenal glands have been called the "*fight-or-run*" glands. The adrenals quicken the clotting time of blood – to reduce loss if bloodshed ensures. "The proper functioning of the medulla is thus of the greatest importance for the individual's survival and for his adjustment to an everchanging and sometimes hostile environment." (Blair et al., 1966, p. 27).

The sexglands or gonads. The Sex glands function both as organs of internal secretion and external secretions. As duct glands their function is reproduction. As ductless glands they play an important role in the development of personality and behaviour. The female glands are known as ovaries and the male glands s testes. The almond-shaped ovaries lie on either side of a woman's lower abdomen, and you know perfectly well the location of the male sex glands—the testes. The ovralries secrete a hormone known as oestrogen and a second hormone—progesterone. The testes secrete the hormone testosterone. Inadequate functioning of these glands in either boys or girls may make normal development of the secondary sexual characteristics impossible. Dysfunction of the sex glands may have a damaging impact on the lives of adolescent boys and girls. At the time of puberty, inadequate flow of oestrogen will not result in the resculptring of a girl's body into that of a woman. Inadequate flow of test osterone shall not produce a virile male out of a young adolescent boy but change him into the safest of watchmen of a young adolescent boy but change him into the safest of watchmen of a Women's hostel. Adolescents are extremely sensitive to differences which exist between them and their older friends. "Either precocious sexual development or greatly retarded development is a source of great concern and anxiety to them and may have far-reaching effects upon their adjustment to school and to other life situations." (Ibid, p. 27).

Other endocrine glands. The parathyroid glands are lying on the posterior surface of the thyroid glands, but have no known connection with the thyroid activity. Deficiency in the functioning of the parathyroids, in extreme cases, may cause texnus which may result in the death of a individual. Less marked deficiency of function of these glands cause several disorders such as hyperexcitability, irritability, mental depressions and others. The pineal gland, located at the base of the brain, and the *thymus gland*, located in the upper thorax, both produce hormones whichhelpto regulate the rate f bodily growth and th eonset of puberty. Underfunctionign of th epancreas which secrete insulin, causes diabetes. The liver also possesses endocrine functions which are of great value in supplying energy to working muscles.

Te endocrine glands do not work unrelated and independently of one another. They seem to function in a team and for similar purposes. For example, the hormones secreted by the pituitary, pineal, thyroid and sex glands control growth very definitely. The joint actions of the sex, pituitary, pineal, thymus, adrenal and thyroid glands, influence sex development. Endocrine glands maintain the chemical balance of the body. Health and growth are dependent upon them. Our mental and emotional lives are controlled by their joint actions. Therefore, teachers should be alert in detecting disorders in the endocrine glands of the children. If they find any disorder in any pupil, they should refer the child to a doctor for treatment or do so through the parents.

Physical and Sensory Defects and mental Disorders

There are many other physical and sensory defects or disorders, some of which congenital, which greatly influence the learning and adjustment of school children. Among these are the following: poor eyesight, defective hearing, physical deformities, defective speech organs, skin blemishes and so on and so forth. Physical anomalies of various types cause a lot of emotional disturbance in adolescent boys and girls.

Children with defective vision, hearing or speech organs are not able to learn things as normal children do.

"Genes play a role in some of the behaviour disorders. There is some evidence of a genetic basis for manic depressive psychosis and schizophrenia. This evidence comes from the analysis of concordance rates for MZ and DZ Co-twins" (Morgan & king, 1975, p. 57).

These children need special education which shall be discussed in greater detail in later chapters, particularly on exceptional children.

Mental Traits and Personality

"It is not known to what extent mental traits are inherited" 9blair et al., 1966, p. 17). Very true; but all the same, that heredity forms a basis of both intelligence and personality is evident from the following statements.

"In so far as intelligence is concerned, "few psychologists nowadays would be inclined to contest the mere fact of mental inheritance' (Burt, 1958). It is when weaks about the mode of transmission of the genetic factor and the proportion of the population variance which can be attributed to it that we find controversy" (Wright et al., 1971, p. 64). And again :'...... Cattlell used the junior version of his own 16 Personality Factor Test and found that some of the personality dimensions were mainly a function of environment and others of heredity, and that the pattern varied depending on whether the focus was upon differences between families or upon differences within families" (ibid, p. 65).

"From the studies of twins reared apart it does seem that in spite of different environmental influences the twins develop similarly in a number of aspects" (Sorenson, 1977 p. 121). "Genealogical studies show that there is a decided tendency for intellectual inferiority or superiority to follow family lines. Correlational studies indicate that the closer the degree of blood relationship between pairs of people the greater is their similarity in intellectual level...Experimental studies have demonstrated that the family from which a child comes, influences his level of intllectual functioning," write Sawrey and Telford (1964), pp. 44.45). And Morganand Kind (1975, p. 57) state: "Studies of the genetics of personality and temperament indicate that such traits as sociality, emotionality, and activity may have a genetic basic." We shall return to these discussions, later, in chapters on Intelligence and personality.

Environmental Basis of Behaviour

Why do people differ from one another? Do they differ because their heredity is different or because they have had different environments? "The basis of individual differences is to be found in each individual's hereditary background and the environmental conditions under which he has developed," says Anastasi (1958, p. 57). Woodworth and Marquis (1968, pp. 152-154) state: "The numerous specific factors that cause people to differ can be traced back to heredity and environment....The relation of heredity and environment is not like addition, but more like multiplication. The individual does not equal heredity + environment but does equal heredity ×environment. He is a product of the two factors, not a sum of certain parts due to heredity and other parts due to environment. We may represent heredity by the base of a rectangle, environment by the altitude, and the environment by the area of the rectangle, the product of base and altitude."

Environment means the sum total of every influence with which the individual comes into contact after the hereditary pattern has been received through the germ cells of the parents. "Psychologically, environment consists of the sum total of the stimulation the individual receives from conception until death. This is an active concept of environment, i.e., the physical presence of objects does not include itself constitute environment unless the objects serve as stimuli for the individual" (Anastasi, 1958, p. 64). The heredity of a plant is contained in the seed. The soil, moisture, sunlight, weeds, insects, and other things constitute the environment.

There goes on a continuous interaction between biological

inheritance and environmental factors. The individual brings about changes in the environment; and the environment produces change sin him and his behaviour. What ever his hereditary endowments be, he cannot grow and develop in the desired direction unless the environment is also favourable. For the muscles to grow in the children is a hereditary tendency; but this shall not result unless the environment provided them with food and ample opportunity to exercise their muscles. Environmental and Cultural factors exert a great influence on the behaviour of children, the nature of their attitudes and the mode of their adjustment, and therefore on their training, learning and motivation. Teachers should be fully conscious of the working of environmental factors upon individual children.

Environmental is the sum total of the effect of the home and neighbourhood, of the school and church, of the playground and the hospital, of the climate and geographical location, training and learning, and anything else that stimulates the individual in anyway. Our day-to day observations make us fully aware of the environmental influences upon the life situations of the individuals. Children of an agricultural community differ in their dress and habits from children of an industrial community. The fashion of life of people living in cold climates is different from the people living in hot climates. A farmer's boy develops a different temperament from that of a merchant's son. In India, the customs and manners of people differ from region to region.

But these are all acquired characteristics, which cannot be transmitted from parents to offspring. A mother who had her choice hair style in a beauty shop cannot transmit it to any of her children – her daughters. The questions asked are : To what extent environmental conditions influence hereditary characteristics? Does unfavourable environment retard an excellent biological inheritance and a favourabel environment improve an inferior hereditary characteristic? For the psychologists, the determination of the relative influence of heredity and environment upon human behaviour is a formidable problem. Solutions to this problem have been sought through a number of studies. No only is this problem difficult to solve but it is also equally delicate. To study the effect of heredity, individuals of different heredity should be exposed for a prett long time to identical environmental and to study the effect of environment, individuals of identical heredity should be exposed to different environment.

These two types of experiments have been conducted on plants and animals; but in so far as humans are concerned, thorough-going experimentation is hardly possible. Ethical and legal implications creep in when one wants to conduct such experiments on human subjects. Yet, psychologists have tried their best to investigate byway of wide scale research and experimentation in this area. Some of the noted studies and their results have been discussed in the rest of this chapter.

Effect of the Environment on Prenatal Development

Most of the psychologists are of the opinion that actually the environment begins to effect the course of development of the individual as soon as he is conceived. Jordan (1959, p. 45) goes to say “”From our discussion thus far it seems clear that structure is inherited...But even the structure itself is not entirely independent of environmental influence” Crow and Crow 91964, p. 43), report on some of the disturbing influences on the developing organism during the prenatal period, as listed by Schwesinger (1933, Heredity and Environment, pp. 331-332). These conditions are “ (1) Excessive malnutrition of the mother’s organism (2) Mothers suffering from wasting diseases such as diabetes; (3) Mothers suffering from infectious diseases, particularly syphilis; (4) Toxic poisons in the body of the mother; (5) Endocrine imbalance in the mother; (6) Injuries on the soft skull of a fetus resulting from the use of obstetrical instruments; and (7) Mother experiencing a severe emotional shock

Is Intelligence Inherited?

Is intelligence inherited? But what is intelligence? Perhaps no term in psychology is so generally used with functional meaning and yet is so difficult to define operationally, as the term intelligence. Some equate intelligence with learning ability, some others with achievement and still some others with adjustment. There is no common agreement about what constitutes intelligence. A well known, if extreme, operational definition of intelligence is: "Intelligence is scores on × Intelligence text," or "intelligence is what × intelligence test ensures". While Binet believed intelligence to be a unitary characteristic, Thurstone thought it as an aggregate of highly specific abilities. However, psychologists have constructed "Intelligence Tests" to measure Intelligence", be it of a unitary characteristic or an aggregate of highly specific abilities.

Unfortunately, all the intelligence tests so far designed are not purported to measure inherited intelligence. It is impossible to get any accurate measure of an individual's inherited intellectual capacity. The Tests devised so far yield a single score for each individual. The best we can do is to use scores from intelligence tests as indications o a child's intellectual advancement. As Jordabn (Ibid, pp. 45-46) points out: "The question actually studied, then, is not "Does environment change substantially an individual's inherited intelligence?" but rather the question has resolved itself into "Does environment change substantially an individual's I. Q. ?" The chief quarter among psychologists now is not as to whether the I.Q changes but as to the amount of change. Some hold that the change is moderate, say, 5.10 points : Others say that under very unusual circumstances the I.Q. may be raised 35.40 points".

The intelligence tests yield a single score – the Intelligence Quotient, or IQ for each individual. The studies of human intelligence that we shall consider in the sections that follow are for the most part based on IQ scores from these tests. And what is IQ ? the intelligence quotient or I.Q., is a ratio between the mental age (M.A.) and the chronological age (C.A.). The intelligence quotient (IQ) is an index of the rte of mental development. A child's mental age (MA) is a measure of his level of mental maturity. And chronological age is the period from the date on which he was born, up-to-date, that is, birth age or calendar age. The mental are of a child is obtained from his score upon a test of scaled items. IQ = MA/ CA × 100. If the level of mental maturity of the child is normal or average, his MA will just equal his CA and his IQ will be 100. If on the other hand his MA lagged behind his CA, his IQ would be less than 100. Conversely if his MA developed more rapidly than his CA advanced, his IQ would be greater than 100. If a child who is eight years old has a mental age of twelve, his IQ would be 12/8 ×100 or 150. This would be an unusually bright child—hear genius or even genius. Another child who is eight years old and has an MA of only six, his IQ would be 6/8×100 or 75, an IQ, far below average.

A number of investigations, ranging from 1923 to 1963 have been conducted to study how mental growth is facilitated or retarded by factors present in the environment, and referred to in a number of standard tests on Educational Psychology ad General Psychology. Of particular interest are those studies which have been made of children reared in foster homes, children reared in impoverished environments, twins raised together and identical twins raised apart.

Studies of children reared in foster homes

Studies of foster children were an attempt to relate the changes in environment to changes in intellectual level. Such changes are made in the lives of orphans and foster children. In general, adopted children are taken from very poor home environments and become members of homes in which the environment is from good to excellent. The question now resolves itself into : "What is the effect on a child's IQ of his living in an excellent home for four to eight years after having lived some of his life in a very poor one?"

Jordan (Ibid, pp. 47-48) reports about two very important investigations conducted in this direction—ore by Freeman and others (1928), and the other by Burks (1928). These studies were undertaken to find out the beneficial effects upon IQs of children who have been taken from poor homes and placed in superior adoptive homes.

Freeman and his associates discovered 74 children living poor homes. They found the median IQ to be 91.2 of these children by the Binet test of intelligence. After the children had remained an average of four years in their adopted homes, when they were tested again, their median IQ was found to be 93.7. That is, four year's residence in a home environment much superior to the one they had previously experienced had brought about a change of 2.5 IQ- points. When these children we a again tested after their residence for about eight years, it was found that those children who were placed in the better homes, had earned again of 5.3 points; and those children who were placed in relatively poorer homes, had a gain of only 0 1 point. Similarly, Burks found that the median I.Q., of children of average parents placed in a good environment for several years was 107.4 or a gain of 7.4 points, the average IQ being 100.Thus these two investigations are in substantial agreement on the influence of changed environment on the IQ.

Studies of children reared in backward and isolated communities

Studies of underprivileged children have consistently shown that an impoverished environment depresses the intellectual level of children living in it. The depressing effect shows up as an IQ level that diminishes with age.

One such very important study, and reported in several text books on educational psychology, is by Hugh Gordon (1923), of English gypsies and canal boat children. In describing the 76 English canal boat children he studied, he says, "the Canal Boat population as a rule, is born, lives, and dies on the boats". These people lived very isolated lives with very little social intercourse and the children attended school about once a month for one to perhaps two and a half days".

Gordon tested 76 English canal boat children ranging in ages from 4 to 14. Fro this purpose he used the Stanford

Binet Scale intelligence test). The test revealed that the entire group was very much mentally retarded—the average IQ being 69.6. In the second place it was found that the extent of the dullness was proportional to the age of the child. Younger children who had spent fewer years in this impoverished environment had higher IQs than their older brothers and sisters. This means, with increasing age, the average IQs of the children dropped further and further. The correlation between chronological age and IQ is usually Zero, but for the canal boat children it was --. 755, meaning that the older the child the lower the IQ. In so far as the canal boat children are concerned. Age and IQ are negatively correlated.

A study was made by E.J. Asher (1935) on children reared in isolated and socially impoverished communities in the mountains of eastern Kentucky. The study has shown that the average IQ of the children drops steadily with increase in chronological age. In the Kentucky group the median IQ dropped steadily from 84 at seven years to 60 at 15 years. Jorban (Ibid, p. 49) conducted a study on the children of mill workers in an economically and educationally depressed community. His study showed decrease in average IQ from 100 at age six years to 85 to 13 years. He concludes that if the children have not developed an average linguistic ability, miss one of the most potent influences for mental development.

Correlational Studies of Identical Twins

The final study of the effect of environment on mental development is taken from investigations of children who pair by pair have identical heredity. When identical twins are raised together, we have the phenomenon of identical heredity and almost identical environments. When identical twins are raised apart, we have the phenomenon of identical heredity but dissimilar environment. It is clear that under these conditions which makes persons more or less unlike can be directly attributed to the influence of the environment.

The approach to the problem of elative contributions of heredity and environment in determining intelligence is a correlational one. The correlational method determines quantitatively the degree of similarity between persons related in various ways. A coefficient of correlation is a numerical index used to indicate the degree of correspondence between two sets of paired measurements. The most common kind is the product-moment coefficient designated by r, and also known as Pearsonian r. A perfect positive correlation is represented by + 1.00 perfect negative by – 1.00. and no relationship whatever by a correlation 0.00. In between plus or minus 1.00 and 0.00 various degrees of relationships are expressed by numbers such as 0.10, 0.32 and 0.83. To give one example, we could correlate the IQ scores of pairs of identical twins. First, we would give an IQ test to all the twins. Then we would calculate the correlation coefficient to see how closely the IQ scores of the pairs of identical twins agreed with each other.

In the case of identical twins reared together it was fund that environment had very little effect on certain basic physical characteristics, the correlations ranging from 0.91 to 0.98 and the average being 0.95. But environment had more effect on knowledge acquired, the correlations ranging from 0.91 to 0.95, the average being o.93 (Source, After Horatic et al., 1937).

Investigations on identical twins reared apart, and one study conducted on 19 pairs of identical twins whose home environment was quite different (Newman et al., 1937), revealed the following facts as reported by Jordan (Ibid (Ibid, p. 51), who writes : "When all 19 pairs are taken together, the average I.Q. difference is 8.2 pints on the Stanford. Binet individual test and 8.0 points on the Otis group test. To get the full meaning of these scores they must be compared with 10.6 points average difference found in the case of 297 fraternal twins and a difference of 4.75 in the case of 231 identical twins raised together. It we compare the difference of 4.75 I.Q. points of identical twins raised together. If we compare the difference of 4.75 I.Q. points of identical twins raised together with 8.2 points. Of identical twins raised apart, we discover the influence of the environment...when heredity and environment are most nearly the same the differences are smallest (average difference=4.75); when heredity is the same but the environment differs, the differences are next in size (average difference=8.2); and when heredity is different and environment much the same the differences are greatest (average difference=10.6).

Effects of the Environment upon Personality

Personality is dynamic it refers to integrated behaviour. It represents an interaction between inherited potentialities and environmental influences. Environmental factors, of course have much to do with the type of character and personality an individual shall develop.

In the field of personality differences, Cattell and his associates have developed a "Multiple Abstract variance Analysis or M.A.V.A." approach (Cattell et al., 1955) and referred to by Wright et-al., (Ibid, p. 65 & p. 535). This is a technique for handling a variety of familiar comparisons at the same time and calculating the ratios of the variance due to genetic and environmental differences. Cattell administered the junior version of his own 16 personality Facto Test on a large number of children of varied hereditary and environmental similarity. Cattell and his associates obtained scores on twelve personality factors which earlier research had established significant. Wright et-al., (Ibid, p. 535) write: "The main findings of this study are summarized below:

(1) In five factors...environmental factors appear to play the dominant role....

(2) Four factors.....seem to be equally influenced by both heredity and environment...

(3) In three factors the role of hereditary factors is clearly the most important". The experimental findings shall be discussed later, in detail.

This experiment, therefore, establishes the fact that some

of the personality dimensions are mainly a function of environment and others of heredity.

A study of three primitive tribes living in the New Guinea islands is really amusing (Mead, 1935).

The Arapesh tribe lives in the mountain regions. These people are highly, co-operative, peaceful and can be easily trained and controlled. Their children seldom show temper tantrums or steal and lie. The river-dwelling Mandugumor tribe lives one hundred miles away from the mountain-dwelling arapesh tribe. These people are highly competitive, suspicious of one another, aggressive and violent. Among the lake-dwelling Tchambuili tribe, the roles of men and women are completely reversed. The women do the farming, fishing, hunting and other heavy work. The men stay at home, look after the children and devote themselves to artistic pursuis. The women thus develop typically masculine personalities and the men appear effeminate. These differences in temperment and personality among the peoples the three tribes can easily be traced back to their respective systems of social organisation and methods of child rearing.

Environmental factors, therefore, not only play a most important role in the mental development of the individual but have also much to do with the type of character and personality he will develop.

Heredity and Environment in the Classroom

The teacher should be aware of the fact that the individual child is a product of both heredity and environment. Also he should know that a favourable environment can modify to some extent biological inheritance while an unfavourable environment shall retard it. In order to understand, control and predict the behaviour of a child, the teacher should know the physical condition of the child, his needs and abilities, and the environmental facts, the social and cultural forces acting upon him.

The task of the school is to develop the character and

personality of the child, his health and intellectual ability. A good school, therefore, should have good health service and teachers should be watchful of the health needs of the child. A school with good discipline, control and morale can do much in the development of character and personality of the child. Good teaching can help the pupils acquire greater knowledge and information.

Growth and Development

For some, growth denotes a progressive change in quantity, size or volume. The heart grows in size. It becomes bigger and bigger. The bones grow longer, thicker and heavier. In general, the body grows measuring more inches in height and more pounds in weight. These authors say that growth ca be measured quantitatively in points, inches or pounds. Development also indicates increase but refers primarily to progressive changes resulting I improved quality, character and composition. For instance, bones grow in size, but they also develop when they change their composition and form. The brain cells grow larger but also develop by undergoing chemical changes.

Thus development indicates more advancement, unfoldment, progressive changes both in quantity and quality and a going forward to greater maturity. But this is only one point of view. Growth and Development are very closely related terms which, more often than not, overlap. But the whole fun is that each author wants they should mean exactly what he wants them to mean. To quote some of the statement s that are noteworthy: "Growth in an organism is that structural change which increases its level of functioning in specific ways," say Wilson et al., (1969, p. 165). In so far as Jordan (1956, p. 40) is concerned, "Growth on the other hand will emphasize that progress toward maturity which is a result of inner maturity and environmental influences." And Woodworth and Marquis (1968, pp. 271-72) are of the opinion that "thus growth of any organism from an immature to a mature state is called maturation", and "development consists both growing and learning". "Development is a process resultant from a constant flux or interchange of energies within an organism and energies within its environment," says MC Growth in the text edited by Skinner (1964, p. 166). Helen Thompson (1968, p. 293) remarks: "Meredith (1945) concluded that the three terms, growth, development and maturation which are used in contradictory ways by different workers serve no useful and significant distinction' as their proponents had claimed. He proposed using the terms interchangeably, giving preference to growth as being shortest of the three terms."

From the discussions carried on so far, the present author concludes thus: Growth in human beings may be an inherited capacity and human development gets determined by a complex of inherited and environmental forces; but these two are closely related concepts—so closely related that though they may be distinguished in idea, they cannot be separated in actual performance. Each of these two shares in the process of helping an individual in his progress towards becoming the kind of adult that he eventually will be. What he is as an adult depends on how well he has grown and also on what he has learned. Therefore, the safest course to take is to use the terms interchangeably as Meredity suggests.

Principles of Growth and Development

Human Development is Determined by a Complex of Inherited and Environmental Forces: In the fourth chapter of this text it was explained how an individual at any stage of his development is the product of hereditary and environmental factors working simultaneously upon him. Also it was explained how an individual reacts and behaves in all life situations in response to those two interacting forces. The child behaves as he does because he is a human child with an array of needs demanding satisfaction. He is surrounded by socio-cultural forces which determine how these needs should be satisfied. The endocrine glands shape his mental and emotional life primarily, and so on. Therefore, this principle of growth and development does not need an elaborate discussion here.

Growth is gradual and Continuous: People generally divide the process of growth into different stags such as : Infancy, Childhood, Pre-adolescence, Adolescence and Adulthood. This does not mean that there is a gap in the process of growth between one stage and another. Growth does not leap from one state to another. It is not that a boy grows three feet in height, then his growth stops for sometime and then suddenly the boy begins to grow again in height and reaches a height of four feet six inches. Growth is gradual and continuous. At each moment of life any individual is in the process of changing into something a little different from what he now is. Life begins as a single celled organism but by cell division grows into millions of cells' and the organisation of bodily cells become more and more complicated. The mental and the speech abilities of the human child grow slowly but continuously. Everyday the child acquires knowledge of different kinds in different degrees. At first, the baby babbles and gurgles, but gradually he begins to talk and then read. As the human child grows, his behaviour pattern grows more and more complex in nature. When the baby is hungry and milk is not given to it, naturally, it would cry and roll on the floor. But an adolescent even through food is not given to him when he is hungry, shall not cry and roll on the ground. He shall express his resentment in a different way. This is because the adolescent has made an advancement over the baby, both emotionally and socially.

(c) *The Rate of Growth is not Even*: Of course, growth is gradual and continuous; but, it is more rapid at some periods that at others. In infancy the rate of general physical growth is more rapid than at any other stage of development. The organs of the body mature at different rates. Legs grow faster than arms. Brain grows faster than sex organs. The sex glands grow at a different rate from the adrenals or the thymus. Hence one individual differs from another on account of differing states of development reached at by the bodily organs.

Different traits of an individual develop at different rates and reach the limits of development at different times. In the same individual various components of personality may grow at different rates. These differing patterns of growth in the same individual are referred to as "*ages*". The child has many ages. He may be ten years old chronologically, have a mental age of 12, and a social age of 14. He may have an emotional age of 13 and an educational age of 11.

The rate of maturation differs from individual to individual. Maturation refers to the inner changes that occur in the individuals as a result of heredity and irrespective of environmental conditions. In whatever environmental conditions they may be, at first the babies are not able to sit but a time comes when they sit up without assistance. And another time comes when they begin to walk and talk. It is on account of the process of maturation that such things happen.

Differing rates of maturation and unevenness of growth are of great educational significance as they account for individual differences. In our country, our greatest drawback in the field of education is that we overlook individual differences in growth and development. We admit pupils to different classes on the basis of their chronological age and ignore their respective levels of development, mental, emotional social and physical. While admitting him into a class we do not consider the different "ages" of the child. We do not group children for instruction according to their level of mental development. As a result, the children face a lot of difficult in adjusting themselves to school instruction and environment. The bright boy doesn't like the mode of our instruction and the dull boy is unable to follow what we teach.

Each child grows at his own unique rte. Therefore, uniform treatment of children at any level or in any subject is quite unsound. Children respond differently to the same learning activity or the same subject matter or the same teaching procedure. Therefore, individualized instruction is a necessity. Curriculum and teaching procedures must suit individual children. Only an efficient and skillful teacher can do this.

One should not expect the same level of achievement at the end of a teaching-learning course. The achievement of each child shall depend upon the forces working within him and the forces acting upon him from without. Also the nature of personal-social \emotional adjustment of children vary both in kind and degree. Therefore, to treat all the children alike in a teaching-learning situation is educationally unsound and unwholesome. Some suggest the classification and grouping of children on the basis of their IQs. Others do not prefer the classification of children on the basis of their mental age. They prefer "individualized instruction" to "ability grouping. The reason for this is that children grouped under the basis of mental age may widely differ in their emotional age or reading age or social age. If the teacher wants "ability grouping," he has to classify children in one way for one purpose and in other ways for other purposes. Therefore, "individualized instruction" is the safest course they argue.

The Rate of Growth is Rapid in the Early years of Life : The rate of general physical growth is more rapid in infancy than at any subsequent stage of development. During the first six months of life the rate of growth is most rapid. In the early years of life the growth of body makes a rapid progress, then the rate of growth slowers down and again when the individual is about 14 years old, the body begins to grow very rapidly. But the time the child is about 2 to 3 years old, his sense organs function very well. When he is six years old, his nervous system is nine-tenths of the adult weight at birth its weight being one-fourth of the adult weight. As studies by Thurstone and Thorudike show (Skinner, 1959, pp. 1777-78), mental development is very rapid during the early years of life.

Raid development during the early years of life has some educational significance. As a number of functions develop together in the early years of life, the young child wants to do a number of things he is capable of doing. Therefore, the school should engage children in a number of activities that the children are ready to perform. In order to encourage children to display all the capacities they have developed, the school should provide them with a rich environment. While the children are young, they should be helped to have better personal and social adjustment, through a variety of activities they shall be engaged in.

Each Species follows Common General pattern of Development: Each one of us is an organism. We belong to the human species. Qualities and characteristics grow and develop in us in orderly succession. The orderly succession of the growth of traits in us does to differ from individual to individual. The infant lifts its head first, then its chest and then its stomach. The baby sits, crawls, stands alone and then walks in that order. When he is 5 years old, a boy can copy a square and reproduce a diamond when he is seven. If he cannot do the former at five, he cannot do the latter at seven. When a small cube is presented to infants who are 16 weeks old, they shall only gaze at the object. But if the cube is presented to them when they are 40 weeks old, 85 percent of them shall surely try to touch it. The sequence of development is orderly and predictable. If you find a particular trait has developed in a child, you can tell what shape it shall take in future.

The Direction of Growth is from General to Specific: In the early stages of human growth, the direction is from general to specific or from mass to individualism. In the beginning, there is a total movement of the body. Gradually specific actions follow and the total movement stops. After they are born, infants for about 10 to 15 days move their whole body to stretch or sneeze. After sometime, when infants try to lift their heads, they exercise all the muscles of the body. But when they being to walk after a few months, they use only a few muscles. They walk with the legs and use hands for other activities.

The behaviour of the neonate is a mass activity in which the whole body participates; but gradually, specific parts of the body are used for specific purposes. At first, the responses of the baby are generalized. In course of time generalized responses give place t specific responses. For instance, the cry of the baby in the beginnings a generalized response. His cry becomes a specific response when he cries only when he is hungry. The baby uses the word "Daddy" to greet most of the male members of the family. This is a generalized response. It becomes specific when the baby uses the word Daddy" to greet his father only.

(g) *Development is a Process both of Differentiation and of Integration*

The direction of growth from general to specific or from mass to individuation is the process of "differentiation" But development takes place through the process of "integration' also. "Many activities as children grow older are integrations of specific processes already acquired" says Jordan (1956, p. 63).

"Walking' is an excellent example to show that development is a process of integration. Simpler habits of the arm control leg control, control of body movements and balancing are combined into the integrated activity of walking. In games of skill, there is an integration of many learned habits. For example, in a game of football, quick starting, swift running and stopping, easy control of the round object by the right foot or the left and many other specific processes are integrated and arranged into one organized whole, a complex pattern of skill.

Growth is of the Total Organism: Growth relates to the whole organism—the total personality. It is the total child who grows. Physical, emotional, mental, social and moral development occur simultaneously and interact upon one another. They are interrelated and interdependent. However, physical growth is fundamental forming the base. Along with the body the nervous system grows. Mental development depends upon the growth of the brain. Language development is dependant upon the growth of the brain, eyes and ears and the vocal organs. Language development shall get hampered if the brain and the sense organs have not developed well and do not function properly. If his language development gets hampered, it would cause emotional disturbances in a child. Children with physical defects and deficiencies are emotionally disturbed and find it difficult for personal – social adjustment. Even they may not get accepted by the same age group.

Growth is of the total individual and the function of education is to elevate the entire personality of the child. Teachers should provide the most favorable environment to stimulate the growth of the whole child. They should engage children in varied and novel activities to draw out the inherent potentialities of the latter.

Design of Development is Individualistic : Individuals differ at birth. Each child possesses his own growth and development pattern which tends to remain constant from infancy to maturity. Children who are tall or short in the early years of life continue to remain as such till adulthood. The dull or bright continue to be dull or bright. Each child grows at his own unique rate and even though environmental conditions change, the rate of growth remains relatively constant. This trend in growth and development pattern is a of great educational significance.

It is possible to predict the extent to which mental development shall take place in a child as he grows older and older. Also it is possible to telling advance the kind and degree of education the child shall fit into. A study of the child's present behaviour will tell us the nature of his behaviour in future and what course it is likely to take. This principle, if they are aware of it, helps teachers to shape the behaviour of children.

Behavioural changes Result from Learning and Maturation Operating Together: Changes in behaviour result from learning and maturation, both in important amounts. Maturation stands for the genetically determined growth. It refers to that phase of growth which relates to the unfolding of whatever characteristics are incorporated in the genes. Babies sitting up, crawling, waling and the bladder and bowel control are products mainly of maturation.

"Learning is a process or operation inferred from relatively permanent changes in behaviour that result from practice. On the other hand, relatively permanent changes in behaviour that result from maturation and temporary changes that result from drugs, fatigue, and the like are not considered to be learning" (Klausmeier Q Ripple, 1971, pp. 7-8).

All the children, stand upright, walk or run rather than walk when the time comes, without practice or instruction. Such things as these result on account of maturation rather than learning. But take into consideration a young boy learning the skill of riding a bicycle or a young lady learning the skill of waling on a rope in circus. The boy and the lady mastered the skills as a result of learning. Learning is the result of reinforced practice. A 6-year old child cannot recognize any of the twenty words in his First Reader. He receives instruction and practices. Six months later he recognizes all the words. Eh could recognize all the words as a result of reinforced practice. There fore, reinforced practice is the cause of learning and learning is the result.

However, maturation and learning are so closely related that their influence cannot be isolated. They operate as dual forces in all cases of behavioural change. Children grow into learning. In the case of an immature, still-growing individual, it is too difficult to make a distinct on between maturation and learning. As a result of reinforced practice, the young boy is able to learn the skill of riding a bicycle; but he cannot learn this skill until his bodily organs have reached the required level of maturity for learning this skill. Therefore, the developing child learns while he grows and grows while he learns. In the early stages of development learning and maturation go hand in hand.

Maturation provides the necessary physiological foundation for learning. It is considered as an essential prerequisite for learning. Performance of different school tasks require different levels of maturation in children. But it is not possible to hasten the process of maturation and make the children ready to learn certain school tasks that the teacher desires they should learn. However, reinforced practice has its own value in he early years of development. In the first place, such practices result in increased self—confidence and the second place, children feel proud when they perform a task successfully after considerable practice. This makes them learn desirable motives and interests.

The teachers should be cautious in so far as these issues are considered. Certainly, a considerable portion of a child's readiness for learning depends upon maturation. On the other hand, environment also play sits own part. Earlier it was discussed how an unfavourable environment causes permanent set back to maturing intellectual functions and a rich environment boosts upmental maturation during early years of development. The teacher need not always wait the child to be ready for learning in the normal course. He can motivate the child to learn certain tasks providing a rich and favourable environment. Practice in the development of certain skills during the early ages is a necessity. For example, language skills and particularly learning a foreign language, can be profitably accomplished at a much earlier age than at the high school level. Practice of reading skill is necessary for the normal child during the early years of development. Certain mathematical concepts can be developed much earlier than was once thought possible. Therefore, teachers, by all means, should encourage children to practice the performance of tasks.

Study of Physical Growth

"Growth in intellect, personality and character can be adequately understood only in relation to physical growth". (Pressey et al., 1967,p. 9) A child's mental and personality development, and his success in school, depend to a large extent upon his health, energy, rate of growth and general physical fitness. Knowledge about a child's physical nature may be revealing in studying his behaviour in his home and at school. "Only in relation to the physiological changes going on in childhood and adolescence can we interpret changes in interest and attitudes during this period". (Ibid., p. 9).

The physical appearance of a child is of much importance to him. The child whose level of physical development is at variance with that of his friends' may feel insecure and ashamed. Any physical abnormality exerts as tremendous influence upon a young person's emotional reactions.

A sound knowledge of physical development and the normal variations may help the teacher in guiding the social and personal adjustment of the child and the adolescent. It may also provide a base for curriculum construction, determination of teaching procedures and proper utilization of learning equipment.

Trends in Physical Growth after Birth

A number of studies in child development have resulted in definite conclusions concerning trends of physical growth after birth. The general growth trend of the body is pictured as follows. (1) Growth is rapid in Infancy (from birth up till age two). (2) It slows down in early and middle childhood (from ages two to eight); (3) An increased growth rate begins between the ages 8 and 10 and continues till adolescence, that is, ages 17 and 18. (4) From this time on, there is a tapering off of growth to maturity (ages 24 and 25). As educators, we are mostly concerned with child development form birth to maturity. Adulthood or maturity—from ages 25 to 60—can be regarded as the period of life during which the individual can utilize whatever powers and potentialities he has achieved during his earlier stages of development. Old age stars after 60 during which the powers and strength gradually decline.

Aspects of Physical Development There are two aspects of physical development—Anatomic and Physiologic Anatomic refers to skeletal growth, including the growth of bones structure, changes in height and weight and changes in body proportions. Physiologic includes developmental changes in the nervous, circulatory, respirative, digestive and excretory systems and also muscular and glandular systems. Life depends upon the proper functioning of these systems.

Specific Growth Changes

(a) Growth in Height and Weight

Eighty-five percent of the new-born infants weigh between 6 and 9 pounds and vary between 17 and 22 inches in height. On the average, a boy is about 20.5 inches in height and 7.5 pounds in weight whereas a girl is about 20.3 inches and 7 ponds. The weight of an infant doubles in the first 6 months. The height of an infant increases by about 50 percent during the first year of life and the weight triples. The rate of growth gradually decreases from the second year till age 12 or 13.

Upto puberty, the male child is larger in all body measurements than the female child. The girls reach puberty when they are about 11 to 12 years old, about two years earlier than boys; and during this period the girls surpass the boys in total size. However, the growth spurt of the adolescent girls is less intense and shorter than that of the adolescent boys. When they are about 14 years old, boys begin to grow faster that girls in height and weight. The average age at which the adolescents reach adult height is approximately 16 for girls and 18 for boys. A youngman is about 4 inches taller and about 25 pounds heavier than a young women. From ages 6 to 18, during these 12 years, boys increase over one-half in height and over 3 times in weight. Adolescent girls prefer the company of adolescent boys, older, stronger and bigger than them as they feel very secure and happy in the company of these boys. Ultimately this results in younger girls carrying older boys.

There are wide variations in height and weight for men and women. In height men may range from the little dwarf to the tall giant and in weight from the midget to the fat man of the circus. Norms for height and weight in Indian conditions are lacking. Sufficient research has not yet been conducted in this area. However, boys and girls of India are less tall and weight less than their counterparts in European countries. In our country, standard height and weight charts for use in schools and colleges are not available. However, teachers should encourage children to have physical exercise and good food for an excellent body build. Underourishment and improper functioning of endocrine glands result in stunted growth which may cause emotional disturbances in children, particularly adolescents. When teachers come across such cases, they may advise the parents to consult a doctor for treatment to bring about some improvement in the physical build of these children. Teachers should be aware of the fact that relative height and weight are necessary in so far as they are indicative of good physical health and do not deviate greatly from the average making the child emotionally upset. Indians do not bother much about height and weight and I am an Indian.

(b) Changes in Body Proportions and Contours

Physical growth is from the head downward and from the trunk outward. Infants, children, adolescents and adults differ in their body proportions. A new-born infant's head is approximately one-fourth of its total body length and that of an adult is about one-tenth. The trunk is about three-eights the total length of the body at birth which remains approximately the same at adulthood. At birth, the legs are three-eighths the body length but at adulthood they are one-half. From infancy up to puberty, head growth is slow, limb growth rapid and trunk growth intermediate. As the child grows older, while the proportion of the head decreases, that of the legs increases correspondingly. As he years pass by, all he parts of the body grow larger; but at adulthood, the arms and legs are proportionately longer.

Body contours also change with increasing physical maturation. The infant has a small flat nose which grows and becomes prominent when he reaches adolescence. Before the onset of puberty, difference in body contours between boys and girls is very little. When they reach the early years of adolescence, their body contours become significantly different. Adolescent boys have broad shoulders, narrow hips and straight leg-lines. On the other hand, girls have narrow shoulders, wide hips and curved leg-lines. Gradually, the bodies of boys and girls get resculptured into that of young men and young women.

(c) *Skeletal Changes*

Anew-born infant has 270 bones. They are small, spongy, pliable and loosely connected. He has soft spots in his skull which usually get closed before the end of his second year When he is about 13 to 14 years old, the human individual has 350 bones which have become hardened, with increased mineral content and changed chemical content During the processes of osification (hardening of bones), some of the smaller bones fuse together. Therefore, at adulthood, the number of bones is reduced to 206. The bony structure of human beings follows a relatively regular growth pattern but on account of ossification and nutrition, individual differences in the bony structure are occasionally noticed. In connection with skeletal growth, reference also may be made to dentition. The infant is born toothless but gradually the first set of "baby teeth" appear. As the child grows older, the "baby teeth" fall one by one and get replaced during childhood by a second set of "permanent teeth". With proper care and good food, the second set of teeth serve the individual throughout life.

(d) *Physiological Development*

The growth of the skeletal structure and the internal organs of the body are closely related. Both develop from birth onward; but the internal organs mature at different rates. In its rate of growth, each internal organ may vary from any or all others.

The musculature system increases both in weight and in its power to control the skeletal movement. Muscles constitute 23 to 25 percent of the total body weight in infancy, 27 per cent at age 8, 44 per cent at age 16, and in an adult about 45 per cent. In general, men have greater muscular power than women.

The heart is 5 times as large at age size at birth. From

age six to puberty, it grows more slowly. From age 12 to age 18, within six years, it doubles in weight and volume. During the embryonic and fetal periods, there is evidence of frequent but feeble heart beat. Respiration starts after birth. During the first month of life, the heart beats 140 times per minute. As its size increases, the heart beats more and more slowly. The blood pressure in the arteries increases. At age size, the rate of heart beat is 100 times per minute, and at age 12, eighty-five times. For an adult, the normal rate of heart bat is about 72 times per minute.

At birth, the infant possesses his full number of neurons (nerve cells). The neural structure is approximately what it shall be in future life. The neurons strengthen rapidly. The nervous system reaches its finalize by the time the child is 12 years old. The maturation of certain nerve cells in eh brain makes it possible for certain mental developments in later life.

The lymphatic system eliminates body wastes and destroys bacteria. It increases rapidly for the first 12 years of life. The activity of the lymphatic system decreases rapidly after this age.

The function of the endocrine glands was discussed earlier. Different endocrine glands grow at different rates. The thymus and the pineal glands are very active during childhood and do not allow sex glands to mature early. These two glands turn less active during adolescence. The thyroid and pituitary glands grow faster compared to other glands.

In the life of a boy or girl, sexual maturity is of great importance. The genitals grow very slowly during childhood. They being to grow rapidly with the onset of puberty and the reproductive cells—sperm and ova—get secreted in the testes and ovaries of boys and girls respectively. Also the six glands secrete hormones that develop the secondary sex characteristics in boys and girls. Girls being to menstruate when they are about 12 to 13 years old. During the years 12 to 14, their breasts develop, hair grows, on the public triangle and the facial contour changes. The boys mature later than girls, the average age being 14.Inth boys, hair grows in the public region and the arm pits, the shoulders broaden, the voice deepens, beard grows on the face, the facial contour changes and the sweat glands under the arm pits become active and odorous. As menstruation in girls, in the boys nocturnal emissions follow the development of secondary sex characteristics.

Motor Development

Those bodily movements that result from the coordinated functioning of nerves and muscles are usually referred to as moter activities. Motor development is necessary for the survival of the human child. Motor skills serve individuals in their day-to-day living.

Motor activities involve physical strength, the movement of gross and finer muscles, in well co-ordinated fashion and dynamic strength that causes the whole body movement. Gross movements of the body are needed in such activities as running and bicycling. Dynamic strength is needed for such activities as swimming and gymnastics. Writing, painting, the use of different kinds of tools and appliances need finer muscular coordination.

Movements after birth are mainly reflex action and largely automatic. With the nervous system and musculature becoming mature, the child gain s control over different motor functions. Maturation determines the rate and pattern of early motor responses. Later motor development depends on both maturation and practice. Experience and training.

(a) Early Motor Development

Motor growth takes an orderly sequence. Motor control begins in the head region of the infant. At first tries to hold its head erect and fixate the eyes. Next, it develops precision in reaching for and grasping objects that interest it.

For the first month of life the baby lies on its back, at the end of which it begins to lie on its stomach; It is difficult for the infant at this stage to change its position from the prone to the prone posture. By the fourth month it sits with support and by the seventh month, sits alone and erect. When it is 8 months old, it stands up when helped, at the 9th month stands up holding an article of furniture, at the 11th month walks when led, pulls itself up to stand by furniture when it is 12 months old, at the 13th month tries to climb up steps, stands alone by the 14th month and walks alone when it is 15 months old. The infant begins to creep when it is about 8 to 10 months old.

Individual differences are noticed in the method of locomotion. Some infants crawl on all fours while others crawl with their buttocks on the floor. Some infants prefer crawling to walking even after they have learned to take steps. With some encouragement they shift from crawling to walking. Those infants who crawl early, are likely to learn walking also early. Given good health, play space and sufficient number of toys, the infant shall exercise its muscles to gain motor control. Normal motor development may get hampered on account of physical defects and ill health. Parents should not try to hasten the individual maturational motor or process. They should allow the infant to develop at its own rate the motor coordinations.

Physical strength is estimated from the strength of the grip. Ability to grasp depends both upon physical strength and muscular coordination. The grasping movement of the infant is a reflex and is feeble. When the baby is about one year old, grasping with the thumb and fore finger begins and continues through adulthood.

At first, the movements of the infant are awkward and fumbling. It is unable to manipulate the objects in the physical environment well. His arm and movements develop in a consistent pattern through the first six years of life of the child. Gradually the infant begins to manipulate the play things, drinking equipment and other objects. This helps he child to develop specific skills in gaining control of objects by the time he enters into formal schooling.

(b) Later Motor Development

In the elementary and secondary schools, much time and attention is given in developing motor skills in children. They are engaged in a variety of activities that demand correct motor responses. Some of the most important activities are " penmanship. Drawing dancing, cooking, sewing, laboratory experiments, and various games. All these activities need motor control. Strength, speed, precision, rhythm, timing and finer muscular co-ordination are the most important aspects of motor execution. Long periods of training and practice are needed to develop these abilities in children. During the practice periods, errors are eliminated and correct responses are established. Not only intense practice but a desire to succeed and a confidence that successful performance can be attained are also essential for the development of motor skills.

There are wide differences in strength of grip among children. Variations in strength of grip are directly related to differences in ages at which puberty occurs and the accompanying increases in weight appear. Boys are found to be superior to girls in strength of grip. This superiority increases after age 14 and affects the whole personality of adolescent boys and girls in a variety of ways.

There are a number of motor activities such as dancing, playing different games and stenography, which depend upon the co-ordination of and integration of smaller muscles. Co-ordination of movements is necessary to learn handwriting. When they are about six years old, children are able to control movements better. From this time on improvement in motor control and regularity of movement makes legible handwriting possible.

Speed of response is needed for hitting or kicking a ball. Rhythm is closely associated with music and dancing. Timing is important for such complex responses as striking a golf ball or hitting a base ball. Playing Cricket is an excellent example. It involves all these aspects of motor execution. Any single act we perform involves muscular co-ordination.

If the muscles and nerves do not work together in proper combination, we do not get the result aimed at.

From age six onward improvements in the finer motor co-ordinations take place in children. They learn games involving running, throwing, hitting, kicking and balancing in space. Boys are superior to girls in playing games which involve running, hitting and kicking. In motor performances that depend upon finger dexterity and flexibility of wrist movement, girls tend to be superior to boys. Therefore, girls are found to dress themselves earlier than boys and show proficiency in such activities as knitting and needle work and stenography.

Dynamic strength stands for that strength which moves the whole body in a defined direction. Most of the outdoor games such as swimming and gymnastics depend much upon the dynamic strength of the individual. Activities such as climbing and broad jump also need dynamic strength. Boys are found to be superior to girls in the display of dynamic strength and perform such activities as broad jump, distance throw and vertical jump much better than the girls. Biological differences, differences in cultural expectation, motivation and practice are perhaps responsible for the widening differences between adolescent bys and girls in such activities as running, jumping and throwing.

Some individuals are right-handed, some others left-handed and still some others who are right-handed for certain activities are left-handed for others. It is not possible to tell the proportions of right-handed, left-handed and neither right nor left-handed individuals. There are many theories to account for the handedness. Some think the let-handed are born as such. Others claim that it stems out of the chance use of left hand in the early years of life Still some others explain it as a result o the dominance of the right hemisphere of the cerebulum. Also there are others who think that it is on account of the training given in using the left hand in the early years of life. Therefore, there is no universally accepted position about handedness. Teachers may encourage children to be right handed but on no account try to change handedness if it is likely to upset the child emotionally or may resulting the child feeling insecure. Even though they are left-handed, there are individuals who areas dexterous and efficient as their right handed cuter parts.

Significance of Physical Growth

Pressey and others (19670, p. 9), sum up the educational significance of physical growth in the lines that following and neglected fact in education is growth. Mot important, because the first requirement through the school years should be that healthy growth be achieved; mot helpful because the plasticity and vigour of the growth period greatly aid education; most deceiving, because education frequently mistakes as its own accomplishment what is actually the result of maturing; most confusing, because growth involves constant change; most neglected, because growth is so usual and yet so complex and often subtle."

Physical growth influences learning, personality and adjustment of children. Some of the physical and sensory defects and disorders that adversely affect the learning and adjustment of both children and adolescents and present a lot of psychological problems are defective vision, defective hearing and speech organs, physical deformities, chronic illness and malnutrition.

A dominant motive in the life of an adolescent is to be like others and gain approbation of both youngsters and adults. Any shift in physical proportions which seems to the adolescent boy or girl to make him or her different from others, plunges them into an ocean of worries. It is the social implication of any physical conditions that affects the emotional balance of the adolescents. Physical defects and deviations, therefore, present a lot of psychological problems for the teachers to resolve.

Besides physical deviations and sensory defects, there are other hazards the children meet with, Children meet with accidents. They are severely burne or run over by automobiles or drowned. If they survive, they are confined to the hospital for a pretty long time and come out of the hospital, invalid, disabled, disfigured or with mental aberrations, Interruption of school work, unwholesome personal-social relationships, and a lot of other troubles creep in on account of these incidents. Illness and accidents are so common during childhood and adolescence that they have to be reckoned with.

Physically handicapped children deserve special attention and extra help. Their learning difficulties have to be diagnosed and determined. Remedial teaching to meet the nature and extent of their learning difficulties should be given to them. The negative attitude they have developed should be slowly but surely removed and self confidence should be built up in them. Materials which are interesting and in the right proportion to the children's readiness should be collected and used. Close attention should be paid to these children and necessary guidance in new teaching—learning situations should be given to them. They should be given early opportunities to use and demonstrate their newly learned skills. However, children, who are receiving remedial teaching, should not be engaged in any competition. It may undermine their growing confidence.

Physical disorders such as unusual fatness, thinness and malnutrition can be rectified by diet control, proper nutrition, exercise and rest. Poor food habits, strenuous exercise and fatigue should be avoided. Good nutrition has good effects on the temperament of the child.

As safety education for children I necessary to help them avoid fatal accidents, health education is necessary to form in them good habits of health and hygiene and also a positive attitude towards health practices. Children should be encouraged to abide by the rules of the road and form other desirable habits in their day-to-day living. Constant medical check-up of the boys and girls would not only reveal their health condition but also their personal problems. For the treatment of chronic illness, parents should be advised to consult doctors.

There are certain physical indisositions and sickness that are psychological in origin. They result from the fruistration of psychosocial needs in children. Teachers should try to find out' the causes of such aiments and try to reduce the emotional stress the children suffer from by being sympathetic towards them. The teachers should try to make children realistic and self confident. Most of speech disorders such as stammering and stuttering arise from psychological stress. Teachers dealing with such children should provide them with situations in which their sense of worth whileness would be built up. Dynamic strength integrated with motor control and co-ordination have a very high value in our civilization. Athletic ability has a prestige value in the present-day society. Children who are unable to participate in different games on account of their inadequacies fele themselves insecure and inferior as a result of which their emotional-social adjustment gets affected. Therefore, a physical education programme in the schools is a necessity.

The primary aim of any physical education programme in a school should be to develop physical fitness in children and should be conceived as a series of planned developmental experiences. Athletics, too strenuous is not conducive to optimum physical growth. Competitive sports are too severe for those who are at the formative period of life. Therefore, everything should be "moderate" for children and adolescents.

11

The Juvenile Justice: Care Protection and Delopment of Children

The Government of India, having ratified the Convention, has found it expedient to re-enact the existing law relating to juveniles bearing mind the standards prescribed in the Convention on the Rights of the Child, the United Nations Standard Minimum Rules for the Administration of Juvenile Justice, 1985 (The Beijing Rules), the United Nations Rules for the Protection of Juveniles Deprived of their Library (1990), and all other relevant international instruments. To achieve this objective the Juvenile Justice (Care and Protection of Children) Bill was introduced in the Parliament. To provide for the care, protection, treatment, development and rehabilitation of neglected or delinquent juveniles and for the adjudication of certain matters relating to, and disposition of, delinquent juveniles the Juvenile Justice Act, 1986 (53 of 1986) was enacted by Parliament. Several provisions of the Constitution including clause (3) of Article 15, clauses (e) and (f) of Article 39, Articles 45 and 47 also impose on the State a primary responsibility of ensuring that all the needs of children are met and that their basic human rights are fully protected. On 20th November, 1989 General Assembly of the United Nations adopted the convention on the Rights of the

Child wherein a set of standards to be adhered to by all State Parties in securing the best interests of the child has been prescribed. The Convention emphasises social re-integration of child victims, to the extent possible, without resorting to judicial proceedings.

Act 56 of 2000

The Juvenile Justice (Care and Protection of Children) Bill having been passed by both the Houses of Parliament received the assert of the President on 30th December, 2000. It came on the statute Book as The Juvenile Justice (Care and Protection of Children) Act, 2000 (56 of 2000).

The Juvenile Justice (Care and Protection of Children) Act, 2000

(56 of 2000) (30th December, 2000)

An Act to consolidate and amend the law relating to juveniles in conflict with law and children in need of care and protection, by providing for proper care, protection and treament by catering to their development needs. And by adopting a child-friendly approach in the adjudication and disposition of matters in the best interest of children and for their ultimate rehabilitation through various institutions established under this enactment.

Whereas the Constitution has, in several provision, including clause (3) of Article 15, clauses (e) and (f) of Article 39, Article 45 and 47, impose on the State a primary responsibility of ensuring that all the needs of children are met and that their basic human rights are fully protected;

And Whereas, the General Assembly of the United Nations has adopted the Convention on the Rights of the Child on the 20th November, 1989.

And Whereas, the Convention on the Rights of the Child has prescribed a set of standards to be adhered to by all State Parties in securing the best interests of the child;

And Whereas, the Convention on the Rights of the Child

emphasizes social reintegration of child victims, to the extent possible., without resorting to juicial proceedings;

And whereas, the Government of India has ratified the Convention on the 11th December, 1992.

And Whereas, it is expedient to re-enact the existing law relating to juveniles bearing in mind the standards prescribed in the Convention on the Rights of the Child. The united Nations Standard Minimum Rules for the Administration of Juvenile Justice. 1985 (the Beijing Rules), the United Nations rules for the Protection of Juveniles Deprived of their Liberty (1990), and all other relevant international instruments.

Be it enacted by Parliament in the Fifty-first Year of the Republic of India as follows:-

CHAPTER 1

PRELIMINARY

1. *Short Title, Extent and Commencement*—(1) this Act may be called the Juvenile Justice (Care and Protection of Children Act, 2000).

   (2) It extends to the whole of India except the State of Jammu and Kashmir.

   (3) It shall come into force on the such date as the central government may, by notification in the Official Gazette appoint.

2. *Definition*: In this Act, unless the context otherwise requires:—

   (a) "advisory board" means a Central or a State advisory board of district and city level advisory boar as the case may be constituted under such a 62.

   (b) "begging" means—

   (i) soliciting or receiving aims in a public place or entering into any private premises for the purpose of soliciting or receiving aims, whether under any pretence;

(ii) exposing or exhibiting with the object of obtaining or extorting aims, any sore, wound, injury, deformity ' r disease, whether of himself or of any other person or of an animal;

(c) "board" means a Juvenile Justice Board constituted under Section 4;

(d) "child in need of care and protection" means a child—

(i) who is found without any home or settled place or abode and without any ostensible means of subsistence.

(ii) who resides with a person (whether a guardian of the child or not) and such person—

(a) has threatened to kill or injure the child and there is a reasonable likelihood of the threat being carried out, or

(b) has killed, abused or neglected some other child or children and there is a reasonable likelihood of the child in question being killed, abused or neglected by that person,

(iii) who is mentally or physically challenged or ill children or children suffering from terminal diseases or incurable diseases having no one to support or look after,

(iv) who has a parent or guardian and such parent or guardian is unfit or incapacitated to exercise control over he child.

(v) who does not have parent and no one is willing to take care of or whose parents have abandoned him or who is missing and run away child and whose parents cannot be found after reasonable injury,

(vi) who is being or is likely to be grossly abused, tortured or exploited for the purpose of sexual abuse or illegal acts,

(vii) who is found vulnerable and is likely to be inducted

into drug abuse or trafficking.

(viii) who is being or is likely to be abused for unconscionable gains,

(ix) who is victim of any armed conflict, civil commotion or natural calamity;

(e) "children's home" means an institution established by a State Government or by Voluntary Organisation and Certified by that Government under Section 34;

(f) "committee' means a Child Welfare Committee constituted under section 29;

(g) "competent authority" means in relation to children in need of care and protection a Committee and in relation to juveniles in conflict with law a Board;

(h) "fit institution" means a governmental or a registered non-governmental organisation or a voluntary organisation prepared to own the responsibility of a child and such organisation is found fit by the competent authority;

(i) "fit person" means a person, being a social worker or any other person, who is prepared to own the responsibility of a child and is found fit by the competent authority to receive and take care of the child;

(j) "guardian', in relation to a child, means his natural guardian or any other person having the actual charge or control over the child and recognised by the competent authority as a guardian in course of proceedings before that authority;

(k) "juvenile' or 'child" means a person who has not completed eighteenth year of age;

(l) "juvenile in conflict with law" means a juvenile who is alleged to have committed an offence;

(m) "local authority' means panchayats at the village and Zila Parishad at the district level and shall also include a Municipal Committee or Corporation or a Cantonment Board or such other body legally entitled to function as local authority by the Government;

(n) "narcotic drug" and "psychotropic substance" shall have the meanings respectively assigned to them in the Narcotic Drugs and Psychotropic Substances Act 1985 (61 of 1985);

(o) "observation home" means a home established by a State Government or by a voluntary organisation and certified by that State Government under Section 8 a as observation home for the juvenile in conflict with law;

(p) "offence' means an offence punishable under any law for the time being in force;

(q) "place of safety" means any place or institution (not being a police lock-up or jail), the person in charge of which is willing temporarily to receive and take care of the juvenile and which, in the opinion of the competent authority, may be a place of safety for the juvenile;

(r) "prescribed means prescribed by rules made under this Act;

(s) "probation office" means an officer appointed by the State Government as a probation officer under the Probation of Offenders Act, 1958 (20 of 1958)

(t) "public place" shall have the meaning assigned to it in the Immoral Traffic (Prevention) Act, 1956 (104 of 1956);

(u) "shelter home means a home or a drop-in-centre set up under Section 37;

(v) "special home" means an institution established by a State Government or by a Voluntary Organisation and Certified by that government under Section 9;

(w) "special juvenile police unit" means a unit of the police force of a State designated for handling of juveniles or children under Section 63;

(x) "state government", in relation total Union Territory,

means the Administrator of that Union Territory appointed by the President under article 239 of the Constitution;

(y) all words and expressions used but not defined in this Act and defined in the Code of Criminal Procedure, 1973 (2 of 1974), shall have the meanings respectively assigned to them in that Code.

3. *Continuation of Inquiry in Respect of Juvenile who has Ceased to be a Juvenile.*—Where an inquiry has been initiated against a juvenile in conflict with law or a child in need or care and protection and during the course of such inquiry the juvenile or the child ceases to be such, then, notwithstanding anything contained in this Act or in any other law for the time being in force, the inquiry may be continued and orders may be made in respect of such person as if such person had continued to be a juvenile or a child.

CHAPTER II

JUVENILE IN CONFLICT WITH LAW

4. *Juvenile Justice Board.*—(I) Notwithstanding anything continue in the Code Criminal Procedure, 1973 (2 of 1974), the State Government may, by notification in the Official Gazette, constitute for a district or a group of districts notification, one or more Juvenile Justice Boards for exercising the powers and discharging the duties conferred or imposed on such Boards in relation to juveniles in conflict with law under this Act.

(2) A Board shall consist of a Metropolitan Magistrate or a Judical Magistrate of the first class, as the case may be, and two social workers of whom at least one shall be a woman, forming a Bench and every such Bench shall have the powers conferred by the Code of Criminal Procedure, 1973 (2 of 1974), on a Metropolitan Magistrate or, as the case may be, a Judicial Magistrate of the first class and the Magistrate on the Board shall be designated as the principal Magistrate.

(3) No Magistrate shall be appointed as a member of the Board unless he has special knowledge or training in child psychology or child welfare and no social worker shall be appointed as member of the Board unless he has been actively involved in health, education, or welfare activities pertaining to children for at least seven years.

(4) the term of office of the members of the Board and the manner in which such member may resign shall be such as may be prescribed.

(5) The appointment of any member of the Board may be terminated after holding inquiry, by the State Government, if—

(i) he has been found guilty of misuse of power vested under this Act.

(ii) he has been convicted of an offence involving moral turpitude, and such conviction has not been reversed or he has not been granted full pardon in respect of such offence.

(iii) he fails to attend the proceedings of the Board for consecutive three months without any valid reason or he fails to attend less than three-fourth of the sittings in a year.

COMMENTS

The State Government has been authorised to constitute for a district or a group of districts one or more Juvenile Justice Boards for exercising the powers and discharging the duties, conferred or imposed on such Boards in relation to Juveniles in conflict with the law under this Act. The Board shall consist of a Metropolitan Magistrate or a Judicial Magistrate of the first class, as the case may be, and 'two social workers of whom at least one shall be a woman.

5. *Procedure, etc., in relation to Board*: (1) The Board shall meet at such times and shall observe such rules of procedure in regard to the transaction of business at its meetings, as may be prescribed.

(2) A child in conflict with law may be produced before an individual member of the Board, when the Board is not sitting.

(3) A Board may act notwithstanding the absence of any member of the Board, and no order made by the Board shall be invalid by reason only of the absence of any member during any stage of proceedings;

Provided that there shall be at least two members including the principal Magistrate present at the time of final disposal of the case.

(4) In the event of any difference of opinion among the members of the Board in the interim of final disposition, the opinion of the majority shall prevail, but where there is no such majority, the opinion of the principal magistrate shall prevail.

COMMENTS

A child in conflict with law can be produced before an individual member of the Board, when the Board is not sitting.

6. *Powers of Juvenile Justice Board.*—(I) Where a Board has been constituted for any district or a group of district, such Board shall, notwithstanding anything contained in any other law for the time being in force but save as otherwise expressly provided in this Act, have power to deal exclusively with all proceedings under this Act relating to juvenile in conflict with law.

(2) The powers conferred on the Board by or under this Act may also be exercised by the High Court and the court of Session, when the proceeding comes before them in appeal, revision or otherwise.

7. *Procedure to be followed by a Magistrate not empowered under the act:* (1) When any Magistrate not empowered to exercise the powers of a Board under this Act is of the opinion a that a person brought before him under any of the provisions of this Act (other than for the purpose of giving evidence), is a juvenile or the child, he shall without any delay record such opinion and forward the juvenile

or the child and the record of the proceeding to the competent authority having jurisdiction over the proceeding.

(2) The competent authority to which the proceeding is forwarded under sub-section (1) shall hold the inquiry as if the juvenile or the child had originally been brought before it.

8. *Observation homes*: (1) Any State Government may establish and maintain either by itself or under an agreement with voluntary organisations, observation homes in every district or a group of districts, as may be required for the temporary reception of any juvenile in conflict with law during the tendency of any inquiry regarding them under this Act.

(2) Where the State Government is of opinion that any institution other than a home established or maintained under sub-section (1), is fit for the temporary reception of juvenile in conflict with law during the tendency of any enquiry regarding them under this Act, it may certify such institution as an observation home for the purposes of this Act.

(3) The State Government may, by rules made under this Act, provide for the management of observation homes, including the standards and various types of services to be provided by them for rehabilitation and social integration of a juvenile, and the circumstances under which, and the manner in which, the certification of an observation home may be a granted or withdrawn.

(4) Every juvenile who is not placed under the charge of parent or guardian and is sent to an observation home shall be initially kept in a reception unit of the observation home for preliminary inquiries, care and classification for juveniles according to his age group, such as seven to twelve years, twelve to sixteen years and sixteen to eighteen years, giving due considerations to physical and mental status and degree of the offence committed, for further induction into observation home.

COMMENTS

State Governments have been empowered to establish and

maintain either by themselves or under an agreement with voluntary organisations, observation homes in every district or a group of districts, as may be required for the temporary reception of any juvenile in conflict with law during the pendency of any inquiry regarding them. State Governments have also been empowered to certify any institution, other than a home established or maintained by themselves or under an agreement with voluntary organisations, as an observation home for the purposes of this Act.

9. *Special homes.* (1) Any State Government may establish and maintain either by itself or under an agreement with voluntary organizations, special homes in every district or a group of districts, as may be required for reception and rehabilitation of juvenile in conflict with law under this Act.

(2) Where the State Government is of opinion that any institution other than a home established or maintained under sub-section (1), is fit for the reception of juvenile in conflict with law to be sent there under this Act, it may certify such institution as a special home for the purposes of this Act.

(3) The State Government may, by rules made under this Act, provide for the management of special homes, including the standards and various types of services to be provided by them which are necessary for re-socialisation of a juvenile, and the circumstances under which and the manner in which, the certification of special home may be granted or withdraw.

(4) The rules made under sub-section (3) may also provide for the classification and separation of juvenile in conflict with law on the basis of age and the nature of offences committed by them and his mental and physical status.

COMMENTS

State Governments have been empowered to establish and maintain, either by themselves or under an agreement with voluntary organisation, special homes in every district or a group of districts for the reception and rehabilitation of juvenile in conflict with law. State Governments have also been empowered to certify any institution, other than a home established or maintained by themselves or under an agreement with voluntary organisations, that it is fit for the reception of juvenile in conflict with law.

10. *Apprehension of Juvenile in Conflict with Law*: (1) As soon as a juvenile in conflict with law is apprehended by police, he shall be placed under the charge of the special juvenile police unit or the designated police officer who shall immediately report the matter to a member of the Board.

    (2) The State Government may make rules consistent with this Act,-

    (i) to provide for persons through whom (including registered voluntary organisations) any juvenile in conflict with law may be produced before the Board.

    (ii) to provide the manner in which such juvenile may be sent to an observation home.

COMMENTS

When a juvenile in conflict with law is apprehended by police, he has to be placed under the charge of the special juvenile police unit or the designated police officer who shall immediately report the matter to a member of the Board.

11. *Control of custodian over juvenile*: Any person in whose charge a juvenile is placed in pursuance of this Act shall, while the order is in force have the control over the juvenile as he would have if he were his parents, and shall be responsible for his maintenance, and the juvenile shall continue in his charge for the period stated by competent authority, notwithstanding that he is claimed by his parents or any other person.

COMMENTS

When any juvenile is placed in the charge of a person he

shall have the control over the juvenile as he would have if he were his parents, and shall be responsible for his maintenance and the juvenile shall continue in his charge for the period stated by the competent authority.

12. *Bail of juvenile:* (1) When any person accused of a bailable or non-bailable offence, and apparently a juvenile, is arrested or detained or appears or is brought before a Board, such person shall, notwithstanding anything contained in the Code of Criminal Procedure, 1973 (2 of 1974) or in any other law for the time beginning force, be released on bail with or without surety the shall not be so released if there appear reasonable grounds for believing that the release is likely to bring him into association with any known criminal or expose him to moral, physical or psychological danger or that his release would defeat the ends of justice.

    (2) When such person having been arrested is not released on bail under sub-section (1) by the officer incharge of the police station, such officer shall cause him to be kept only in an observation home in the prescribed manner until he can be brought before a Board.

    (3) When such person is not released on bail under sub-section (1) by the Board it shall, instead of committing him to prison, make an order sending him to an observation home or a place of safety for such period during the pendency of the inquiry regarding him as may be specified in the order.

13. *Information to Parent, Guardian or Probation Officer:* Where a juvenile in arrested, the officer incharge of the police station or the special juvenile police unit to which the juvenile is brought shall, as soon as may be after the arrest, inform –

    (a) the parent or guardian of the juvenile, if he can be found, of such arrest and direct him to be present at the Board before which the juvenile will appear; and

    (b) the probation officer of such arrest to enable him to obtain information regarding the antecedents and family background of the juvenile and other material circumstances likely to be of assistance to the Board for making the inquiry.

COMMENTS

When any juvenile is arrested, the officer in charge of the police station or the special juvenile police unit to which the juvenile is brought, as soon as may be after the arrest, has to inform the parent or guardian of the juvenile about his arrest and direct him to be present at the Board before which the juvenile will appear and he has also to inform the probation officer of such arrest to enable him to obtain information regarding the antecedents and family background of the juvenile.

14. *Inquiry by Board regarding juvenile*: Where a juvenile having been charged with the offence is produced before a Board, the Board shall hold the inquiry in accordance with the provisions of this Act and may make such order in relation to the juvenile as it deems fit:

    Provided that an inquiry under this section shall be completed within a period of four months from the date of its commencement, unless the period is extended by the Board having regard to the circumstances of the case and in special cases after recording the reasons in writing for such extension.

15. *Order that may be Passed Regarding Juvenile*: (1) Where a Board is satisfied on inquiry that a juvenile has committed an offence, then, notwithstanding anything to the contrary contained in any other law for the time being in force, the Board any, it thinks so fit,—

    (a) allow the juvenile to go home after advice or admonition following appropriate inquiry against and counselling to the parent or the guardian and the juvenile;

    (b) direct the juvenile to participate in group counselling and similar activities;

    (c) order the juvenile to perform community service;

(d) order the parent of the juvenile or the juvenile himself to pay a fine, if he is over fourteen years of age and earns money;

(e) direct the juvenile to be released on probation of good conduct and placed under the care of any parent, guardian or other fit person, on such parent, guardian or other fit person executing a bond, with or without surety, as the Board may require, for the good behaviour and well-being of the juvenile for any period not exceeding three years;

(f) direct the juvenile to be released on probation of good conduct and placed under the care of any fit institution for the good behaviour and well-being of the juvenile for any period not exceeding three years;

(g) make an order directing the juvenile to be sent to a special home.

(i) in the case of juvenile, over seventeen years but less than eighteen years of age for a period of not less than two years;

(ii) in case of any other juvenile for the period until he ceases to be a juvenile:

"Provided that the Board may, if it is satisfied that having regard to the nature of the offence and the circumstances of the case it is expedient so to do, for reasons to be recorded, reduce the period of stay to such period as it thinks fit."

(2) The Board shall obtain the social investigation report on juvenile either through a probation officer or a recognised voluntary organisation or otherwise, and shall take into consideration the findings of such report before passing an order.

(3) Where an order under clause (d), clause (e) or clause (f) of sub-section (I) is made, the Board may, if it is of opinion that in the interests of the juvenile and of the public, it is expedient so to do, in addition make an order that the juvenile in conflict with law shall remain under the supervision of a probation office

named in the order during such period, not exceeding three years as may be specified therein, and may in such supervision order impose such conditions as it deems necessary for the due supervision of the juvenile in conflict with law:

Provided that if at anytime afterwards it appears to the Board on receiving a report from the probation officer or otherwise, that the juvenile in conflict with law has not been of good behaviour during the period of supervision or that the fit institution under whose care the juvenile was placed is no longer able or willing to ensure the good behaviour and well-being of the juvenile it may, after making such inquiry as it deems, fit, order the juvenile in conflict with law to be sent to a special home.

(4) The Board shall while making a supervision order under sub-section (3), explain to the juvenile and the parent, guardian or other fit person or fit institution, as the case may be, under whose care the juvenile has been placed, the terms and conditions of the order and shall forthwith furnish one copy of the supervision order to the juvenile, the parent, guardian or other fit person or fit institution, as the case may be, the sureties, if any, and the probation officer.

16. *Order that may not be passed against juvenile*: (i) Notwithstanding anything to the contrary contained in any other law for the time being force, no juvenile in conflict with law shall be sentenced to death or life imprisonment, or committed to prison in default of payment of fine or in default of furnishing security:

Provided that where a juvenile who has attained the age of sixteen years has committed an offence and the Board is satisfied that the offence committed is of so seriousin nature or that his conduct and behaviour have been such that it would not be in his interest or in the interest of other juvenile in a special home to send him to such special home and that none of the other measures provided under this Act is suitable or sufficient, the Board may order the juvenile in conflict with law to be kept in such place of safety and in such manner as it thinks fit and shall report the case for the order of the State Government.

(2) On receipt of a report from a Board under sub-section (1), the State Government may make such arrangement in respect of the juvenile as it deems proper and may order such juvenile to be kept under protective custody at such place and on such condition as it thinks fit: Provided that the period of detention so ordered shall not exceed the maximum period of imprisonment to which the juvenile could have been sentenced for the offence committed.

17. *Proceeding under chapter VIII of the Code of Criminal Procedure not competent against Juvenile*: Notwithstanding anything to the contrary contained in the Code of Criminal Procedure, 1973 (2 of 1974) no proceeding shall be instituted and no order shall be passed against the juvenile under Chapter VIII of the said Code.

18. *No joint proceeding of juvenile and person not a juvenile*: (1) Notwithstanding anything contained in section 223 of the Code of Criminal Procedure, 1973 (2 of 1974) or in any other law for the time being in force, no juvenile shall be charged with or tried for any offence together with a person who is not a juvenile.

(2) If a juvenile is accused of an offence for which under Section 223 of the Code of Criminal Procedure, 1973 (2 of 1974) or any other law for the time being force, such juvenile and any person who is not a juvenile would, but for the prohibition contained in sub-section (I), have been charged and tried together, the Board taking cognizance of that offence shall direct separate trials of the juvenile and the other person.

COMMENTS

No juvenile can be charged with or tried for any offence together with a person who is not a juvenile.

19. *Removal of Disqualification Attaching to Conviction*: (i) Notwithstanding anything contained in any other law, a juvenile who has committed an offence and has been dealt with under the provision of this Act shall not suffer disqualification, if any, attaching to a conviction of an offence under such law.

(2) The Board shall make an order directing that the relevant records of such conviction shall be removed after the expiry of the period of appeal or a reasonable period as prescribed under the rules, as the case may be.

20. *Special Provision in Respect of Pending Cases*: Notwithstanding anything contained in this Act, all proceedings in respect of a juvenile pending in any court in any area on the date on which this Act comes into force in that area, shall be continued in that court as if this Act had to been passed and if the court finds that the juvenile has committed an offence, it shall record such finding and instead of passing any sentence in respect of the juvenile, forward the juvenile to the board which shall pass orders in respect of that juvenile in accordance with the provisions of this Act as if it had been satisfied on inquiry under this Act that a juvenile has committed the offence.

21. *Prohibition of Publication of name, etc., of Juvenile Involved in Any Proceeding Under the Act.*: (1) No reporting any newspaper, magazine, news-sheet or visual media of any inquiry regarding a juvenile in conflict with law under this Act shall disclose the name, address or school or any other particulars calculated to lead to the identification of the juvenile nor shall any picture of any such juvenile be published:

"Provided that for reasons to be recorded in writing the authority holding the inquiry may permit such disclosure, if in its opinion such disclosure is in the interest of the juvenile."

(2) Any person contravening the provisions of sub-section

(1) shall be punishable with fine, which may extend to one thousand rupees.

COMMENTS

Newspapers, magazines, news-sheet or visual media have been prohibited to disclose the name, address or school or any other particulars calculated to lead to the identification of the juvenile in conflict with law nor they can public any picture of such juvenile. Any person who contravenes this provision shall be punishable with fine upto one thousand rupees.

22. *Provision in Respect of Escaped Juvenile*: Notwithstanding anything to the contrary contained in any other law for the time being in force, any police officer may take charge without warrant of a juvenile in conflict with law who has escaped from a special home or an observation home or from the care of a person under whom he was placed under this ct, and shall be sent back to the special home or the observation home or that person, as the case may be; and no proceeding shall be instituted in respect of the juvenile by reason of such escape, but the special home, or the observation home or the person may, after giving the information to the Board which passed the order in respect of the juvenile, take such steps in respect of the juvenile as may be deemed necessary under the provisions of this Act.

23. *Punishment for Cruelty to Juvenile or Child*: Whoever, having the actual charge of, or control over, a juvenile or the child, assaults, abandons, exposes or willfully neglects the juvenile or causes or procures him to be assaulted, abandoned, exposed or neglected in a manner likely to cause such juvenile or the child unnecessary mental or physical suffering shall be punishable with imprisonment for a term which may extend to six months, or fine, or with both.

COMMENTS

If any person having the actual charge of, or control over, a juvenile or the child, assaults, abandons, exposes or willfully neglects the juvenile or causes or procures him to be assaulted, abandoned, exposed or neglected in any manner likely to cause such juvenile or the child unnecessary mental or physical suffering, he shall be punishable with imprisonment upto six months, or fine, or with both.

24. *Employment of Juvenile or Child for Begging:* (1) Whoever employs or uses any juvenile or the child for the purpose or causes any juvenile to beg shall be punishable with imprisonment for a term which may extend to three years and shall also be liable to fine.

    (2) Whoever, having the actual charge of, or control over, a juvenile or the child abets the commission of the offence punishable under sub-section (I), shall be punishable with imprisonment for a term which may extend to one year and shall also be liable to fine.

25. *Penalty for Giving Intoxicating Liquor or Narcotic Drug or Psychotropic Substance to Juvenile or Child:* Whoever gives, or causes to be given, to any juvenile or the child any intoxicating liquor in a public place or any narcotic drug or psychotoropic substance except upon the order of duly qualified medical practitioner or in case of sickness shall be punishable with imprisonment for a term which may extend to three years and shall also be liable to fine.

26. *Exploitation of Juvenile or Child employee:* Whoever ostensibly procures a juvenile or the child for the purpose of any hazardous employment keeps him in bondage and withholds his earnings or uses such earning for his own purposes shall be punishable with imprisonment for a term which play extend to three years and shall also be liable to fine.

27. *Special Offences:* The offences punishable under sections 23, 24, 25 and 26 shall be cognizable.

28. *Alternative Punishment:* Where an act or omission constitute an offence punishable under this Act and also under any other Central or State Act, then, notwithstanding

anything contained in any law for the time being in force, the offender found guilty of such offences, shall be liable to punishment only under such Act as provides for punishment which is greater in degree.

CHAPTER III

CHILD IN NEED OF CARE AND PROTECTION

29. *Child Welfare Committee*: (1) The State Government may, by notification in Official Gazette, constitute for every district or group of districts, specified in the notification, one or more child welfare Committees for exercising the powers and discharge the duties conferred on such Committees in relation to child in need of care and protection under this Act.

(2) The Committee shall consist of a Chairperson and four other members as the State Government may think fit to appoint, of whom at least one shall be a woman and another, and expert on matters concerning children.

(3) The qualifications of the Chairperson and the members, and the tenure for which they may be appointed shall be such as may be prescribed.

(4) The appointment of any member of the Committee may be terminated, after holding inquiry, by the State Government, if—

(i) he has been found guilty of misuse of power vested under this Act;

(ii) he has been convicted of an offence involving moral turpitude, and such conviction has not bee reversed or he has not been granted full pardon in respect of such offence;

(iii) he fails to attend the proceedings of the Committee for consecutive three months without any valid reason or he fails to attend less than three-fourth of the sittings in a year.

(5) The Committee shall function as a Bench of Magistrates

and shall have the powers conferred by the Code of Criminal Procedure, 1973 (2 of 1974) on a Metropolitan Magistrate or, as the case may be, a Judicial Magistrate of the first class.

COMMENTS

State Governments have been empowered to constitute for every district or group of districts one or more Child Welfare Committees for exercising the powers and discharge the duties in relation to child in need of care and protection under the Act. The Committee shall consist of a Chairperson and four other members, of whom at least one shall be a women and another an expert on matters concerning children.

30. *Procedure, etc., in Relation to Committee:* (1) The Committee shall meet at such times and shall observe such rules of procedure in regard to the transaction of business at its meetings, as may be prescribed.

(2) A child in feed of care and protection may be produced before an individual member for being placed in safe custody or otherwise when the Committee is not in session.

(3) In the event of any difference of opinion among the members of the Committee at the time of any interim decision, the opinion of the majority shall prevail but where there is no such majority the opinion of the Chairperson shall prevail.

(4) Subject to the provision of sub-section (I), the Committee may act, notwithstanding the absence of any member of the Committee, and no order made by the Committee shall be invalid by reason only of the absence of any member during any stage of the proceeding.

31. *Powers of Committee:* (1) The Committee shall have the final authority to dispose of cases for the care, protection, treatment, development and rehabilitation of the children as well as to provide for their basic needs and protection of human rights.

(2) Where a Committee has been constituted for any

area, such Committee shall, notwithstanding anything contained in any other law for the time being in force but save as otherwise expressly provided in this Act, have the power to deal exclusively with all proceedings under this Act relating to children in need of care and protection.

32. *Production before Committee*: (1) any child in need of care and protection may be produced before the Committee by one of the following persons:

(i) any police officer or special juvenile police unit or a designated police officer;

(ii) any public servant;

(iii) childline, a registered voluntary organisation or by such other voluntary organization or an agency as may be recognised by the State Government;

(iv) any social worker or a public spirited citizen authorized by the State Government; or

(v) by the child himself.

(2) The State Government may make rules consistent with this Act to provide for the manner of making the report to the police and to the Committee and the manner of sending and entrusting the child to children's home pending the inquiry.

33. *Inquiry*: (1) On receipt of a report under section 32, the Committee or any police officer or special juvenile police unit or the designated police officer shall hold an inquiry in the prescribed manner and the Committee, on its own or on the report from any person or agency as mentioned in sub-section (1) of section 32, may pass an order to send the child to the children's home for speedy inquiry by a social worker or child welfare officer.

(2) the inquiry under this section shall be completed within four months of the receipt of the order or within such shorter period as may be fixed by the Committee:

Provided that the time for the submission of the inquiry

report may be extended by such period as the Committee may, having regard to the circumstances and for the reasons recorded in writing, determine.

(3) After the completion of the inquiry if the Committee is of the opinion that the said child has no family or ostensible support, it may allow the child to remain in the children's home or shelter home till suitable rehabilitation is found for him or till he attains the age of eighteen years.

34. *Children's Homes*: (1) The State Government may establish and maintain either by itself or in association with the voluntary organisations, children's homes, in every district or group of districts, as the case may be, for the reception of child in need of care and protection during the pendency of any inquiry and subsequently for their care, treatment, education, training, development and rehabilitation.

(2) The State Government may, by rules made under this Act, provide for the management of children's homes including the standards and the nature of services to be provided by them, and the circumstances under which, and the manner in which, the certification of a children' home or recognition to a voluntary orgnisation may be granted or withdrawn.

COMMENTS

State Governments have been empowered to establish and maintain either by themselves or in association with the voluntary organizations, children's homes in every district or a group of districts for the reception of child in need of care and protection during the pendency of any enquiry and subsequently for their care, treatment, education, training, development and rehabilitation.

35. *Inspection*: (1) The State Government may appoint inspection committees for the children's homes (hereinafter referred to as the inspection committees) for the state, a district and city, as the case may be, for such period and for such purposes as may be prescribed.

(2) the inspection committee of a State, district or of a city shall consist of such number of representatives from the State Government, local authority, Committee, voluntary organisations and such other medical experts and social workers as may be prescribed.

36. *Social Auditing*: The Central Government or Government may monitor and evaluate the functioning of the Children's homes at such period and through such persons and institutions as may be specified by that Government.

37. *Shelter Homes*: (1) The State Government may recognize, reputed and capable voluntary organisation and provide them assistance to set up and administer as many shelter homes for juveniles or children as may be required.

(2) The shelter homes referred in sub-section (I) shall function as drop-in-centres for the children in the need of urgent support who have been brought to such homes through such persons as are referred to in sub-section (1) of section 32.

(3) As far a possible, the shelter homes shall have such facilities as may be prescribed by the rules.

COMMENTS

State Governments have been empowered to recognize reputed and capable voluntary organisations and provide them assistance to set up and administer shelter homes for juveniles or children. These shelter homes shall function as drop-in-centres for the children in the need of urgent support.

38. *Transfer*: (1) If during the inquiry it is found that the child hails from the place outside the jurisdiction of the Committee, the Committee shall order the transfer of the child to the competent authority having jurisdiction over the place of residence of the child.

(2) Such juvenile or one child shall be escorted by the staff of the home in which he is lodged originally.

(3) The State Government may make rules to provide for the traveling allowance to be paid to the child.

39. *Restoration*: (1) Restoration of and protection to a child shall be the prime objective of any children's home or the shelter home.

(2) The children's home or a shelter home, as the case may be, shall take such steps as are considered necessary for the restoration of and protection to a child deprived of his family environment temporarily or permanently where such child is under the care and protection of a children's home or a shelter home, as the case may be.

(3) The Committee shall have the powers to restore any child in need of care and protection to his parent, guardian, fit person or fit institution, as the case may be, and give them suitable directions.

Explanation: For the purposes of this section "restoration of child" means restoration to—

(a) parents;

(b) adopted parents;

(c) foster parents.

CHAPTER IV

REHABILITATION AND SOCIAL REINTEGRATION

40. *Process of Rehabilitation and Social Reintegration*: The rehabilitation and social reintegration of a child shall begin during the stay of the child in a children's home or special home and the rehabilitation an social reintegration of children shall be carried out alternatively by (i) adoption, (ii) foster care, (iii) sponsorship, and (Iv) sending the child to an after-care organisation.

41. *Adoption*: (I) The primary responsibility for providing care and protection to children shall be that of his family.

(2) Adoption shall be resorted to for the rehabilitation of such children as are orphaned, abandoned, neglected and abused through institutional and non-institutional methods.

(3) (3) In keeping with the provisions of the various

guidelines for adoption issued from time to time by the State Government, the Board shall be empowered to give children in adoption and carry out such investigations as are required or giving children in adoption in accordance with the guidelines issued by the State government from time to time in this regard.

(4) The children's home, or the Stage Government run institutions for orphans shall be recognized as an adoption agencies both for scrutiny and placement of such children for adoption in accordance with the guidelines issued under sub-section (3)

(5) No child shall be offered for adoption—

(a) until two members of the Committee declare the child legally free for placement in the case of abandoned children.

(b) Till the two months period for reconsideration by the parent is over in the case of surrendered children, and

(c) Without his consent in the case of a child who can understand and express his consent.

(6) The Board may allow a child to be given in adoption—

(a) to a single parent, and

(b) to parents to adopt a child of same sex irrespective of the number of living biological sons or daughters.

42. *Foster Care*: (1) The foster care may be used for temporary placement of those infants who are ultimately to be given for adoption.

(2) In foster care, the child may be placed in another family for a short or extended period of time, depending upon the circumstances where the child's own parent usually visit regularly and eventual after the rehabilitation, where the children may return to their own homes.

(3) The State Government may make rules for the purposes of carrying out the scheme of foster care programme of children.

43. *Sponsorship*: (1) the sponsorship programme may provide supplementary support to families, to children's homes and to special homes to meet medical, nutritional, educational and other needs of the children with a view to improving their quality of life.

(2) The State Government may make rules for the purposes of carrying out various schemes of sponsorship of children, such as individual to individual sponsorship, group sponsorship or community sponsorship.

44. *After-care Organisation*: The State Government may, by rules made under this Act, provide—

(a) for the establishment or recognition of after-care organisations and the functions that may be performed by them under this Act;

(b) for a scheme of after-care programme to be followed by such after-care organisations for the purpose of taking care of juveniles or the children after they leave special homes, children homes and for the purpose of enabling them to lead an honest, industrious and useful life;

(c) for the preparation or submission of a report by the probation officer or any other officer appointed by that Government in respect of each juvenile or the child prior to his discharge from a special home, children's home, regarding the necessity and nature of after-care of such juvenile or of a child, the period of such after care, supervision thereof and for the submission of report by the probation officer or any other officer appointed for the purpose, of the progress of each juvenile or the child;

(d) for the standards and the nature of services to be maintained by such after care organisations;

(e) for such other matters as may be necessary for the purpose of carrying out the scheme of after-care programme for the juvenile or the child;

Provided that any rule made under this section shall not provide for such juvenile or child to stay in the after-care organisation for more than three years:

Provided further that a juvenile or child over seventeen years of age but less than eighteen years of age would stay in the after-care organisation till he attains the age of twenty years.

45. *Linkages and Co-ordination*: The State government may make rules to ensure effective linkages between various governmental, non-governmental, corporate and other community agencies for facilitating the rehabilitation and social reintegration of the child.

CHAPTER V

MISCELLANEOUS

46. *Attendance of Parent or Guardian of Juvenile or Child:* Any competent authority before which a juvenile or the child is brought under any of the provisions of this Act, may, whenever it so thinks fit, require any parent or guardian having the actual charge of or control over the juvenile or the child to be present at any proceeding in respect of the juvenile or the child.

47. *Dispensing with Attendance of Juvenile or Child:* If, at any state during the course of an inquiry, a competent authority is satisfied that the attendance of the juvenile or the child is not essential for the purpose of inquiry, the component authority ay dispense with his attendance and proceed with the inquiry in the absence of the juvenile or the child.

48. *Committal to Approved Place of Juvenile or Child Suffering from Dangerous Diseases and his Future Disposal:* (I) When a juvenile or the child who has been brought before a competent authority under this Act, is found to be suffering from a disease requiring prolonged medical treatment or physical or mental complaint that will respond to treatment, the competent authority may send the juvenile or the child to any place recognised to be an approved

place in accordance with the rules made under this Act for such period as it may think necessary for the required treatment.

(2) Where a juvenile or the child is found to be suffering from leprosy, sexually transmitted disease, Hepatitis B, open cases of Tuberculosis and such other diseases or is of unsound mind, he shall be dealt with separately through various specialised referral services or under the relevant laws as such.

49. *Presumption and Termination of Age*: (1) Where it appears to a competent authority that person brought before it under any of the provisions of this Act (otherwise than for the purpose of giving evidence) is a juvenile or the child, the competent [authority shall make due inquiry so as to the age of the person and for that purpose shall take such evidence as may be necessary (but not an affidavit) and shall record a finding whether the person is a juvenile or the child or not, stating his age as nearly as may be.

(2) No order of a competent authority shall be deemed to have become invalid merely by any subsequent proof that the person in respect of whom the order has been made is not a juvenile or the child, and the age recorded by the competent authority to be the age of person so brought before, it, shall for the purpose of this Act, be deemed to be the true age of that person.

50. *Sending a Juvenile or Child outside Jurisdiction*: In the case of a juvenile or the child, whose ordinary place of residence lies outside the jurisdiction of the competent authority before which he is brought, the competent authority may, if satisfies dafter due inquiry that it is expedient so to do, send the juvenile or the child back to a relative or other person who is fit and willing to receive him at his ordinary place of residence and exercise proper care and control over him, not withstanding that such place of residence is outside the jurisdiction of the competent authority; and the competent authority exercising

jurisdiction over the place to which the juvenile or the child is sent shall in respect of any matter arising subsequently have the same powers in relation to the juvenile or the child as if the original order had been passed by itself.

51. *Reports to be Treated as Confidential*: The report of the probation officer or social worker considered by the competent authority shall be treated as confidential:

Provided that the competent authority may, if it so thinks fit, communicate the substance thereof to the juvenile or the child or his parent or guardian and may give such juvenile or the child, parent or guardian an opportunity of producing such evidence a may be relevant to the matter stated in the report.

52. *Appeals*: (1) Subject to the provisions of this section, any person aggrieved by an order made by a competent authority under this Act may, within thirty days from the date of such order, prefer an appeal to the Court of Session:

Provided that the Court of Session may entertain the appeal after the expiry of the said period of thirty days if it is satisfied that the appellant way prevented by sufficient cause from filing the appeal in time.

(2) No appeal shall lie from—

(a) Any order of acquittal made by the Board in respect of a juvenile alleged to have committed an offence; or

(b) Any order made by a Committee in respect of a finding that a person is not a neglected juvenile.

(3) No second appeal shall lie from any order of the Court of Session passed in appeal under this section.

53. *Revision*: The High Court may, at any time, either of its own motion or on an application received in this behalf, call for the record of any proceeding in which any competent authority or Court of Session has passed an order for the purpose of satisfying itself as to the legality or propriety

of any such order and may pass such order in relation thereto as it thinks fit:

Provided that the High Court shall not pass an order under this section prejudicial to any person without giving him a reasonable opportunity of being heard.

54. *Procedure in Inquiries, Appeals and Revision Proceedings*: (1) Save as otherwise expressly provided by this Act. A competent authority while holding any inquiry under any of the provisions of this Act, shall follow such procedure as may be prescribed and subject thereto, shall follow, as far as may be, the procedure laid down in the Code of Criminal Procedure, 1973 (2 of 1974) for trials in summons cases.

(2) Save as otherwise expressly provide by or under this Act, the procedure to be followed in hearing appeals or revision proceedings under this Act shall be, as far as practicable, in accordance with the provisions of the Code of Criminal Procedure, 1973 (2 of 1974).

55. *Power to Amend Orders*: (1) Without prejudice to the provisions for appeal and revision under this Act, any competent authority ay, on an application received in this behalf, amend any order as to the institution to which a juvenile or the child is to be sent or as to the person under whose care or supervision a juvenile or the child is to be placed under this Act:

Provided that there shall be at least two members and the parties or its defence present during the course of hearing for passing and amendment in relation to any of its order.

(2) clerical mistakes in orders passed by a competent authority or errors arising therein from any accidental slip or omission may, at any time, be corrected by the competent authority either on its own motion or on an application received in this behalf.

56. *Power of Competent Authority to Discharge and Transfer Juvenile or Child*: The competent authority or the local authority may, notwithstanding anything contained in this Act, at any time, order a child in

need of care and protection or a juvenile in conflict with law to the discharged or transferred from one children's home or special home to another, as the case may, be, keeping in view the best interest of the child or the juvenile, and his natural place of stay, either absolutely or on such conditions as it may think fit to impose:

Provided that the total period of stay of the juvenile or the child in a children's home or a special home or a fit institution or under a fit person shall not be increased by such transfer.

57. *Transfer between Children's Homes, Under the Act, and Juvenile Homes, of like Nature in Different Parts of India:* The State Government or the local authority may direct any child or the juvenile to be transferred from any children's home or special home outside the State to any other children's home, special home or institution of a like nature with the prior intimation to the local Committee or the Board, as the case may be, and such order shall be deemed to be operative for the competent authority of the area to which the child or the juvenile is sent.

58. *Transfer of Juvenile or Child of Unsound Mind or Suffering from Leprosy or Addicted to Drugs:* Where it appears to the competent authority that any juvenile or the child kept in a special home or a children's home or shelter home or in an institution in pursuance of this Act, is suffering from leprosy or is of unsound mind or is addicted to any narcotic drug or psychotropic substance, the competent authority may order his removal to a leper asylum or mental hospital or treatment centre for drug addicts or to a place of safety for being kept therefore such period not exceeding the period for which the is required to be kept under the order of the competent authority or for such further period as may be certified by the medical officer necessary for the proper treatment of the juvenile or the child.

COMMENTS

If any juvenile of the child kept in a special home or children's home or shelter home or in an institution, is suffering from leprosy or is of unsound mind or is addicted to any narcotic drug psychotropic substance, the competent authority a can order his removal to a leper asylum or mental hospital or treatment centre for drug addicts or to a place of safety for being kept there.

59. *Release and Absence of Juvenile or Child on Placement:*

(1) When a juvenile or the child I kept in a children's home or special home and on a report of a probation officer or social worker or of government or a voluntary organsation, as the case may be, the competent authority may consider, the release of such juvenile or the child permitting him to live with his parent or guardian or under the supervision of any authorised person named in the order willing to receive and take charge of the juvenile or the child to educate and train him for some useful trade or calling or to look after him for rehabilitation.

(2) The competent authority may also permit leave of absence to any juvenile or the child, to allow him, on special occasions like examination, marriage or relatives, death of kith and kin or the accident or serious illness of parent or any emergency of like nature to go on leave under supervision, for maximum seven days, excluding the time taken in journey.

(3) Where a permission has been revoked or forfeited and the juvenile or the child refuses or fails to return to the home concerned or juvenile to which he was directed so to return, the Board may, if necessary, cause him to be taken charge of and to be taken back to the concerned home.

(4) The time during which a juvenile or the child is absent from a concerned home in pursuance of such permission granted under this section shall be deemed to be part of the time for which he is liable to be kept in the special home:

Provided that when a juvenile has failed to return to the special home on the permission being revoked or forfeited, the time which elapses after his failure so to return shall be excluded in computing the time during which he is liable to be kept in the institution.

60. *Contribution by Parents*: (1) The competent authority which makes an order for sending a juvenile or the child to a children's home or to a special home or placing the juvenile under the care of the fit person or fit institution may make an order requiring the parent or other person liable to maintain the juvenile or the child to contribute to his maintenance, if able to do so, in the prescribed manner according to income:

(2) The competent authority may direct, if necessary, the payment to be made to poor parent or guardian by the Superintendent or the Project Manager of the home to pay such expenses for the journey of the inmate or parent or guardian or both, from the home to his ordinary place of residence at the time of sending the juvenile as may be prescribed.

61. *Fund:* (1) The State Government or local authority may create a Fund under such name as it thinks fit for the welfare and rehabilitation of the juvenile or the child dead with under this Act.

(2) There shall be credited to the Fund such voluntary donations, contributions or subscriptions as may be made by any individual or organisation.

(3) The Fund created under sub-section (1) shall be administered by the State Advisory Board in such manner and for such purposes as may be prescribed.

COMMENTS

State Governments or local authorities have been empowered to create Funds for the welfare and rehabilitation of the juvenile or the child. Such funds may be created with voluntary donations, contributions or subscriptions as may be made by any individual or organisation. Such funds are to be administered by the State Advisory Boards.

62. *Central, State, District and City Advisory Boards*: (1) The Central Government or a State Government may constitute a Central or a State advisory board, as the case may be, to advise that Government on matter relating to the establishment and maintenance of the homes, mobilisation of resources, provision of facilities for education, training and rehabilitation of child in need of care and protection and juvenile in conflict with law and co-ordination among the various official and non-official agencies concerned.

(2) The Central or State Advisory Board shall consist of such persons as the Central Government or the State government, as the case may be, may think fit and shall include eminent social workers, representatives of voluntary organisations in the file of child welfare corporate sector, academicians, medical professionals and the concerned Department of the State Government.

(3) The district or city level inspection committee constituted under Section 35 of this Act shall also function as the district or city advisory board.

63. *Special Juvenile Police Unit*: (1) In order to enable the police officers who frequently or exclusively deal with juveniles or are primarily engaged in the prevention of juvenile crime or handling of the juveniles or children under this Act to perform their functions more effectively, they shall be specially instructed and trained.

(2) In every police station at least one officer with aptitude and appropriate training and orientation may be designated as the juvenile or the child welfare officer' who will handle the juvenile or the child in co-ordination with the police.

(3) Special juvenile police unit, of which all police officers designated as above, to handle juveniles or children will be members, may be created in every district and city to co-ordinate and to upgrade the police treatment of the juveniles and the children.

64. *Juvenile in Conflict with Law Undergoing Sentence at*

Commencement of this Act: In any area in which this Act is brought into force, the State Government or the local authority may direct that a juvenile in conflict with law who is undergoing any sentence of imprisonment at the commencement of this Act, shall, in lieu of undergoing such sentence, be sent to a special home or be kept in fit institution in such manner as the State Government or the local authority thinks fit for the remainder of the period of the sentence; and the provisions of this Act shall apply to the juvenile as if he had been ordered by the Board to be sent to such special home or institution or, as the case may be, ordered to be kept under protective care under sub-section (2) of section 16 of this Act.

65. *Procedure in Respect of Bonds*: Provisions of Chapter XXXIII of the code of Criminal Procedure, 19973 (2 of 1974) shall, as far as may be, apply to bonds taken under this Act.

66. *Delegation of Powers*: The State Government may, by the general order, direct that any power exercisable by it under this Act shall, in such circumstances and under such conditions, if any, as may be prescribed in the order, be exercisable also by an officer subordinate to that Government or the local authority.

67. *Protection of Action Taken in good Faith*: No suit or legal proceedings shall lie against the State Government or voluntary organisation running the home or any officer and the staff appointed in pursuance of this Act in respect of anything which is in good faith done or intended to be done in pursuance of this Act or of any rules or order made there under.

68. *Power to make Rules*: (1) The State government may, by notification in the Official Gazette, make rules to carry out the purposes of this Act.

(2) In particular, and without prejudice to the generality of the foregoing powers, such rules may provide for all or any of the following matters, namely:-

(i) the term of officer of the members of the Board

and the manner in which such member may resign under sub-section (4) of Section (4);

(ii) the time of the meetings of the Board and the rules of procedure in regard to the transaction of business at its meeting under sub-Section (1) of section 5;

(iii) The management of observation homes including the standards and various types of services to be provided by them and the circumstances in which and the manner in which, the certification of the observation home may be granted or withdrawn and such other matters as are referred to in Section 8;

(iv) the management of special homes including the standards and various types of services to be provided by them and the circumstances in which and the manner in which, the certification of the special home may be granted or withdrawn and such other matters as are referred to in Section 9;

(v) persons by whom any juvenile in conflict with law may be produced before the board and the manner of sending such juvenile to an observation home under sub-section (2) of Section 10:

(vi) matters relating to removal of disqualifications attaching to conviction of a juvenile under Section 19;

(vii) the qualifications of the Chairperson and members, and the tenure for which they may be appointed under sub section (3) of Section 29;

(viii) the time of the meetings of the committee and the rules of procedure in regard to the transaction of business at its meeting under sub-section (I) of Section 30:

(ix) the manner of making the report to the police and to the Committee and the manner of sending and entrusting the child to children's home pending the inquiry under sub-section (2) of Section 32;

(x) the management of children's homes including the standards and nature of services to be provided by them, and the manner in which certification of a children's home or recognition to a voluntary organisation may be granted or withdrawn under sub-section (2) of Section 34;

(xi) appointment of inspection committees for children's homes, their tenure and purposes for which inspection committees may be appointed and such other matters as are referred to in Section 35;

(xii) facilities to be provided by the shelter homes under sub-section (3) of Section 42;

(xiii) for carrying out the scheme of foster care programme of children under subsection (3) of Section 42;

(xiv) for carrying out various schemes of sponsorshp of children under sub-secton (2) of section 43;

(xv) matters relating to after-care organisaiton under Section 44;

(xvi) for ensuring effective linkages between various agencies for facilitating rehabilitation and social integratin of the child under Section 45;

(xvii) the purposes and the manner in which the Fund shall be administered under sub-section (3) of section 61;

(xviii) any other matter which is required to be, or may be, prescribed.

(3) Every rule made by a State Government under this Act shall be laid, as soon as may be after it is made, before the Legislature of that State.

69. *Repeal and savings*: (1) The Juvenile Justice Act, 1986 (53 of 1986) is hereby repealed.

(2) Notwithstanding such repeal, anything done or any action taken under the said this Act.

Power to Remove Difficulties: (1) If any difficulty arises in giving effect to the provisions of this Act, the Central Government may, by order, not inconsistent with the provisions of this Act, remove the difficulty;

Provided that no such order shall be made after the expiry of the period of two years from the commencement of this Act.

(2) However, order made under the section shall be laid, as soon as may be after it is made, before each House of Parliament.

Bibliography

adatoo, C.P. (1958), Ego Reintegrtion Observed in Analysis of Late Adolescents, *Int, J. Psa*, xxxix.

Bakwin, H. and Bakwin, R.M. *Behaviour Disorders in Children*, London: W.B. Saunders Co., 1972

Barton, Len (Ed), *School Pupils and Deviance*, England: Nafferton, 1979.

Benjamin, J. (1950), Methodological Considerations in the Validation and Elaboration of Pscychoaalytical Personality Theory, Am, J. *Orthopsychiat*, XX.

Burt, C. *The Young Delinquent*, London: University of London Press, 1925

Bose, K. Prsonality Patterns of Delinquents, CIE, *Studies in Education and Psychology*. Delhi: C.I.E. University of Delhi, 1966.

Blumberg, L. Thelma, "Transforming Low Achievement and Disruptive Adolescents into Model Students," *The School Counselor*, Vol, 34 No. 1, Sept. 1986.

Channabasavana, S.M. et. al. "Juvenile Delinquency: A Socio Demographic Study," The Indian Journal of Criminalogy and Criminalistics. Vol. 1, No. 1, March, 1981.

Dollard, J. et. al. Frustration and Aggression, New York, Heaven, Comm., Yale University Press, 1939.

Friedlander, K. *The Psycho-analytical Approach to Juvenile Delinquency*. London: Kegan Paul, 1947.

Glueck, S. & Glueck, E.t. One Thusand Juvenile Delinquents - Their Treatmetn by court an dClinic, Harward University press, cambridge, Mass, 1934.

Herr, L. Edwin, "The Reevant Conselor," *The School Counsellor* Vol, 34, No. 1, Sept. 1986.

Hall, Baston M.B. *Psychiatric Examination of the School Child*, London: Edward Arnol Co. 1947.

Joshi, S.D. "Problems of Educaiton of the Weaker Sections of Society: the Weaker Sections in Baroda District (Gujarat state) - (176.

Jeyasingh, V.J. "Juvenile Recidivism: Socio-Psychological View" Indian Journal of Criminology & Criminalistics, Vol. 1, No. 4, December, 1981.

Kvaraccous, W.C. *Juvenile Delinquency*, Washngton: Naional Education Association, 1958.

Memta, P.H. "Guidance Services in India Toards the End of 1981," *Report of a Status Survey, Indian Education Review*, Vol. 18, No. 2, April, 1983.

Merril,M.A.*Problem of Child Delinquency*, Boston: Houghton Mifflin Co. 1947.

Nye, I.F. *Family Relations and Delinquent Behaviour*, New York: John Wiley, 1958.

Powers, Edwin and Witmer, *Experiements in Prevention of Delinquency*, New York: Columbia Univrsity Press, 1951.

Rao, V.N. & Parthasarathy, R. "Teacher as Counsellor," *The Educational Review*, Vol. XC, No. 12, December 1984.

Shankar, U. *Problem Children: Based on case Studies of Indian Children*, Delhi: Atma Ram & Sons, 1958.

Seetharaman, A.S. "Education in Slums - A Study of the Utilisation of Educational facilities by Slum Dwellers of Bangalore in Relation to their social and Economics Background. Un-published thesis, Bangalore Institute of Social and Economic Change, 1980.

Shea, T.M. *Teaching Children and Youth with Behaviour disorders*, Saint Louis: The C.V. Mosby Co., 1978.

Shanmugam, T.E. Quoted by Somasundaram & Polhaya, in "Jucenile Delinquency inGirls- The Role of Mild Mental Retardation," *Indian Journl of Criminology*, 7, 1964.

Shaw, C.r. and Mckay, H.D. *Juvenile Delinquency and Urban Area, Chicago*: University of Chicago Press, 1942.

Verma S.C. *The Young Delinquent: A Sociological Enquiry*, Lucknow: Pustak Kendra, 1969.

Wittels, F. (1949), TheEgo of the Adolescent, In: Searchights on Delinquency, Ed. K.R. Eissler. New York: International Universities Press.

Woody, R.H. *Behaviural Problem Children in the Schools: Recognition, Diagnosis and Behavioural Modifcation*, New York: Appleton Century 0 Crofts, 1969.